ETHNICITY AND NATIONALISM IN ITALIAN POLITICS

DAMES

Dansk Center for Migration
og Etniske Studier

**EUROPEAN RESEARCH CENTRE
ON MIGRATION & ETHNIC RELATIONS**

Ethnicity and Nationalism in Italian Politics

Inventing the *Padania*: Lega Nord and the northern question

MARGARITA GÓMEZ-REINO CACHAFEIRO
Universidad de Salamanca, Spain

Ashgate

Aldershot • Burlington USA • Singapore • Sydney

Published by
Ashgate Publishing Limited
Gower House
Croft Road
Aldershot
Hampshire GU11 3HR
England

Ashgate Publishing Company
131 Main Street
Burlington, VT 05401-5600 USA

Ashgate website: http://www.ashgate.com

British Library Cataloguing in Publication Data
Gómez-Reino Cachafeiro, Margarita
 Ethnicity and nationalism in Italian politics : inventing
 the Padania : Lega Nord and the northern question. -
 (Research in migration and ethnic relations series)
 1.Nationalism - Italy, Northern 2. Ethnicity - Italy,
 Northern 3.Italy - Politics and government - 1994-
 I.Title
 320.9'45

Library of Congress Control Number: 2001091558

ISBN 0 7546 1655 X

Printed and bound by Athenaeum Press, Ltd.,
Gateshead, Tyne & Wear.

Contents

List of Tables

Acknowledgements

This book is mostly based on a dissertation—only chapter 4 was added to the original manuscript written at M.I.T. First of all, I would like to thank my advisor, Suzanne Berger, and the other members of my dissertation committee, Richard Locke, Anthony Messina and Torben Iversen, for their comments, criticisms and suggestions throughout the years. In this book I attempted to respond to their final suggestions and criticisms. I hope I have somehow done it, although it was always hard to meet their standards. I also would like to thank the Massachusetts Institute of Technology and the Harvard-Center for European Studies for their financial support to conduct my research in Italy in 1995 and 1996. In Cambridge I thank my colleagues and friends Inger Weibust, Phineas Baxandall and Jonathan Schleffer for their comments and criticisms on many drafts. I would also like to thank my colleagues in the reading group of the Department of Anthropology of Harvard University for their suggestions and criticisms about my writing. Special thanks to the Abby Collins and the Center for European Studies at Harvard University for the two wonderful years I spent there as an affiliate. In Italy I would like to thank the Facolta di Studi Politci e Sociali at Universita Statale de Milano for an institutional affiliation in 1995-1996. My friend and colleague Francesco Zucchini deserves special thanks for his generous help on collecting data and understanding Italian politics. I also would like to thank the members of Lega Nord for their time and information, although I keep them anonymous here. In the Netherlands I would like to thank Karen Phalet and Meindert Fenemma for their comments on part of this manuscript. In Belgium I also would like to thank Marc Swyngedouw for his criticisms on parts of this manuscript and for providing the institutional space to finish this book in the Department of Sociology at Katolieke Universiteit Leuven. I am grateful to my friends and families in Spain, Italy and the United States for their support and encouragement. This book is dedicated to Bill 'Patley' Jones, *in memoriam*.

Margarita Gómez-Reino Cachafeiro
Salamanca

1 Perspectives on Peripheral Nationalism in Europe

Introduction

The erosion of the traditional cleavages that structured West European party systems (class, religion) has become an uncontroversial fact in the study of political change in Europe. Over the past two decades, scholars have studied electoral de-alignment and provided new analytical frameworks to explain the sources of political change and the creation of new cleavages. In the 1970s the main novelty in European politics was the rise of Green parties and ecological issues. In the past decade, a new family of parties, the alternatively labeled new radical right, new extreme right or populist right, with an agenda based on anti-migrant rhetoric and tax issues, became politically visible. Yet during the 1990s political change in Europe went far beyond the question of new party mobilisation and the emergence of new cleavages. This past decade brought economic and political changes that today reinforce new images of disintegration of nation-states and national political economies. The end of Cold War alignments and the relaunching of European integration have accelerated socio-economic transformation of the European continent at a major scale. A revival of nationalism in a variety of forms dominated political debates in Eastern Europe and the ex Soviet Union, but also in the pluralist democracies of Western Europe. At stake are the redefinition of categories of belonging and solidarity, and the politics of inclusion and exclusion in the construction of a European polity.

This book examines an unexpected political development: the rise of new parties in Northern Italy claiming self-government upon the basis of a national and cultural distinctive North. By all accounts *peripheral* nationalism is an old political conflict (the center-periphery or ethno-territorial cleavage in European party systems) but also it is, as this book shows, a political breakthrough, a new product of recent trends.[1] The Italian North had been without political parties advancing claims of national political autonomy and self-determination in the past. Party mobilisation was limited to those cultural and linguistic communities in the 'special' regions of the North, the Trentino-Alto Adige, Val d'Aosta and Friuli-Venezia Giulia.[2] However, in the 1980s and early 1990s political mobilisation diffused to most of the Northern 'ordinary' regions of Italy. In short, this book investigates the rise of Lega Nord and the political revolt of the Italian North.

The study of new party mobilisation in Northern Italy allows us to address current debates on the direction and scope of political change in European politics. Scholars writing on political change in European party systems associate new political mobilisation in Northern Italy with three related issues. First, Lega Nord's claims of nationhood and demands of self-determination and secession from the Italian state are linked to a global revival of nationalism after 1989. During the 1990s nationalism became again a major driving force in politics worldwide. The breaking-up of the Soviet Union and Yugoslavia provided closer images of the destructive powers of the national idea in contemporary politics. Today, some scholars even argue, as Seyla Benhabib writes: 'the negotiation of identity and difference is the political problem facing democracies on a global scale' (Benhabib, 1996, p. 3). Second, the rise of Lega Nord is tied with a political backlash in European societies manifested by the success of new radical right-wing parties and the spread of xenophobic, ethnocentric and racist sentiments against new migrants. Le Pen's Front National, the Flemish Vlaams Blok, and Haider's FPÖ are today well-known examples of the political successes of anti-migrant mobilisation. Third, Lega Nord's demands for political autonomy are also analysed within a new institutional scenario in the European Union that undermines both the political and economic unity of nation-states. European integration allegedly strengthens the viability of national sub-units in their pursuit of economic and political autonomy from central governments. Thus, the rise of Lega Nord is at the center of crucial debates not only about the creation of new cleavages in European party systems, but also, and more broadly, about the very sustainability of traditional nation-state boundaries as we know them.

Why did new political mobilisation emerge in Northern Italy? Why do new parties advance claims of nationhood and self-government, and why now? The rise of new political mobilisation in Italy is a puzzle for traditional analysis of the alternatively labeled ethno-territorial, regional or center-periphery cleavage. First, the rise and success of Lega Nord is cast as an anomaly. Theories on *ethno-territorial* political mobilisation read off the emergence of political parties from a necessary condition: the existence of a bounded collectivity—whether defined in objective or subjective terms—which is characterised by cultural traits. Academic emphasis on the uniqueness of the Italian experience derives from the lack of previously defined *ethnic* identities in the regions of Northern Italy (Diani and Melucci, 1992; Rusconi, 1993). Scholars stress the absence of both objective and subjective differences—whether in the form of distinctive languages or regional self-identifications in the North of Italy—to sustain the new regional revolt. Thus, for some scholars the nationalism of Lega is a 'nationalism without a nation' (Melucci and Diani, 1992, p. 168). Second, in European party systems, the so-called ethno-territorial cleavage was characterised by the specialisation of voters' appeals: it was a marginal cleavage in light of its limited electoral relevance (constrained by the size of the minority) and it was narrowly defined by 'cultural' demands. Yet the electoral success of Lega Nord in the early 1990s made the Northern question in Italy a mass phenomenon. Lega Nord preceded and survived a major upheaval that changed in fundamental ways the Italian party system. Surprisingly, this on-going electoral persistence has taken place despite arguments about a short-term wave of protest vote, and the emergence of a new party system in Italy. This electoral success is quite shocking. Scholars have brought to the fore major shifts in party elite strategies with the alternation of moderation and radicalisation of party demands, the lack of congruence of elite and voters' attitudes (party elites exhibiting more radical attitudes about political independence and about migrants), the apparent *irrationality* of elites and voters in light of the empirical evidence on the absence of subjective self-identifications with a non-existent *Padania*, and the poor institutional performance of Lega Nord's representatives at the local and national level.

The political stability of European party systems was built upon the structuring power of traditional cleavages. Lipset and Rokkan's traditional model of the formation of the European party systems posited that different cleavage configurations developed in each polity as the result of the timing and interaction of conflicts emerging from the national and industrial revolutions (Lipset and Rokkan, 1967).[3] The sequential interaction of four cleavages emerging from these revolutions (center-periphery, state-church, land-industry and workers-owners) gave rise in each state to different party systems. The crucial role played by political parties during the early periods of democratisation shaped the main lines of conflict and stabilised political alignments providing 'enduring relations between specific social groups, organisational networks and ideologies' in European party systems (Bartolini and Mair, 1991, p. 217).

Italian politics—structured around class and religious cleavages—was an outstanding example of the power of these conflicts in structuring the political system and stabilising electoral alignments. The formation of the Italian party system made class and religion the main dimensions of conflict before and after the fascist interlude. In the post-war period, Italian politics evolved around the conflict between the Christian Democratic party and the Italian Communist party. The dynamics of a multiparty system produced fragile coalition governments orchestrated by the Christian democrats.

In the classical path-dependency explanations of the formation of the Italian party system, the timing of cleavages prevented the 'translation' of the

North-South divide as a regional cleavage (Lipset and Rokkan, 1967). In the Italian party system, *ethnicity* was not, as Samuel Barnes writes, a meaningful variable to explain political and electoral alignments (Barnes, 1978). The only recognised ethnic minority within the state boundaries was the German-speaking population of the Bolzano province, which was represented by the SVP. In scholarly writing, territory was, at best, an important element to explain the strength of local—but not *ethnic*— identities. As Barnes put it, 'Italians have a strong attachment to their city or village *(campanilismo)*. The very particularism of their attachments makes the growth of larger identification difficult' (Barnes, 1974: 197). The introduction of a state structure that recognised both special and ordinary regions aimed to pre-empt political mobilisation in the 'special' regions of Trentino-Alto Adige, Val d'Aosta, Sicily, Sardegna and Friuli-Venezia Giulia, and to decentralise some powers to the remaining fifteen 'ordinary' regions—only implemented in the 1970s.

Italy was an anomalous case for modernisation theory. To start with, Italy was not considered a nation-state. One of the common claims by historians and students of Italian politics politics is the 'lack' of an Italian nation (Mack Smith, 1990). The often quoted sentence by one of the architects of Italian unification, Massimo D'Azeglio—*fatta L'Italia, dobbiamo fare gli Italiani*—appears in almost every scholarly work on Italian politics (Putnam, 1993). Italy was not considered a multi-ethnic state either. As mentioned before, other sources of territorial identification—local identities—were, instead, politically salient and resilient (Seggati, 1995).

Territorial dualism between a developed economic North and a backward South was a permanent feature of Italian politics. Socio-economic disparities between North and South in Italy proved historically enduring. Despite the efforts of Italian governments during the post-war period to promote endogenous economic growth in the South, today North and South still exhibit widespread economic differences. In many historical and political accounts of Italian politics, the South has also been the source of most of the pathological characteristics of the Italian political system (clientelism, corruption, Mafia, *trasformismo*) and the wrongdoing of the political class during the post-war period. Recently, Putnam's work on Italian regional governments identified historical cultural differences—patterns of civicness—between North and South to explain variation in the institutional performance of the Italian regions and in rates of regional economic development.

In light of all the overwhelming evidence of the structural nature of the North-South divide, the rise and success of Lega Nord, a party mobilising and exploiting the North-South divide, was, as someone put it to me once, 'rather obvious'. The erosion of traditional cleavages in the Italian party system during the 1980s and the disappearance of Italian political parties in the midst of corruption scandals in the early 1990s allowed the regional cleavage in Italian politics to 'resurface'. Thus, in these views, the resilience of regional disparities between North and South would explain a *cleavage displacement* in the Italian party system.

This book, however, presents an explanation of party mobilisation in the North of Italy that focuses on the less obvious aspects of the politicisation of the territorial divide. First, I argue that a 'translation' of the traditional North-South divide provides a deterministic explanation of what was a *contingent* event and the product of political choices. The packaging of a united North was a difficult political process with many constraints attached—and which became visible throughout the past decade. Second, nationalism and claims of territorial autonomy are not an obvious response to the territorial divide between North and South. The gap between North and South had historically been defined on socio-economic, and not on cultural-national terms. Yet the 'translation' of territorial differences between North and South in the Italian state did not come in the form of a neo-liberal party or an anti-tax revolt *tout court*, but in the form of claims of nationhood and self-determination for the North. Third, if anything, history was reversed in that it was not the traditionally considered *peripheral* South, but the Italian North, the subject of political revolt.

This book explains why and how a new politics of identity emerged in Northern Italy and how a new political party, Lega Nord, constructed the symbolic and political unity of the North. It answers the question of why a territorial identity became the focus of political mobilisation with claims of self-government and cultural distinctiveness. This work explores these questions first, through a historical study of the structure of incentives for political mobilisation and party formation in the Northern Italian regions, and second, through a case study of Lega Nord's style of mobilisation, symbolic politics and party ideology.

The rise of Lega Nord has been analysed in the context of two alternative analytical frameworks and within the universe of two distinctive families of political parties. On the one hand, explanations of the formation of the ethno-territorial cleavage in European party systems consider that new political mobilisation responds to the presence of *ethnic* or national minorities that 'survived' the period of nation-state formation. The resilience of cultural differences is the basis for political mobilisation. The political parties representing national minorities are characterised by the specialisation of voters' appeals—cultural recognition within nation-states. This explanation, in fact, became for some scholars the analytical yardstick to assess and measure what Lega Nord *is not*. On the other hand, some scholars have explained Lega Nord as the Italian manifestation of the rise of a new family of parties in Europe: the new radical right. This second explanation highlights the rise of a new post-industrial cleavage in European party systems generated by crisis and dislocation in the transformation from industrial to post-industrial societies.

The fitness of Lega Nord within one political family or the other has been debated over the past decade. The next section provides an overview of the two alternative frameworks and their explanations for the rise and success of Lega Nord in Italian politics.

The Old Ethno-Territorial Cleavage in European Party Systems

The ethno-territorial, regional or center-periphery cleavage represents political conflict between national and alternative territorial cultures (Lipset and Rokkan, 1967). It is the first cleavage in the developmental sequence of European party systems The formation and consolidation of the ethno-territorial cleavage is path-dependent: the product of historical developments in the process of nation and state formation. Labeled by some scholars as *ethnoregionalist* parties, this family of political parties is defined as those political parties who 'endorse a nationalism whose core is based on *ethnic* distinctiveness as opposed to other kinds of regionalisms' (De Winter and Türsan, 1998, p. 5). De Winter and Türsan single out two common denominators for ethnoregionalist parties: a subnational territorial border and an exclusive group identity (Türsan, 1998, p. 5).

This family of political parties exhibits the following characteristics. First, cultural demands and claims of recognition represent the main aspect of party demands. Until the past decade, most analyses assumed political mobilisation reflects some pre-existing collectivity: cultural differences are embedded in a community and provide the objective basis of collective identification. Second, the ethno-territorial or regional cleavage represents a distinctive axis of electoral competition cutting across the main ideological axis in European party systems.[4] Regionalist parties subordinate all other issues to the territorial claim of cultural distinctiveness.[5] Traditional ideologies are considered of secondary importance to characterise the parties. Third, these are minor and small political parties characterised by the specialisation of voters' appeals. As Urwin put it, their significance in party systems lies in their 'potential disaggregative impact' in the polity (Urwin, 1983, p. 232). Academic attention was directed towards understanding the mechanisms for accommodation in plural societies, and the 'peculiarites' of this type of political party—their free riding and blackmailing power—and the determinants of political conflict or stability, rather than to the analysis of the determinants of their electoral success or failure.[6]

The trajectory of the family of sub-state nationalist political parties in European party systems is marked by three waves of political mobilisation. Rokkan and Urwin identify two different cycles or waves of mobilisation of the ethno-territorial cleavage (Rokkan and Urwin, 1982). The first wave of political mobilisation represents the process of *cleavage formation* and took place with the democratisation of European party systems. Modernisation theorists assumed that the development of the modern nation-state and the process of industrialisation would drive European societies towards cultural homogeneity and incorporated the *peripheries* in national cultures. According to Lipset and Rokkan, 'purely territorial oppositions rarely survive extensions of the suffrage' (Lipset and Rokkan, 1967, p. 12). Instead, the second wave of political mobilisation, the *ethnic* wave of the 1970s, corresponded with the first signs of erosion of the main cleavages in European party systems (Esman, 1977). In the 1960s and 1970s, European nation-states were challenged by a wave of political mobilisation that brought about new claims for autonomy and self-government in France, U.K., Belgium, Italy and Spain. From the rediscovery of ethnic minorities in the 1970s, scholars drew a new analytical map in which Europe was no longer a set of nation-states but was 'multi-ethnic and multi-ethnic structures remain the rule' (Esman, 1977, p. 26). Thus, the second cycle of mobilisation was about *cleavage displacement* with the re-awakening of *ethnic* identities in the 1970s. The third, and contemporary wave of political mobilisation would reflect, according to Müller-Rommel, a 'collective identity mood' mobilised by ethnoregionalist parties (Müller-Rommel, 1998, p. 24). Müller-Rommel also highlights the contemporary potential of these parties as reservoirs of protest votes against the state and governmental parties. Recent scholarship has added resource mobilisation theory and political opportunity structures to explain the determinants of new political mobilisation.

The assumptions of modernisation theory, which portrayed an evolutionary trajectory towards the cultural homogeneity of European nation-states, are no longer part of scholarly research. However, much of our received wisdom in political science stills considers identities as *ethnic* and pre-existing, the legacies of collective traits. For Guy Heraud: 'the *ethnie* is a collectivity presenting certain common distinctive characteristics of language, culture and civilisation' (Heraud, 1963: 23).[7] Among the objective differences identified, the existence of a language provided the most self-evident manifestation of distinctiveness and a clear-cut criterion to identify *ethnic* minorities. According to Heraud, 'the language transmits a culture, reflects a sensitivity, becomes the sanctuary of ethnic values' (Heraud, 1963: 44).[8]

Theories on *ethnic* political mobilisation rely on a previous process of *ethnic* group formation and group solidarity (Hetcher and Levi, 1979).

Hetchter identifies two main processes behind *ethnic* group formation: the existence of a hierarchical cultural division of labor that promotes reactive group formation; and a segmental dimension of the cultural division of labor that leads to interactive group formation (Hetcher, 1975; Hetcher and Levi, 1979). In this sense, 'ethnic entrepreneurs' mobilise a pre-exiting ethnic potential. The relative salience of nationalism—roughly measured by electoral success—provides the basis to further distinguish between *ethnic* and *national* minorities. Anthony Smith illustrates this interpretation: 'within European states there are both ethnies and nations: on the one hand, fully-fledged nations like Catalonia, Scotland and Flanders, and on the other hand, *ethnic* communities like the Galicians in Spain, or the Sorbs in Eastern Germany' (Smith, 1986, p. 129).

Theories on ethno-territorial mobilisation in Europe read-off the emergence of political mobilisation—either movements or parties—from a set of necessary and sufficient conditions that can be explored in given territorial units. A necessary condition is the existence of a bounded collectivity—whether defined on objective grounds as an ethnic group or subjective terms as a collective identity—which is characterised by traits or markers in the form of language, culture or religion. European states were endowed with a set of minorities that survived the impact of modernisation processes and represented a 'feasibility set' for new political mobilisation. The identification of a limited range of ethnic minorities in Europe was the starting point to explain political mobilisation.

A proliferation of scientific taxonomies of European ethnic and national minorities presented as natural and given what was the result of classificatory process. Table 1.1 presents the first mapping of *ethnic* minorities in Europe developed by Guy Heraud in 1963.

Table 1.1 Minorities in Europe

Northern Europe	Lapons
	Feroe Islands
	Finnish Swedes
	German and Danish in Slesvig
	Southern Germany
Western Europe	Galicia
	Euskadi
	Celtic, Scottish, Welsh, Bretton
	Normand Islands
	Frisons
	Flanders and Wallonia
	French Flemish
	Germans in Belgium
	Alsace et Lorraine
	Val D'Aosta
Central Europe	Swiss Jura
	Rheto-Romans
	Croats and Slovenians in Austria
	Slovenians in Italy
	South Tyrol
Southern Europe	Gibraltar
	Catalans
	Occitanias
	Northern Italians
	Corsicans
	Sardinian and Sicilians
	Malta
	Albanians and Greeks in Italy
	Cyprus

Source: Heraud, 1963

Heraud's taxonomy identifies a single criterium to classify European *ethnic* minorities: the presence of linguistic differences. The divisions established between ethnic minorities reflect larger geographical areas in the European continent rather than within European states. In 1963, Heraud had singled out the 'North of Italy' as a cultural unit—the area between the Alps and the Apennines, the old *Gaule Cisalpina*—characterised by the presence of dialects. In Heraud's classification, the Venetian dialect was considered as *purely* Italian and therefore, not an *ethnic* one.[9] Heraud also included in his classification two 'special' regions of the Italian state, Sicily and Sardinia, as *ethnic* minorities in Italy. The introduction of minorities in Northern Italy in Heraud's typology was unique—he is the only academic voice treating the North of Italy as a single cultural and *ethnic* unit. In contrast, the presence of minorities in Southern Italy is widely recognised in social-scientific discourse. Chapter 2 develops this theme and presents alternative classifications of Italian *ethnic* minorities in the 1970s.

The giveness of national minorities, in objective terms, presents unsurmountable analytical and empirical problems. Although these theories look for objective criteria (culture, language), the existence of these collective traits and their implications for processes of collective identity formation is, in fact, extremely problematic, as for example the basic—although contested—distinction between a language and a dialect. Moreover, socio-economic processes in Europe—migration, industrialisation—make extremely difficult to identify geographically *enclosed* minorities. In advanced industrialised societies, the assumption of distinctiveness and affinity between a people, a culture and a territory is less and less evident (Berger, 1977; Linz, 1985).

An alternative solution in social-scientific discourse was to identify *ethnic potential*, that is a set of factors that could eventually lead to identity mobilisation. Table 1.2 shows the classification of European regions with ethnic potential introduced by Gourevitch. The political translation of this potential leads into a typology of strong and weak nationalism.

Table 1.2 Gourevitch's Regions with Ethnic Potential

Strong Nationalism	Weak Nationalism
Catalonia	Brittany
Spanish Basque Provinces	French Basque Provinces
Scotland	French Occitania
Quebec	Alsace
Croatia	Southern Germany
Flanders	Southern Italy
	Galicia, Andalucia
	Montenegro, Macedonia

Source: Gourevitch, 1979: 307

Gourevitch's classification includes the Italian South as a case of weak nationalism, reflecting the traditional view that the South was a *periphery* on its own right. He does not include any reference to the *ethnic* potential identified by Heraud in Northern Italy. In contrast to Heraud, Gourevitch speculated with the possibility of considering Veneto as one of the regions with *ethnic* potential in Italy.

Having singled out the *necessary* condition, scholars provided alternative explanations to assess the *sufficient* condition for political mobilisation in the 1970s: *grievance* potential. In the 1970s and with the well-known exception of Lijphart—who claim that cleavage displacement was the result of economic afluence in Europe—students of the ethno-territorial cleavage emphasise the importance of economic and distributive conflicts as the stimulus for new political mobilisation. The differential impact of economic industrialisation across regions is determinant in all the explanations of the *awakening* of national minorities. Marxist accounts developed a version of dependence theory that emphasised economic backwardness in the *peripheries*. The relative stage of economic development of the region and its exploitation by central governments shaped the salience of regional grievances. Uneven economic development causes relative deprivation in peripheral regions (Nairn, 1977, p. 128), and *internal colonialism* explains a cultural division of labor and the marginality and economic exploitation of the peripheries vis-a-vis the state (Hechter, 1975, p. 9). Regional peripherality in functionalist accounts of regional political mobilisation is the result of the lack of congruence between political and economic factors (Gourevitch, 1979). In the 1970s the processes of internationalisation of the economy and their impact on the position of the regions vis-à-vis central governments was highlighted as the key factor generating new grievances and new efforts to mobilise *peripheries*. For Rokkan and Urwin, these new economic processes modified the structural position of the territory and its cultural, economic and political role within European states (Rokkan and Urwin, 1983).

The implicit assumption underlying the analyses presented above was that successive cycles of mobilisation on the ethno-territorial cleavage would reflect less the salience of cultural differences and territorial identities, and more territorial interests and the regional redistribution of economic resources (Lipset and Urwin, 1983; Urwin, 1982, p. 436). Notice however, that Müller-Rommel links the third wave of political mobilisation with the presence of a 'collective identity mood' in European electorates, and not with the salience of regional economic grievances (Müller-Rommel, 1998). Since the 1970s, however, there are divergent approaches to explain the ethno-territorial revival alternatively as identity and cultural demands, or interests and economic demands.

Analysing the rise of Lega Nord within the traditional family of sub-state nationalist political parties offers two main advantages. First, it rightly situates Lega Nord within the context of nationalism and claims of institutional recognition and self-determination for national minorities within European states. The *genesis* of party moblisation and party formation in Northern Italy was about recognition of new national minorities. We cannot understand the politics of Lega Nord without addressing the question of identity politics and the territorial demands of the party. Second, it provides an analytical basis to explain why the territory becomes the focus of political struggle as economic development and state policies increase the visibility of economic differences within states. Although providing contrasting answers as to why the success of new political mobilisation, it provides ground to theorise about a new political space for nationalism in European party systems.

However, explaining Lega Nord as a ethnoregionalist political party also presents major shortcomings. First, this mode of analysis forces us to construct ex-post the necessary condition for political mobilisation. In the 1990s, classifications of national minorities in Europe were refashioned to accommodate the *latecomers*. For example, today as Italian *ethnic* minorities—Italian regions with ethnically-culturally distinctive groups— appear not only the Tyrolese, but also the Saboyards, Sards, Venetians, Lombards, Ligurians, Friulians and the Sicilians (Budge et al., 1997, p. 106). 'Padanians' have been *ex post* introduced already in the list of European national minorities. In the 1993 revised edition of *L'Europe des Ethnies*, Heraud labels Northern Italy as High Italy or *Mediolanie* to designate the regional dialects spread trough the regions of Piedmont, Lombardy, the Italian Switzerlands, Ligury, the Nordwest of Tuscany, Emilia-Romagna, St Marino and the North of the Marches. The Veneto region is again excluded from Heraud's classification of *ethnic* minorities in Northern Italy (Heraud, 1993, p. 46). The contemporary exclusion of the Venetian region is somehow surprising, since Veneto is the Italian region where the regional dialect is mostly used (Istat, 1995). During the 1990s Veneto became one of the most autonomist region in Italy. Heraud excluded Veneto as part of an homogenous Northern Italy stressing that the center of political mobilisation was in the capital of Lombardy, Milan (Heraud, 1993, p. 48). Second, we cannot explain why claims of nationhood emerged in the absence of *ethnic* potential. Including Lega Nord as part of this family of political parties without addressing the nature of identity politics and the invention of Padania provides no analytical device to understand the nationalism of Lega Nord. Recognising that Lega Nord is the less *ethnic* of these nationalist parties (as De Winter correctly emphasise) leads us to explore differences between old and new politics of identity (De Winter and Türsan, 1998).

Ethnicity is often used as an apscriptive category (see Verkuyten, 1993)—in an evolutionary perspective in which race is substituted by ethnicity and the latter for culture. Moreover, as this book shows, *ethnicity* is also used with the particular meaning attached to one current within nationalism in Europe developed in the 1960s and 1970s by some movements and parties. In Basque nationalism the distinction between nation and *ethnie* marked in fundamental ways the departure of a new Basque nationalism, following theories on *ethnism*, in contrast to the traditional ideological basis traditionally by the PNV. *Regionalism* is not deprived either from specific political meaning. It distinguishes for instance, the family of traditional *peripheral* nationalisms in the Spanish state, and those regionalisms of more recent birth, such as the Partido Andalucista, Partido Aragones Regionalista or Union Valenciana in the Spanish party system.

The impact of the second wave of ethno-territorial mobilisation showed widespread variation across European polities. Overall, as Urwin noted, the *ethnic* wave of the 1970s was rather marginal in electoral terms. Although in the U.K., political parties such as the Scotish National Party was very successful for the first time in its history during the 1970s, in France the Breton movements remained outside the electoral arena (Berger, 1977).

A common assumption in academic writing is that this family of political parties relies fundamentally on cultural demands and traditional ideologies are of minor importance to explain their politics. Müller-Rommel, for example, excludes anti-migrant and fascist parties from the family of *ethnoregionalists*. However, this exclusion is not historically accurate. Flemish and Breton fascist parties emerged in the 1930s. Moreover, his framework excludes in principle one of the political parties in Western Europe, Lega Nord, which is characterised by anti-migrant rhetoric (although there is a chapter on Lega Nord in the same volume edited by De Winter and Tursan).

The different trajectories of peripheral nationalism in European party systems cannot be studied without addressing how ideological differences have played a major role in political competition, providing left versions of nationalist parties (in socialist or Marxist form) and conservative or right-wing versions. The fundamental differences between the two moments of identity mobilisation in European party systems, the 1970s and the past decade, lies in the political and historical context in which new movements and parties emerge and major ideological shifts in European polities. In the 1970s, *ethnicist* theories and *internal colonialism* became part of a new political discourse against imperialism and national liberation and resistance. At stake in the 1990s is a reformulation of cultural collective differences in the form of a European identities, national identities and alternative cultures across European states. The redefinition of cultural groups is inextricably linked to alternative visions of state and market and the scope and depth of the welfare state.

Müller-Rommel rightly distinguishes between the rise and the success of these parties as two separate research questions. He links party success with the emergence of a new cleavage dimension shaped by post-materalist values. The relationship between the electoral potential of these parties as reservoir for votes and the 'collective identity mood' mentioned by Müller-Rommel is unclear. Since the 1970s many studies have shown the extent to which *multiple* or *dual* identifications (in contrast to exclusive identities) are pervasive and need to be reintroduced in the analysis of party mobilisation and success. Empirical analysis about collective identification and voting behavior shows variations in the relationship between self-identification and voting patterns: we can study the extent to which voters are able to shift their votes between different parties and/or elections. Unfortunately, Müller-Rommel offers no analytical tools to explore systematically how identity mobilisation, collective identification and electoral volatility affect the success or failure of these parties in contemporary European party systems.

The Rise of the New Right in European Party Systems

Over the past decade, scholars have studied the rise of a new family of parties in Europe: the alternatively labelled new radical right, populist or extreme right. In his influential and yet much contested analysis of the new radical right, Kitschelt and McGann identified the sources of this new type of political mobilisation in the crisis produced by the transformation of European economies. As Kitschelt and McGann put it:

> The contemporary extreme Right develops in an era of socioeconomic dislocation due to a structural change in production systems, the internationalization of economic competition, and the crisis of the welfare state ... The crisis of the 1980s and 1990s has very uneven effects sectorally and geographically. While some occupational groups, sectors and regions continue to thrive, others within the same countries are caught up in a structural crisis (1995, p. 39).

For Kitschelt, the European new radical right (NRR) is 'commonly associated with two political issues that have become salient since the 1970s and 1980s: the revolt against higher taxes, and the rejection of immigrants from non-Occidental cultures, nationalities and ethnicities' (Kitschelt and McGann, 1995, pp. 19-29). The list includes The National Front parties in Britain, France and Wallonia, the Progress parties in Denmark and Norway, or regional self-identifications in Flanders (Vlaams Blok) and Italy (Lega Nord).

Economic crisis brings about a 'climate of resentment and alienation' permeating Western Europe during the last decade (Betz, 1994, p. 4). The crisis of post-fordism creates a new spatial dimension for electoral competition in European party systems. This dimension has two aspects: economically leftist (redistributive) and politically culturally libertarian (participatory and individualist) positions at one extreme, and economically rightist, free-marketeering as well as political and culturally authoritarian positions at the other (Kitschelt, 1995). In contrast other scholars situate the rise of these parties in the cleavage between materialist and postmaterialist values (Ignazi, 1992; Swyngedouw, 1993).

The demand for authoritarian and rightist parties is not evenly distributed across the population. Kitschelt claims that the demand for this right-wing politics appears in social groups characterised by 'distinctive experiences and deprivations of life chances' (Kitschelt, 1995, p. 5). The electoral success of the new right in Europe is fundamentally associated with losers' constituencies in post-industrial societies.

Beyond the competing values advanced by the new left and the new right, the type of political organisations and styles of mobilisation involved in the New Right are the polar opposite of the democratic and participatory features that characterised the New Left (Kitschelt, 1995, p. 22). These new party organisations have distinctive traits in the form of authoritarian and charismatic leadership.

Kitschelt has provided a typology to assess the differences within the family of new right wing parties in appeals, class composition and attitudes. Kitschelt considers that both Lega Nord and Austria's Freedom party belong to a distinctive category within the extreme right, that of the populist antistatist party.[10] These parties are characterised by their 'appeals directed against big government and the political class' (Kitschelt and McGann, 1995, p. 21). The subtype of populist anti-statist parties is characterised by the moderation of party elites and voters in their attitudes against migrants. Austrian and Italian populist parties can form broader 'negative electoral coalitions' characterised by the mixed composition of their electorates, the result of a political opportunity structure that favors rhetoric against the state and traditional parties. What accounts for the success of the populist antistatist party and makes this strategy an 'electoral winning formula' is the presence of a critical variable, *partitocrazia* or partocracy.[11]

In contrast, some authors consider Lega Nord as a typical example of a new populist right-wing party (Betz, 1994), and others, such as Biorcio, bring together under the label populism the main characteristics of new radical right-wing and Kitschelt's 'populist antistatist' parties (Biorcio, 1991; 1997). Table 1.3 shows how Kitschelt, Biorcio and Betz characterise the supply and demand for Lega Nord.

Table 1.3 New Right, Neopopulism or Populist Anti-Statist?

	Kitschelt	**Biorcio**	**Betz**
Party Label	Populist Anti-Statist	Neopopulist	New Radical Right
Critical Explanatory Variable	Partocracy	Crisis of welfare state	Crisis of welfare state
Demand	A white-collar middle class revolt	Losers' constituencies: Petit bourgeoisie and blue-collar workers	Losers' constituencies: Petit bourgeoisie and blue-collar workers
Supply	Clean government on occasion cater to racist and xenophobic sentiments	Migrants and Taxes	Migrants and Taxes

Source: Kitschelt, 1995; Biorcio, 1991; 1997; Betz, 1994

As the table shows, these authors have different assessments of the supply offered by Lega Nord. Kitschelt's subtype of new populist and anti-statist parties emphasises the moderation of anti-migrant rhetoric. Betz and Biorcio, in contrast, see little variation in the appeals of the party leadership and focus on the centrality of migrants and taxes in the success of Lega Nord.

Kitschelt characterises the success of Lega Nord as a middle class revolt. Biorcio argues that the electoral constituencies of Lega Nord are the 'typical constituencies of neopopulist parties', that is, the petit bourgeoisie and blue-collar workers, yet he has also emphasised the inter-classist nature of Lega Nord's voters (Biorcio, 1997, p. 25). Biorcio also emphasises that the importance of blue-collar workers in the composition of Lega Nord's electoral constituency has been increasing.[12] Already in 1994, survey research showed that workers were the largest component of Lega Nord's electoral support.[13] Thus, by Kitschelt's own criteria, Lega Nord could also be considered as part of other subtypes of the new radical right-wing family, such as the so-called welfare chauvinist party (as Tarchi does in the volume edited by De Winter and Tursan, 1998).

These authors also present different assessments of the relevance of the anti-migrant position of Lega Nord. Kitschelt asserts that the elites and voters of these parties are more moderate on the question of migration, *on occasion* catering to racist and xenophobic sentiments. Biorcio, in contrast, linked the rise of Lega Nord exclusively with the ability of the party to cater to racism—the first party in mobilising against migrants from outside the European community (Biorcio, 1991). Survey data also shows that Lega Nord's voters take a clear and negative position against migrants from outside the European Community. While Lega Nord shares with the new-right wing European parties an emphasis on immigration control, Lega is not the only Italian party that has mobilised against migrants. The ex Movimento Sociale Italiano—today Alleanza Nazionale—also advocates the control of migration flows. The electorates of both parties also show the same negative attitudes towards new immigrants (Biorcio, 1997, p. 158).

Lega Nord has mobilised both against Southerners and new migrants. According to Biorcio, there is a substitution effect in the anti-migrant rhetoric that accounts for Lega Nord's success: the *outsider* was initially the Southerner, but Lega Nord shifted this early emphasis to politicise the question of new migrants in Italy. The Trento study conducted by Sniderman and his colleagues, highlights that prejudice against Southerns is as strong as prejudice against black migrants from Northern Africa and from Eastern Europe (Peri, 2000, pp. 274-275; Sniderman et al., 2000). Chapter 4 discusses Lega Nord's political mobilisation against migrants.

Analysing the rise and success of Lega Nord within the family of the new radical right parties has two main advantages. First, it emphasises the nature of Lega Nord as an anti-migrant party. Beyond the debates about whether this is a form of extreme right, populist or new radical right wing politics, one must address the question of the nature and relevance of the anti-migrant mobilisation to explain the rise and success of Lega Nord. Second, it provides an analytical framework to explain the new cleavage dimensions in European party systems. It offers a parsimonious theoretical model to understand the transformation of European electorates both in light of demand (changing attitudes) and supply (party strategies and political opportunity structures).

Including Lega Nord as party of the family of the new radical right, however, presents three main problems. First, the success of Lega Nord in the areas of the most recent Italian economic miracle cast some doubts on the explanatory power of crisis and social dislocation. It is not in the metropolitan but in the wealthy peripheral provinces of the North where Lega Nord obtains its best electoral results. Far from being hit by a structural crisis, these are thriving territorial economies successfully integrated in global markets. Lega's electoral success draws heavily from the wealthiest areas of Northern Italy, with very high-income rates, the lowest unemployment rates within Italy and a long-term absence of class polarisation. These are the areas of diffused industrialisation based on export-oriented small firms (Trigilia, 1994; Diamanti, 1993; 1996). Moreover, it is not in metropolitan areas—where the presence of migrants is concentrated—but in the small localities of the North—where the presence of migrants is minimal—that Lega Nord has obtained its electoral success (Diamanti, 1993, 1996).

Second, it neglects the question of identity politics. If Müller-Rommel excluded anti-migrant and fascist parties from the family of *ethnoregionalist* parties, scholars studying the new right in Europe emphasise the right-wing agenda of Lega Nord and regard the question of territorial identity as secondary.

Thus, the question of identity in the rise of political mobilisation in Northern Italy is treated as epiphenomenal to political conflict. Scholars drawing sharp distinctions between the ethno-territorial movements and parties in the 1970s and the current wave of territorial mobilisation built their arguments on the distinction between *ethnic* movements and *populist* movements. Thus, for Diani:

> ethno-nationalism and populism exhibited three main differences. First, while populism is characterized by its anti-elitism, ethno-nationalism is based on the resources of local elites. Second, while populism is indifferent to democratic procedures and one of its main feature is the importance of charismatic leadership, ethno-nationalism is not in its main principles, anti-democratic ... populism emphasizes external threats (foreigners, immigrants) while the emphasis of ethno-nationalism is on the ethnic group 'positive diversity' (1993, p. 183).

Many scholars commonly treat the two moments of identity as fundamentally separated by the consideration that the claims for protection and autonomy from the central state in the 1960s and 1970s reflected *ethnic, authentic* identities, and the egoist, racist and xenophobic backlash of the 1990s reflects *invented, populist* identities (Melucci and Diani, 1992). This distinction is based on the *authencity* and *invention* of identity. Thus, typologies are created under the assumption that the differences reflect *substantial* differences in the nature of identity. The analyses, however, leave one central question unanswered. Why nationhood and why the North?

The distinction between ethnonationalism and populism is—as Balibar points out—more factual than analytical (Balibar, 1991). The use of the label populism has three main conceptual problems. First, in the 1970s, populism is associated with *peripheral* nationalism with a very different meaning, in that uneven development and mass politics define a new space for nationalism (Nairn, 1977). Scholars writing within this tradition use the term populism indistinctively to refer to populism as a type of nationalism, and populism as a style of mobilisation (Biorcio, 1991; 1997; Kitschelt, 1995). But they are not the same thing. Third, in Italy the label populist has been used to describe not only Lega Nord, but also Berlusconi's Forza Italia.

The question of identity politics is commonly dismissed on the grounds that the Padania is an *invention* of Lega Nord. Since scholarly work has explored nations as inventions, artifacts of human construction (Gellner, 1983; Hobsbawm, 1990; Anderson, 1991), the question of invention has to be reframed. The claims of nationhood advanced by Lega Nord are invention, funny and/or ridiculous, but they are also a central element both in the genesis of the party and in the strategies of party elites. In short, at the core of Lega Nord's politics is a nationalism that is left unexplained. The anti-tax, anti-party rhetoric and the anti-migrant remarks were filtered through the symbolic construction of a territorial identity. What gave unity to the party in the midst of the substantial political shifts during the 1990s was the politicisation of the Northern question, as the party leadership adapted strategically to different political opportunity structures in the Italian party system. In this book these analytical steps are reversed. First, the question of new peripheral nationalism is explained to explain why new demands of political and cultural recognition. Then, its articulation with old and new politics—whether left or right, whether Green or new radical right—is then analysed.

Finally, under the label of the extreme-right, scholars emphasise the existence of a new spatial dimension of electoral competition. Fenemma has called for efforts to reconceptualise the use of the labels, whether populism, racism or extreme-right (Fennema, 1997). Conceptual problems are particularly salient in the Italian case. Those who include Lega Nord as part of a populist wave, downplay the extent to which new party formations— Forza Italia and Alleanza Nazionale—competed with Lega Nord on the same issues (anti-establishment, free market policies, and the control of migration flows) potentially depriving Lega Nord from its electoral space. Thus, some scholars include Lega Nord as the right-wing populist party in Italy and others, in contrast, considered Alleanza Nazionale as the case in point.

Peripheral Nationalism Reframed

This book studies a controversial new political party, Lega Nord—its genesis, its instrumental uses of ethnicity, nation and culture as a collective attribute, and its style of mobilisation—to explore a new identity politics in contemporary Europe. My analysis of Lega Nord is an inquiry about two main questions. First, I ask why and how nationhood as a collective representation becomes an organisational principle of political action and party formation in contemporary European politics. Second, the study seeks to uncover the ways in which territory, identity and interests are linked in new political mobilisation. Thus, rather than taking groups or minorities as my unit of analysis, the study focuses on how political processes shape the definition and representation of collectivities. This book seeks also to put party mobilisation in Northern Italy in comparative perspective. What follows is an effort to provide the main analytical tools to explain the Italian case within a larger European framework.

Lega Nord's identity politics lie in the uncomfortable boundary between traditional conceptions of *ethnonationalism* and the *populism* of the new right. The book treats political mobilisation in the Northern Italian regions as a political experiment in which political actors used and tried different categorical identities. More importantly, the rise of Lega Nord and the institutionalisation of the North-South territorial divide in Italian politics illustrate a transition in peripheral nationalism in European party systems. The rise of Lega Nord brings together the mobilisation of old *ethnic* (national) minorities in European states and the contemporary political struggle that involves the inclusion and exclusion of new *ethnic* (migrant) minorities in Europe. In short, Lega Nord's *double membership* in these two party families is examined here.

In this book identity is decoupled from any specific content—*ethnicity*. I draw on recent contributions to the study of nationalism and suggest that territorial identities—a subtype of national identities—are historically constructed. Rather than taking identities as given and necessary conditions for political mobilisation, here the causality is reversed by taking the construction of new categorical identities as the outcome of political mobilisation. Identities are not exogenous to the model but are endogenously determined in the political process. Moreover, identity—a territorial identity—is treated not as an ontological reality (a fixed condition of individuals and collectivities) but as a constructed one (a contextually defined and situated definition of individuals and collectivities). This assumption does not imply that there are no pre-existing objective or subjective differences (whether cultural, or economic) in society. It merely states that politics is a major factor in the construction of categories in historical processes.

Constructivist approaches to the study of nationalism have completely modified the terms of traditional debates on *ethnic* groups and nations (Bordieu, 1978; Brubaker, 1996). In these views, identities are not ethnic and identity formation is not about the activation of pre-existing objective differences embedded in a group. Instead of ethnic or primordial, identity is a set of ideas and perceptions about one's belonging to a collectivity. Identities are modern historical constructions in which collective myths, cultures and traditions are made. For constructivist approaches, the traditional analyses of *ethnicity* present a fundamentally a-historical view of processes of identity formation and reproduce the basic claims and ideologies of the parties themselves—a self-representation of the nation or ethnic identity as natural, essential and pre-existing, rewriting the past as a historical precedent to explain present nationhood (Handler, 1988). *Nations* are represented as 'bounded, continuous and homogeneous unit' (Handler, 1988, p. 32).[14]

In contrast, the analytical focus is no longer on nations as substantial entities, but as practical categories (Brubaker, 1996, p. 7). Here cultural differences are no longer objective and substantial but *institutional* and *discursive* (Brubaker, 1996; Bourdieu, 1991). The main implication from this approach is that the politics of identity can be analysed without assuming or dealing with the existence of social groups. In contrast to theories advanced by authors such as Hetcher, or more recently Laitin (1998) in his study of the Russian-Speaking minorities in the ex-Soviet states, this understanding allows the study of categorical identities without the neccesary addition of a theory of the formation of *ethnic* groups. As Calhoun puts it, 'most identity politics involves claims about categories of individuals who putatively share a given identity ... categorical identities can be invoked and given public definition by individuals or groups even where they are not embodied in concrete networks of direct interpersonal relationships' (Calhoun, 1996, p. 26). Thus, the study of the formation and use of categorical identities acquires an independent status in the study of nationalism, providing a solid ground to conduct comparative analysis.

Institutional Analyses and Nationalism

Brubaker considers the nation the main lever for reimagining and reorganising political space since the XIX century (Brubaker, 1996). The emergence of a world-system that institutionalises in international legal provisions the nation as the basic political unit with legitimacy in world politics explains the *structuring power* of this category. Institutional approaches to the study of nationalism seek to explore the role of institutions—in the form of institutional designs, state structures and systems of recognition—as structure of incentives and frameworks with unintended consequences. As Brubaker has shown in the case of the ex Soviet Union, the availability of *ethnicity* and *nationhood* as categories upon which rights are granted provides a *structure of incentives* for new political entrepreneurs to mobilise on cultural and national differences.

The principle of congruence between a territory, a people and a culture is encoded and institutionalised in the international system and provides the legitimacy to claim self-government and political autonomy (Brubaker, 1996; Soysal, 1996). It is upon this principle that nationalism is defined as a theory of political legitimacy holding that the nation and the state should be congruent (Gellner, 1983; Hobsbawm, 1990). Although nation and state are in social science distinctive analytical categories (Weber, Linz, 1967), they are brought together because the principle of congruence is *normative* and not sociological (Soysal, 1996; Brubaker, 1996). *Peripheral* or sub-state nationalism deconstructs the category of nation-states to reproduce the principle of congruence at the sub-national level. The same principle of legitimacy sustains competing alternative claims of congruence between the political and the cultural unit at different levels.

West European states are bounded by both national and international norms for the protection of minorities. In pluralist democracies identity as a categorical statement about one's belonging provides the basis to claim rights and the legitimacy to make social, cultural and economic demands. Since the 1970s European states have accommodated in some form demands for recognition of ethnic and cultural pluralism within their boundaries. Official categories operate as a system of institutionalised differences coupling a collectivity with a culture and a territory. Official categories are not random, but they are arbitrary and reflect the political and institutional conditions of polities (Soysal, 1996). 'Ethnic minorities', 'linguistic minorities', or 'national minorities' *are* different among themselves because they are defined in European states with different criteria to achieve distinctiveness. Whether we identify these collectivities as *ethnic* minorities or groups, national minorities or nations, depends on the different systems of institutional recognition that crystallise the categories and establish the principles of collective and group membership.

In short, institutional systems are explored as independent and/or intervening variables in the rise of nationalism. The transformation of centralised states into regionalised or federal systems in Western Europe in the last wo decades partially reflected the demands of national minorities, but it has also created a political dynamic of its own, they operate as structures of incentives for new claims of recognition. Thus, as we will see, one of the unintended consequences of institutional recognition is that it creates incentives for new political actors to mobilise.

Discursive Practices and Types of Claims

New approaches have also shifted the analytical focus to an understanding of how the categories of *ethnicity* and *nation* become discursive practices and structure social and political interaction (Calhoun, 1994; Herzfeld, 1992). As a political discourse, categorical identities introduce a language that draws boundaries and locates oneself but also locates others as insiders and outsiders (Balibar, 1991). As Herzfeld puts it, the 'dialectics of differentiation' constructs meaning by setting up differences and oppositions (Herzfeld, 1992). Categories of belonging define boundaries of inclusion and exclusion in the collectivity (Balibar, 1986). According to Herzfeld, 'nationalist ideologies are systems of classification .... which define who is an insider and who is an outsider. This system of classification provides a simplification and remaking of an entire people as a unity' (Herzfeld, 1992, p. 109-111).

Identity politics is about boundary-drawing between groups. In the definition of a collectivity, both the markers and the content of cultural difference move center stage. Categories of belonging developed in interaction. Anthropological and sociological accounts tend to place identity formation within group processes. While *ethnicists* are trapped in identity as other-defined, constructivists in turn emphasise identity as self-defined. Yet, categorical identities develop in the interaction that locates *us* and *them* (Barth, 1968).[15] The question of identity as self-defined or other-defined also moves center stage.

The introduction of new categories of belonging is contested and contentious. The politics of identity is about the existence or not of collective differences and their political recognition. Moving beyond debates on identities as *authentic* or *invented*, here we treat authenticity and invention as constituent elements shaping the political struggle for legitimacy and recognition of collectivities. In this struggle, existing institutionalised categories are presented as historical contingencies. New categorical claims, instead, are *essentialised* in political discourse. Beyond authenticity and invention as an institutionalised form, what makes identity categories *real* is their official recognition, whether by international agencies or by state constitutional and legal provisions. Thus, official recognition provides us with a first criterium to define what is legitimate and real, as opposed to invented. Real or fake, authentic or invented, are qualifications attached by observers and experts. Ultimately, as Murray Edelman points out:

> whatever seems real to a group of people is real in its political consequences regardless of how absurd, hallucinatory or shocking it may look to others in different situations or at other times ... People act within the realities they construct for themselves, not in that of a social observer who constructs herself as 'objective' or scientific (1985, pp. 198-199).

Although historical and political processes reify collective differences, paradoxically, the relevance of agency is obscured by the nature of *essentialism*. Discursive practices present as natural and self-evident the consideration of national units as homogeneous and pre-existing, denying the role of agency itself in their construction. As Herzfeld states: 'the distinctive mark of essentialism ... lies in its suppression of temporality: it assumes or attributes an unchanging, primordial ontology to what are the historically contingent products of human or other forms of agency. It is thus also a denial of the relevance of agency itself' (Hertzfeld, 1996, p. 188). Any identity is legitimised in political discourses by the *essentialisation* of differences that are embedded in a collectivity. Thus, while identities are constructed in historical processes, they are presented as essential and natural (Handler, 1992).

Casting the production of Lega Nord as an invention prevents us from exploring what differences exist between past and new constructions. Since sociological and anthropological analyses consider *all* identities as human constructions, we need to explore the *extent of* construction of Padania and the processes that 'make a difference' in the politics of identity and diversity. In contemporary political mobilisation, territorial identities are constructed upon new markers. The main novelties are in the uncertainties upon which the collectivity is defined and the introduction of new differences which are *essentialised*, not only the traditional *ethnic* ones, but also economic and social differences which are reinterpreted as cultural ones. The contemporary unraveling of politics has an impact on classificatory systems. New self-definitions and self-representation are changing the discourses of nationalism. In the contemporary transformation of European politics, the old idea of the nation serves political entrepreneurs for collective boundary drawing to redefine insiders and outsiders.

This book shows the genesis of new political parties in Northern Italy fundamentally and the influence of one specific variant within nationalism, that of the *ethnism* developed in the 1970s by groups and movements across Europe, and the *thirldworldism* typical of the same period. Taking the type of claims as its starting point, the book shows the ways in which new classificatory systems were developed in Northern Italy, and alternative cultures defined and represented since the 1970s.

Political parties claiming the rights for national minorities in European party systems exhibit a striking ideological malleability and floating position with regard to the main dimensions of conflict in European polities (Urwin, 1982). Over time and across space, territorial claims are adapted to different ideological currents. The de-colonisation experience during the 1960s provided a new set of ideas about the position of territorial minorities vis-a-vis central governments. *Thirldworldism* gave new movements an interpretation of political and economic events that explains *ethnic* oppression as a product of internal colonialism. In contrast, the current wave of regional political mobilisation has incorporated the ideological currents and recent debates in European polities. The erosion of welfare state arrangements, the concern with redistributive issues and taking the state out reinforces a neoliberal shift of regionalist parties. Moreover, the impact of fiscal regimes on economic competition and the transformation of existing economic systems provided the context for new regional grievances of the 1990s. Finally, the prospective winners and losers of the process of European integration shape the new demands and programs of regionalist parties.

The position of sub-state nationalist parties in European party systems was originally represented by Lipset and Rokkan with a two dimensional space. One dimension of political space refers to cultural and identity issues: whether broad or narrow versions of nationalism exists; the kind of representations of the collectivity and culture as an attribute. Mobilising on differences is about constructing differences, sameness and diversity within a bounded territory. While boundaries—whether territorially or socially defined—are fuzzy and the content of identity is malleable, the basic claim is a clear-cut distinction between *us* and *them*, and thus, is about creating and enforcing collective boundaries. A second dimension of political space relates to broader conflicts and can be generally represented as the classical traditional left-wing dimension. Alternatively, new cleavages in European party systems are also represented on a vertical dimension (Kitschelt, 1995; Swyngedouw, 1993). The study of the ideological orientations within this family of parties allow us to map ideological differences along the left and right wing dimension, as well as to locate parties along the new cleavage configuration in European party systems.

The literature on *ethnoregionalist* party tends to work under the implicit assumption that there is one political party for each *ethnic* minority, while arguably competition within the sector and patterns of electoral competition play a large role in providing a structure of opportunities for success and failure. It is a common fallacy to identify one party with one minority, while the presence of one single party is a special case, rather than the rule. The mapping out of the nationalist 'sector'—both in its ideological and organisational dimension is crucial to understand patterns of electoral success and failure.

Anti-Migrant Parties and the New Racism in Europe

One of the basic features of the alternatively labeled new radical right, new populist right or new extreme right family of political parties is the presence of a common element: anti-migrant rhetoric. However, beyond the recognition of an anti-migrant agenda, scholars provide different answers to two main questions. First, there are contrasting views about the relative importance of anti-migrant rhetoric in the ideologies and programs of these political parties and the extent to which these parties can be considered 'racist' parties (Mudde, 1995, 2000; Swyngedouw, 1995, 1997). The label *racist* is maintained for those stressing the evolution of traditional biological racism into a new racism that appears without the label *race* (Fenemma, 1997). Second, there are also visible changes in public opinion with regard to attitudes against migrants (Swngedouw, 1995; Van Der Burg, Fennema and Tillie, 2000). During the past decade, the rise of political parties denouncing the 'dangers' of migrants' invasion into Europe was also accompanied by the spread of negative attitudes towards migrants and the electoral success of new right wing parties. However, neither all anti-migrant parties have been successful in European party systems, nor the relationship between the rise of anti-migrant parties and the increase in negative attitude towards migrants is a clear-cut one.

Conceptually, as TerWal and Verkuyten stress, 'a distinction between racism, prejudice, xenophobia and anti-Semitism is based upon comparisons within a more abstract category such as the construction, portrayal, and treatment of a negative "racial" or ethnic out-group' (TerWal and Verkuyten, 2000, p. 9). In comparative research we can assess the form or articulation of racism in the concrete local, national or historical circumstances and the relative importance of distinctions within an abstract category: the construction of *otherness*.

In studying the relationship between political mobilisation and prejudice, a main distinction is introduced between those scholars that consider the rise of prejudice as an elite-driven process—a function of political manipulation—and those that consider the rise of prejudice as a social process in which political parties only express socially-shared attitudes about migrants. For Van Dijk, 'Bias, stereotyping, and outright ethnic polarisation in the media is the product of journalists, or of the politicians they use as reliable sources, and hence, also an elite phenomenon. The same is true for biased text books and scholarly research' (Van Dijk, 1998, p. 176). If Van Dijk is a clear example of an approach that emphasises the role of political elites, other scholars have broadened the scope of actors and actions involved in racism. Racism has a multi-faceted nature in contemporary Europe (TerWal and Verkuyten, 2000). As Balibar states:

> racism, a true 'total social phenomenon', inscribes itself in practices (forms of violence, contempt, intolerance, humiliation and exploitation), in discourses and representations which are so many intellectual elaborations of the phantasm of prophylaxis or segregation (the need to purify the social body, to preserve 'one's own' or 'our' identity from all forms of mixing, interbreeding or invasion in

which are articulated around stigmata of otherness (name, skin colour, religious practices) (Balibar, 1991, pp. 17-18).

The extent to which the process is elite-driven or social prejudices are given is a research question on its own. Political parties are chanels for the expression of socially-shared prejudices, but also active participants in the definition, construction and reproduction of otherness in the political arena. Despite the pervasiveness of racism in a variety of social and political contexts, here we narrow the focus to the role of political parties in the expression, active production and reproduction of prejudices. The new radical right wing parties provides an avenue to express—but also to shape in new ways—attitudes against migrants.

Scholars introduce a distinction between ideological racism and everyday or common racism. As Balibar points out, 'racist thinking does not always assume a systematic form' (Balibar, 1991, p. 54). The expression of prejudices against other groups does not *per se* constitute an ideology: only the articulation of a coherent set of political principles and axioms permits the identification of an ideological system. Although we can observe the emergence of a set of recurrent statements and themes in political mobilisation against migrants, their elaboration into an systematic ideology about collective differences cannot be taken for granted. However, it should also be stressed that the representation of 'others' with commonsensical statements is instrumental: a strategy to define those expressions as part of a common language diffused and shared in society.

During the past decade two main novelties in the relationship between politics and prejudice emerged: the politicisation of the question of migration in European countries, and the development of new ideologies about collective differences, the by now well-known *cultural differentialism*. As Fennema points out, there have been major problems in the conceptualisation of anti-immigrant parties (Fennema, 1997). Anti-migrant parties are sometimes wrongly characterised as 'single-issue' parties (DerBrug, Fennema and Tillie, 2000). Fennema introduced a typology to distinguish between protest parties, racist parties and extreme-right parties. Protest parties are anti-party and anti-establishment, racist parties are single-issue parties and extreme-right parties provide an ideological articulation of specific themes: *ethnic* nationalism, anti-materialism, anti-democratic and conspiration theory (Fennema, 1997). Mudde has recently rejected racism as a distinctive feature of this family of parties, yet he included xenophobia and anti-migrant rhetoric in their core ideology. The parties included in his study did not formally use the word *race*. Mudde shows the absence of an openly expressed belief in hierarchy of races and anti-semitism is clearly visible in the case of German parties but not in Flemish or Dutch parties (Mudde, 2000, p. 172).

In his study of the ideology of the extreme-right in Europe, Mudde finds out that

> most attention in the xenophobic party literature is paid to the threat of (mass) immigration and the creation of a multi-cultural society. All parties portray an image of a flow of immigrants which is out of control and which is kept hidden by the 'Establishment'. Immigrants are seen as competitors, since they take away jobs, money and houses from the 'own people'. They are also linked to every other threat or problem in the country ... such as rising crime and moral decay (Mudde, 2000, p. 173).

Although Mudde prefers the label *xenophobic*, other scholars retain the label *racist* to describe the same 'anti-migrant rhetoric. The main features of the new racism in the construction of the 'other' replicate old models without the explicit recognition of race as a collective marker. Scholars identify in the theory of cultural incompatibility the modern version of racism (Balibar, 1991; Fenema, 1997). The distinguising features and what marks this theory as explicity *racist* derives from the use of culture as a *quasi-biological* attribute. As Etienne Balibar puts it:

> It is a racism whose dominant theme is not a biological heredity but the insurmountability of cultural differences, a racism, which at first sight, does not postulate the superiority of certain groups or peoples in relation to others but 'only' the harmfulness of abolishing frontiers, the incompatiblity of life-styles and traditions; in short, it is what P.A. Taguieff has rightly called a *differentialist* racism (Balibar, 1991, p. 21).

The other central element in racist thinking is the establishment of hierarchies with the attribution of negative features to other groups. Balibar highlights a reworking of old hierarchies: the presentation of a main division of humanity in two groups: 'one assumed to be universalistic and progressive, the other irremediably particularistic and primitive' (Balibar, 1991, p. 25).

Two considerations about conceptualisation are made in advance. First, the category of *racism* is also used as a political tool given its negative connotations. As Fennema points out, 'the concept of racism is highly loaded. To be called racist has seriuos political, if not legal consequences' (Fennema, 1997, p. 474). Second, anti-migrant parties have a 'spoiled identity', they are stigmatised by political elites with accusations of racism and mainstream parties refuse—individually or collectively—to form political and electoral alliances with these parties (Van der Brug, Fennema and Tillie, 2000, p. 82).

In exploring the relationship between politics and different forms of prejudice, the role of different actors should be kept distinctive (party elites, party militants and voters), as well as the different levels in which discourse and representation take place (party documents, party programs and public speeches). In this book the relationship between the expression of prejudice in forms and style (party moblisation) and the political construction of otherness in party ideology is analysed. We distinguish between anti-migrant political parties, public opinion and attitudes towards migrants, and more strictly speaking 'racist' or anti-migrant voters. We focus on party leaders because as Fennema points out, 'party leaders integrate the different elements of a political discourse into a logical coherent political ideology' (Fennema, 1997, p. 486).

Political Processes and Identity Politics

Studying ethnicity and nationalism in party mobilisation, this book seeks to explain first, the introduction of new ideas about collective belonging, and second, why and how identity politics moves from a marginal and neglected issue in political mobilisation to become part of mainstream politics. The approach followed here focuses on three analytical steps: the structure of incentives that lead to new mobilisation; the timing and sequence of mobilisation; and the political opportunity structures that allowed the advancement of new claims. The emphasis on the political processes involved in the politicisation of new national demands allow us to acomplish two main goals. First, analytically, the strenght of territorial identifications, sentiments or grievances is decoupled from its direct 'translation' into political outcomes. The focus is primarily on processes, actors and strategies, and only secondarily on the intensity of feelings or grievances. For example, institutional properties of the French state and French party system go a long way towards explaining why Breton, Occitan and Corsican parties are minor players in French politics as measured exclusively by electoral success. In the Italian case, we will see how, regardless of the potential of the Veneto region as a site for successful new party mobilisation, the timing and sequence of mobilisation tied the fate of the first Venetian parties to the broader Lega Nord, later undermining efforts of territorial mobilisation during the 1990s in Veneto. Thus, the construction of cultural differences is inserted in specific historical and political process.

Second, political processes mediate between ideas and political outcomes. Categories of ethnicity, nationhood and race are articulated in different contexts in distinctive ways. This book seeks to illuminate the concrete processes through which certain ideas about collective identity— and not others—came to dominate political discourse (Thelen and Steinmo,

1992). As Thelen and Steinmo argue, exogenous changes can produce shifts in the goals or strategies being pursued within existing institutions, shaping new outcomes as old actors adopt new goals (Thelen and Steinmo, 1992, p. 17). Recent scholarship on historical institutionalism emphasises the importance of timing and sequence to explain divergent political outcomes in comparative analyses (Thelen and Steinmo, 1993). The central claim here is that specific patterns of timing and sequence in political mobilisation matter. Under the label of path dependency, social and political theory explain different trajectories in economic—industrialisation—and political processes—nation and state formation (Lipset and Rokkan, 1967). Paul Pierson conceptualises path dependence—political development punctuated by critical moments or junctures which shape social life—as a process better defined as 'increasing returns' (Pierson, 1997: 1). As Pierson writes:

> The investigation of increasing returns can provide a more rigorous framework for developing some of the key claims of recent scholarship in historical institutionalism: that specific patterns of timing and sequence matter; that a wide range of social outcomes are often possible; that large consequences may result from relatively small and contingent events; that particular courses of action, once introduced, can be virtually impossible to reverse; and that consequently, political development is punctuated by critical moments or junctures which shape the basic contours of social life (Pierson, 1997, p. 1)

Processes of political mobilisation and party formation are characterised by entry or start-up costs. Collective action is the solution as well as the problem to solve by new political entrepreneurs. Cooperation and coordination help to overcome entry-costs. In the sequence and timing of political mobilisation that redefined the dimensions of electoral competition in the Italian party system, the dynamics of collective action—the cooperative strategies of the party leaders in the Northern regions—defined the future politics of territorial conflict in Northern Italy. The construction of the Northern question was open-ended, small events—a forgotten pact between party leaders in a small town of Northern Italy—had large consequences for explaining the trajectory of territorial conflict in Northern Italy. The fall of the Berlin Wall was the exogenous factor that marked the disarray of traditional electoral alignments in the Italian party system. Increasing returns of self-reinforcing patterns implied that the trajectory of political change took a specific pattern that, once introduced, was very difficult to reverse.

New Party Mobilisation: Styles of Mobilisation and Organisation

Explaining party formation—its genesis, ideological evolution and organisational resources, this book follows a traditional approach to study party politics. However, it also seeks to apply new tools to study party mobilisation. Debates in the literature conceive social movements and political parties as different types of political actors. Scholars distinguish between social movements and political parties along the lines of a *functional* division of labor. For Kriesi,

> Parties and interest groups are specialized in political representation. They have sufficient amounts of resources—in particular, institutionalized access, authority, and expertise—which means that they normally do not have to have recourse to the mobilization of their constituents. While parties and interests groups also mobilize their constituencies from time to time, this is not essential to their activities, which are typically carried out by an elite. Moreover, this mobilization usually takes place within established routines (Kriesi, 1996, p. 153).

For new political parties, however, mobilisation is essential. Thus, the book explores the rise of Lega Nord as a challenger to traditional Italian parties. Social movement's literature is better equipped to understand how new political actors mobilise. From current social movement theory, I borrow the three main concepts that are increasingly used in the political science literature: political opportunity structures, mobilising structures and frame alignment. The concept of political opportunity structure became a major contribution of theorists of political process. The idea is that collective mobilisation does not depend on the intensity of grievances, but on the changes in the institutional structure and power relations that affect the conditions for collective action (Doug McAdam, John D. McCarthy, Mayer N. Zald, 1996, p. 2). Mobilising structures refers to the organisations and networks that sustain collective action. Framing processes refer to the collective processes of interpretation, attribution, and social construction that mediate between opportunity and action. For McAdam, McCarthy and Zald, 'mediating between opportunity, organisation and action are the shared meanings and definitions that people bring to their situation' (McAdam, McCarthy and Zald, 1996, p. 5). The concept of political opportunity structure is often criticised for its lack of precision. As Gamson and Meyer point out, the concept of political opportunity structure, 'used to explain so much, it may ultimately explain nothing at all' (Gamson and Meyer, 1996, p. 275). Political opportunity structure is used in the literature as a set of independent variables—dynamic aspects of the political environment that change— as a holder for intervening variables—such as institutional structures and rules of representation—and as dependent variable. Here political opportunity structure is treated as an intervening variable (McAdam, McCarthy, Zald, 1996).[16] A restrictive definition of political opportunity structures along two dimensions is used here: the patterns of party competition and the rules of electoral representation (McAdam, McCarthy, Zald, 1996). The aim is to show the interaction of structure and agency, the opening and closing of political space with party's strategic choices.

Party Resources

While the erosion of mass party organisations has been analysed by many scholars, the ideal type of mass party still provides a yardstick to assess 'strong' or 'weak' party organisations: their organisational capacities and styles of societal penetration. Instead, here the focus is on two party resources: political partcipation and activism.

Political participation creates what Pizzorno defines as an 'area of equality', a system of political solidarity, and symbolic resources, a common collective. Identity and solidarity and normative considerations prevail over utilitarian ones. Collective identities are about the boundaries that separate *us* from *them*. Solidarity incentives are crucial to motivate people to participate in politics. Direct participation and membership in the party organisation also involves the adoption and use of party symbols. According to Kertzer, 'the individual comes to feel a part of a political organisation by adopting the symbols associated with it, but, just as important, he also comes to be recognised as a fellow member by others in the organisation' (Kertzer, 1988, p. 17). Commitment to the party organisation translates into a few main tasks that party members perform. Lange's study of Communist party sections in Italy distinguished between celebratory and proselytising tasks of local party sections (Lange, 1975). Kertzer's research on Communist and Catholics in a Bolognese neighborhood considered that both celebratory and proselytising tasks could be combined as basically the same (Kertzer, 1980).

Collective rituals are a specific type of political mobilisation. Rituals make people appear as a solidarity unit (Kertzer, 1988).[17] Rituals can be defined with Kertzer, as a 'means by which we express our social dependence, what is important in ritual is our common participation and emotional involvement, not the specific rationalisations by which we account for the rites' (Kertzer, 1988, p. 67). Rituals produce bonds of solidarity without requiring uniformity of belief and by representing the group as a solidarity unity (Kertzer, 1988, p. 67). Rituals work by providing structured and standardised sequences. They are enacted at certain places and times that are themselves endowed with special meaning. Ritual action is repetitive and redundant, but these factors serve, 'as important means of channeling emotion, guiding cognition and organising social groups' (Kertzer, 1995, p. 9).[18]

As Koopmans suggests in his study of political claims-making against racism in Germany and Britain, the success of challengers attempting to mobilise in the public sphere depends on their ability to achieve three strategic aims: visibility, resonance and legitimacy (Koopmans and Statham, 2000). As theatrical and dramatic events, rituals are effective to win media attention and political visibility (Gamson and Meyer, 1996, p. 288).

By challenging the political establishment with controversial statements Lega Nord achieved the party extensive media coverage. The content of what Lega Nord could not pass unnoticed, and obtained public reactions carrying the message to a wider public. The political symbolism of the movement focused on nationhood and democracy, providing media attention, legitimacy to movement participants and access to a wider public.

New political entrepreneurs focus on framing alternative understandings of politics.[19] Framing is a dynamic process and a collective endeavor. As Zald put it:

> framing contests occur in face-to-face interactions and through a variety of media—newspapers, books, pamphlets, radio, television. Movement activists may debate in coffeehouses, in bars, or in meeting halls, but they have to change and mobilize bystander publics, many of whom may only know of the movements and its issues as portrayed in various media (1996, p. 270).

As Snow and Benford state, 'by rendering events or occurrences meaningful, frames function to organise experience and guide action, whether individual or collective' (Snow and Benford, 1986, p. 464).[20] Objective conditions do not change so much. The real changes are in the way the situation is defined and experienced (Snow and Benford, 1986, p. 474).

Here we study symbolic resources to explain the mechanisms to achieve visibility, resonance and legitimacy. In particular the book shows how symbolic resources were used for challenging traditional understandings of political reality. As Laitin argues, this task requires both symbolic interpretations of meaning but also the systematic enumeration of political resources. Analysing political symbolism, we seek to re-introduce the importance of symbols in political manipulation. This task is necessary to explain party mobilisation, yet it departs from the mainstream agenda in political science[21] (Edelman, 1985).

Extra-institutional action is better than institutional action in creating controversy. The latter is, in turn, a way to gain visibility through the mass media. As Gamson and Meyer point out:

> Creating controversy is a way to increase opportunity by opening media access to movement spokespersons. Extrainstitutional action is better than institutional action in creating controversy. The more popular and visually oriented media in particular emphasize spectacle in collective action. Spectacle means drama and confrontation, emotional events with people who have fire in the belly, who are

extravagant and unpredictable. This puts a high premium on novelty, on costume and on confrontation (1996, p. 288).

For new resource-poor parties, the use of symbolic resources to create controversies provides the opportunity to gain mass coverage without mass mobilisation.[22]

The New Italian Party System and Electoral Change

This book concentrates on political mobilisation: party formation, style of mobilisation and party ideology. This book focuses on party leadership and party mobilisation—studying party resources and political participation. Although this book does not investigate the main characteristics of Lega Nord's voters, two questions must be mentioned. First, a label for a party leadership or a party program might or might not correspond to a label for the party voters. Typical of this scenario is the case of the Flemish Vlaams Blok (Swyngedouw, 1998). Party elites are described as 'racists', but not party voters (Swyngedouw, 1998). Second, during the 1990s several studies have address the question of 'protest' vote, providing a wealth of evidence to show that voters are rational in their party choices and party programs play a large role in explaining why people vote for these parties.This book places the emphasis on party mobilisation. The underlying assumption is that what new parties say and do to attract voters is very relevant. The explanation of the early electoral success of Lega Nord is *overdetermined* because of the presence of conjectural factors and a critical juncture that marked the collapse of Italian traditional parties in the midst of corruption scandals. Political protest played a central role in the first phase of expansion. However, the ability to create 'negative electoral coalitions' (in Kitschelt's formulation) might be considered a short-term effect for new parties. A decade after the events that led to the dissappearance of Italian traditional parties, Lega Nord has achieved a brandname among Northern Italian voters and despite common arguments about the disappearance of the party, they have retained an electoral base.

New parties do not simply adapt to changing divisions in the electorate, but actively participate in the forming of these divisions by politicising issues and molding public opinion (Iversen, 1994, p. 183). As Przeworski and Sprague, quoting Gramsci, we count votes at the end of the process:

> .... this is a process of creating images of society, of forging collective identities, of mobilizing commitments to particular projects for the future. Class, religion, ethnicity, race, or nation, do not happen spontaneously as reflections of objective conditions in the psyches of individuals. Collective identity, group

solidarity, and political commitment are continually transformed—shaped, destroyed, and molded anew—as a result of conflicts in the course of which political parties, schools, unions, churches, newspapers, armies, and corporations strive to impose a particular form of organization upon the life of society (1990: 8).

The presence of external political opportunity structures in European party systems is crucial to explain the rise of new political parties in the last two waves of *ethnic* political mobilisation in the 1970s and in the 1990s. 'Entry costs' in the political system are difficult to overcome but critical junctures offer the opportunity to redefine the main dimensions of political conflict.

The Argument in Brief

The book takes first the rise of Lega Nord and a united North, a categorical territorial identity as the dependent variable. The making of a united North—Padania is inserted within a larger context of moblisation of multiple territorial identities in Northern Italy. Rather than fostering *stereotypical* ideas about the territorial divide between North and South, this book shows the making of a united Italian North and Padania as the outcome of a process of political mobilisation. In contrast to the 'obviousness' of the translation of the territorial divide in Italy, the political exploitation of the North-South divide was a problematic political outcome. Moreover, the book shows— through variation in the electoral success of the party and the conflicts evolving around the definition of the territorial question—the profound *disunity* of the Italian North. The salience of the Northern question in Italy relied on the strategic efforts and manipulation of political entrepreneurs, not on a growing unsustainable gap between North and South.

Studying new political mobilisation in Northern Italy provides us with the unique opportunity to explore within-country comparisons. The rise of Lega Nord in Northern Italy is located within a larger framework to understand the wave of political mobilisation that preceded the rise of Lega Nord: the formation of regional parties in Veneto, Lombardy and Piedmont in the late 1970s and early 1980s. First, a comparison of the background conditions for regional political mobilisation—in the classical form of *ethnic* and *grievance* potential—and the determinants of party formation in the Northern Italian regions is presented. New regional parties in Piedmont, Lombardy and Veneto emerged in the same period. We explore their similarities and differences in terms of programs, strategies and resources. This type of design allows us to isolate the determinants of party formation and party success and failure while controlling for other variables (state formation, party system, and institutional frameworks). The dependent variable here is party formation.

The *structure of incentives* to mobilise in the Northern Italian regions was provided by the institutional design of the Italian state: the distinction between 'special' and 'ordinary' regions and the institutional recognition of *ethnicity* by the Italian state as a principle for granting political and economic rights. Why the North? The book argues that the rise of the Northern question in Italy was endogenous to the political process. The selection of the Italian North as the relevant territorial unit was the result of the cooperative strategies of a set of minor parties whose leaders decided to coordinate their efforts against the Italian state and to form a new party. The rise of the Northern question in the Italian party system was a *contingent* event.

A critical juncture marked the unraveling of Italian politics: the fall of the Berlin wall was the exogenous shock that initiated a profound transformation of the Italian party system. The symbolic demise of the Communist *threat* provided a crucial strategic opening for new political parties. After 1989 the erosion of the major divisions that structured the Italian party system during the post-war period provided a favorable opportunity structure for the reconfiguration of electoral alignments. The timing and sequence of mobilisation—as the new political actors adjusted their behavior, ideas and goals to these changing conditions—led to a new dimension of territorial politics in the Italian party system and the Italian North as the relevant territorial unit.

Rather than stressing North and South differences I aim to show the different layers in which the *old* and the *new* were articulated in the categorical remaking of Italians by Lega Nord. Prejudices against Southerners are as old as the Italian state. However, brand new was the creation of a hierarchy of cultures was for the first time tied to claims of nationhood and cultural distintiveness for a united North. Old stereotypical definitions of the North-South divide in Italy framed a public discourse and a common understanding of the failure of public policies to develop the South. Paradoxically, the stereotypical ways in which the North-South divide was packaged by Lega Nord became *old* fashioned as *new* territorial divides within Italy, in particular, within Northern Italy, became politically visible over the past decade.

The book shows how *ethnicity* and *nationhood* were talked and written about by Lega Nord's elite and party activists. The articulation of *ethnicity* and nationhood, their boundaries, content and markers are explained. What characterises new political mobilisation in Northern Italy is not the *invention* of a national distinctiveness. What is characteristic is the extent to which invention is built upon new collective markers and a new cultural differentialism that developed in Europe as a new and central component of the new racism (Balibar, 1990; Swyngedow, 1997; Fenemma, 1997). Initially identities in party mobilisation were *ethnic* and language provided for collective distinctiveness. The content of identity changed (from ethnic essentialism to economic and *civic* essentialism), as well as the territory bounding the collectivity (from the existing ordinary regions to a new North with fuzzy territorial boundaries).

Lega Nord is commonly used as an example and manifestation of the demise of nation-states, the previous disunity of Italy representing one of the factors that explain the success of Lega Nord. Some scholars argue that there is no revival of nationalism or national sentiment, the Italianness being regarded as 'a relic from the past' (Peri, 2000, p. 272). However, there are signs that the opposite is true. In the 1990s in Italian politics have also rearticulated Italian national unity in new ways.

The second part of the book is a case study of Lega Nord, the style of mobilisation and elite strategies. The rise and success of Lega Nord shows that under conditions of political instability and uncertainty, nationhood is still a very contemporary principle of political organisation to define new lines of inclusion and exclusion. Nationhood offers a principle of legitimacy to define the acquisition of rights—as well as the obligations avoided, for example fiscal arrangments—in contemporary politics. At the turn of the century, it should be noted that the availability of nationhood as a widely used category is also accompanied by the discredit of nationalist as the terrain for demagogues and human irrationality. This is a fundamentally transformed political scenario to the efforts of political inclusion, democratic pluralism, recognition and incorporation that dominated debates on national minorities in the 1970s.

The study of Lega Nord illuminates a range of crucial issues for all scholars interested in political change in Europe. While many theories on political change in Europe focus on system-level changes, this study shows the importance of political processes in explaining divergent trajectories of political change. While the conditions under which political parties exercise their role have profoundly changed in European politics, this study of Lega Nord suggests that what parties do play a large role in redefining and in reproducing conflicts they themselves are actively shaping.

Research Sources and Evidence

This book used a variety of archival sources and documentation from the party organisations and party journals. Archival work at Widener Library at Harvard—always an invaluable source—and the help of Roberto Gremmo and Aureli Argemi from Ciemen in Barcelona allowed me to uncover, after much time and effort, the origins of the spread of new ideas in the North of Italy in the *ethnic* wave in the 1970s. Journals and books from that period helped me identify the main ideas and actors in these organisations.

The study is also based on a set of open-ended interviews with party organisers and representatives conducted over the course of thirteen months of fieldwork in Northern Italy. I was in Italy from September 1995 to September 1996. I followed my research with four weeks in January 1997. The interviews lasted from one to six hours and were conducted in different regions of Italy. The survey, a set of 55 open-ended semi-structured interviews was designed to sample key actors in the political process: party activists in the regions of Piedmont, Lombardy and Veneto; and party representatives in all levels of political institutions: local, provincial, regional and national.

I also rely on party documents, and a variety of primary sources— including data on Lega Nord's membership—provided by party organisers. Sources also include the press coverage of the Italian Northern question in mainly two Italian newspapers: *Il Corriere della Sera* and *L'Indipendente*. A variety of secondary sources was also used: electoral results, economic indicators and survey evidence from Italian pollsters. The analysis of symbolic structures—Pontida demonstrations and the Parliament of the North—relied on data from the party organisation and Italian newspapers and from my own personal attendance to these events.

I benefited from widespread academic interest on Lega Nord. When I arrived to Italy in 1995 I talked to several Italian scholars who studied the Lega throughout the 1990s. I would like to thank Giacomo Sani, Renato Mannheimer, Marco Maraffi, Ilvo Diamanti, Paolo Segatti, Mario Diani, Alberto Melucci and Gianni Riccamboni for their time and exchange of ideas. From them and from the press, I obtained the image of Lega Nord from outside: Lega Nord as *other-defined*. In approaching Lega Nord, I wanted to get the image of Lega Nord as *self-defined*, from party activists and elite.

Who I was

I told Lega Nord's organisers that I was a Ph.D. student from MIT. My Spanish citizenship, my gender (in many, but not all situations) and my friendly attitude towards them prevented suspicious minds and conspiracy theories about my presence within the organisation. I told them that my family came from Galicia, one of the historically recognised nationalities in the Spanish state and that also helped to overcome their questions about my intentions in studying Lega Nord. Unfortunately, I could not control suspicious minds from preventing my access to Lega Nord's headquarters in April 1996. A rumor started at the federal secretariat of the party labeling me as a CIA agent and risked the position of the people within the organisation who helped me through my fieldwork. Party organisers kindly provided the sources used in this study and I asked specifically their permission to use them in my research.

I do not share Lega Nord's party agenda. I decided to embark on this project to understand and explain a phenomenon without casting Lega Nord as a social pathology. Murray Edelman summarises the tensions that arise from this endeavor as follows:

> The common form of involvement in politics springs from sharing the immediate interests or feelings of others that are concerned ... A radically different kind of involvement characterizes people who try to understand in historical perspective, and so self-consciously distance themselves from immediate interests and passions as best as they can. This is not objective detachment, for objective detachment is a rationalization for self-assurance, nor an attainable posture. This second form of involvement is rather, a strategy for achieving a particular form of involvement—that of the analyst who looks for patterns in the role-taking of those who are directly involved ... The distinction between the perceptions that arise from direct involvement in a political issue and those that stem from self-conscious distancing is analytical, not empirical. This is a way of classifying situations, not a contrast between concerned people and detached people (1985, pp. 208-209).

Notes

[1] I use *peripheral* nationalism to refer to claims of nationhood advanced for national minorities within European states. In contrast to the first conceptualisation of the term grounded in sociological positivism (Linz, 1967; Gourevitch, 1979), here 'periphery' does not refer to any empirical reality. It merely signals the distinction between state nationalism and sub-state nationalism.

[2] The Italian constitution introduced a two-tier regional framework that provided for the creation of 'special' and 'ordinary' regions. The regionalisation of the Italian state created five special regions (Sicily, Sardinia, Val d'Aosta, Trentino-Alto Adige—established in 1948 and Friuli-Venezia-Giulia—established in 1963) and fifteen ordinary regions created in 1970 after an agreement between the two main parties, the DC and the PCI. See M. Rousseau and F. Zariski, *Regionalism and Regional Devolution in Comparative Perspective* (New York: Praeger Publishers, 1987).

[3] In Lipset and Rokkan's model, cleavages do not 'translate' directly into party oppositions. Translation mechanisms in their model are defined as organisation and electoral strategy, that is, the conditions for the expression of protest and the representation of interests. Martin

S. Lipset and Stein Rokkan, *Cleavage Structures, Party Systems and Voter Alignments* (1967).

[4] Regional parties are located on a vertical dimension cutting the main dimension of conflict in a polity. Lipset and Rokkan's adaptation of the Parsonian AGIL scheme represented a two dimensional space with two axes. The vertical axis represents the cleavage formed by the process of nation-formation. This is defined as a cultural cleavage. The horizontal axis is the functional dimension of interests and represents distributional conflict. Seymour M. Lipset and Stein Rokkan (1967), *Cleavages Structures, Party Systems and Voter Alignments: An Introduction.*

[5] As Urwin put it: 'Regionalist parties are more disparate in the specificity of their demands. There is little in the way of a common economic policy or common view of the structure of society. Few if any, could be said to have a Welanschauung'. Derek Urwin, 'Harbinger, Fossil or Fleabite? Regionalism and the West European Party Mosaic', in Peter Mair ed. *Western European Party Systems* (Beverly Hills: Sage Publications, 1983: 227).

[6] The opportunism' of this type of political parties derives from their special position within a polity. These parties can 'free ride' in national political systems because their agenda is limited to the interests of the population they claim to represent. Collective goods, if any, will accrue to them. They cooperate with other political actors as long as they are offered selective incentives.

[7] Heraud included race or 'biological' traits as ethnic traits in the first edition of *Europe des Ethnies* in 1963. These traits were eliminated in the 1993 edition of the book.

[8] As Fontan put it: 'the linguistic index is the expression of a differentiation of character and mentality, the synthetic result of radical social, economic and political development of humanity which has operated in different ways depending on the territories'. F. Fontan, *Ethnism. Vers un Nationalisme Humaniste* (Bagnols: Librerie Occitaine, 1961), 16.

[9] As Heraud put it 'L'Italie du Nord, entre les Alpes et les Apennins, correspond a l'ancienne Gaule Cisalpine. Et les invasions germaniques—Lombards, Ostrogoths—y ont laissé une empreinte plus forte que dans la péninsule. Cela se traduit de nos jours par le maintien de dialectes gallo-romains, distincts du Toscan et des autres dialectes proprements Italiens. Le Piémontais, le Lombard, le Ligurien, l'Emilian sont de ce type. Seul dans le bassin du Pö, le Vénitian compte comme purement italien. Le Piémontais est le plus typé et le plus homogène de ces parlers. Possédant une forme écrite unifié, il manifeste de nos jours une grande vitalité, et, seul dans son cas, conférre une certaine base culturelle au regionalisme local' (Guy Heraud, *L'Europe des Ethnies*, 1963:217).

[10] Kitschelt's defines political populism as: 'the effort to destroy established institutions of interest intermediation and elite control and to put in their place some kind of direct voice of the people, embodied in the leader of the populist party'. H. Kitchell and A. McGann, *The New Radical Right in Western Europe* (Ann Arbor, MI: The University of Chicago Press, 1995), 160.

[11] Kitschelt defines partocracy as: 'a term used to indicate the fusion of state, party and economic elites in politico-economic networks characterised by patronage, clientelism, and corruption'. H. Kitschelt and A. McGann, *The New Radical Right in Western Europe* (Ann Arbor, MI: The University of Chicago Press, 1995), 161.

[12] Survey evidence from 1991, 1994 and 1996 analysed by Biorcio shows that the percentage of artisans and shopkeepers supporting Lega Nord has been rather stable over time (24%, 26.5%, and 23.9% in 1991, 1994, 1996). In contrast, the support of blue-collar workers has increased over time (16.6%, 21.4%, and 31.2% for the same years). Surveys from Eurisko, Cirm, Abacus, Roberto Biorcio, *La Padania Promessa* (Milano: Il Saggiatore, 1997), 252. The survey shows that employees (19%), blue collar workers

(25.7%) and the self-employed (16.3%), are overrepresented within Lega Nord's electorate compared to the electorate of the Italian parties (16.8%, 21.5%, and 14.8%). Survey Ispo 1996, Ilvo Diamanti, *Il male del Nord. Lega, Localismo, Secessione* (Roma: Donzelli Editore, 1995), 119.

[13] The result of this survey showed that, out of 100 Lega Nord's voters, 30.1% were blue collar workers, while the percentage of PDS voters was 25.8%. Gabriele Calvi and Andrea Vanucci, *L'Elettore Sconosciuto. Analisi Socioculturale e Segmentazione degli orientamient politici nel 1994* (Bologna: Il Mulino, 1995).

[14] See Eric Hobsbawm and Terence Ranger eds., *The Invention of Tradition* (Cambridge: Cambridge University Press, 1978); Benedict Anderson, *Imagined Communities: Reflections on the Origin and Spread of Nationalism* (London: Verso, 1991); Richard Handler, *Nationalism and the Politics of Culture in Quebec* (Madison: The University of Wisconsin Press, 1988). For a critical assessment of the constructivists for opening up the space to contest the authenticity and legitimacy of identities, see Charles L. Briggs, 'The Politics of Discursive Authority in Research on the 'Invention of Tradition", *Cultural Anthropology 11* (No.4 1996):435-469. On essentialism, see the essay by Craig Calhoun in *Social Theory and the Politics of Identity* (Cambridge: Blackwell Publishers, 1994); Michael Herzfeld, *The Social Production of Indifference. Exploring the Symbolic Roots of Western Bureaucracies* (Chicago: The University of Chicago Press, 1992).

[15] Frederik Barth's theory of ethnic groups focuses on interaction. As he states: 'the critical focus of investigation becomes the ethnic boundary that defines the group, not the cultural stuff that it encloses'. Frederick Barth, *Ethnic Groups and Boundaries. The social Organization of Culture Difference* (Boston: Little, Brown and Company, 1968). However, Barth's emphasis is on boundaries as principles of social organisation, while my argument higlights the political and institutional nature of the process of boundary creation.

[16] McAdam has traced the historical origins and evolution of the concept of political opportunity structure. First coined by Eisinger in 1973, political opportunity structure is the central concept in a new 'political process' model of social movement. For this approach, the timing and fate of movements is largely dependent upon the opportunities afforded to insurgents by the shifting institutional structure and ideological disposition of those in power.

[17] Kertzer's definition of ritual is the following: 'ritual is symbolic behavior that is socially standardised and repetitive'. D. Kertzer, *Ritual, Power and Politics* (New Have: Yale University Press, 1988), 9.

[18] Kertzer writes:
The political leader who wants to create the public impression that he is a champion of justice, equity and the general good is far more likely to achieve a deeper and more lasting impression by staging a dramatic presentation of this image than by asserting it verbally. His appearance should be repleted with appropriate symbols and managed by a team of supporting actors. In this way, power holders, or aspiring power holders, seek to promulgate the view of the political situation they would like the general population to hold. The drama not only constructs a certain view of the situation, but it also engenders an emotional response that associates notions of right and wrong with the elements in this view. It is, indeed, a moral drama, not just an instructional presentation (1988, pp. 40-41).

[19] D. McAdam, J. McCarthy and M. Zald define framing as: 'the strategic efforts by groups of people to fashion shared understandings of the world and of themselves that legitimate and motivate collective action'. D. McAdam, J. McCarthy and M. Zald eds, *Comparative Perspective on Social Movements* (Cambridge: Cambridge University Press, 1996): 6. A. Snow, R. Benford, et al., 'Frame Alignment Processes, Micromobilisation and Movement

Participation', *American Sociological Review* vol. 51 (August 1986): 464-481.

[20] As Snow and Benford put it: 'social movements frame or assign meaning and interpret, relevant events and conditions in ways that are intended to mobilise potential adherents and constituents, to garner bystander support and to demobilise antagonists'. A. Snow and R. Benford, 'Ideology, Frame Resonance and Participant Mobilisation', *International Social Movement Research* vol.1 (1988): 198.

[21] As Edelman puts it:

The epistemological tension with the mainstream of political science has produced most of the commentary on the writings about political symbolism; criticism has chiefly been directed to their failure to verify or falsify conclusions about political cognitions according to the logical positivist model of science. In my judgment, this line of criticism is not helpful, because research that satisfied the positivist criterion could not be an inquiry into symbolism at all, but rather, a study of the utterances people have been socialised to express, a more common but wholly different research enterprise (1985, p. 196).

[22] The complexity and uncertainty of meaning of symbols, are for Kertzer, the source of their strength. (Kertzer, 1988, p. 11). Kertzer highlights the importance of three properties of symbols: condensation of meaning—a symbol embodies diverse ideas that are 'simultaneously elicited but also interact'; multivocality—there is a variety of different meanings attached to the same symbol (the same symbol may be understood by different people in different ways); and ambiguity—the symbol has no precise meaning (Kertzer, 1988, p. 11).

2 New Political Mobilisation in Northern Italy

Today the category of *Padania* has become a common point of reference for analyses of the political revolt of the Italian North. However, during the 1980s new political mobilisation in the North of Italy took a very different form. Rather than the North as a distinctive cultural and economic unit, political mobilisation involved the rise of new parties with new claims of *ethnic* and national distinctiveness for the 'ordinary' regions of the North. This chapter investigates the determinants of territorial political mobilisation in the regions of Piedmont, Lombardy and Veneto in the late 1970s and early 1980s. This chapter explains the *incubation* period of political mobilisation in Northern Italy. Most scholars have only payed attention to Bossi's Lega Lombarda, yet others have also written about all the other parties in the 'ordinary' regions of Northern Italy (Diamani, 1993; Biorcio, 1997). The presence of the other political parties is considered of minor importance because they were not relevant parties—in Sartori's sense. The question of which territorial identity—whether Lombard, Venetian or Padanian—is treated as secondary to political mobilisation. Yet this chapter shows that this early process of political mobilisation had crucial implications for the rise of Lega Nord and its political trajectory during the 1990s. To understand the process of political mobilisation in Northern Italy first we have to address the question of party formation: why and how political parties in the Northern Italian regions were created? Which were the party claims, ideologies and programs?

The rise of new political parties in the Northern Italian regions in the early 1980s is surprising for two reasons. First, there is an academic consensus on the lack of *ethnic* identities in *all* the Northern Italian regions of Piedmont, Lombardy and Veneto (Rusconi, 1993). The only officially recognised ethnic minority in Italy was, and is still today, the German-speaking population of South-Tyrol. Scholars, however, commonly refer to three *ethnic* groups in Italy: the French-speaking population of Val d'Aosta, the German-speaking inhabitants of Alto-Adige, and the Slavic minorities along the Yugoslav border (Barnes, 1974: 196). In the 1980s political mobilisation took place despite the *lack* of ethno-cultural differences in all the ordinary regions of the North.

Second, since the 1970s most explanations of the salience of the territorial cleavage emphasise the importance of economic processes—modernisation, globalisation—in generating new territorial grievances. More puzzling, political mobilisation took place in the *core* regions of Italy, not in the *peripheral* South. The core Northern regions of Lombardy and Piedmont were, according to Gourevitch, the least likely to experience *peripheral* mobilisation (Gourevitch, 1979). The consideration of these regions as the *core* of Italy both in political and economic terms—the congruence beween political and economic functions—would have prevented the rise of territorial political mobilisation.

The structural position of the 'ordinary' regions of the North was different. Veneto provided an ideal terrain to mobilise on regional grievances (Diamanti, 1993). The presence of a different socio-economic model in Veneto, part of a distinctive regional economy gaining importance in the global economy, would have made this region the ideal site for a successful process of political mobilisation. The erosion of the ties that linked economic and political networks, center and periphery, in the Veneto region resulted from the weakening of the Christian Democratic elite. As this chapter shows, Veneto offered the best scenario to successfully mobilise on regional economic interests. However, by the end of the 1980s the territorial question had become politically salient only in the Lombard region.

This chapter provides evidence to support the claims of historical institutionalism in the study of nationalism: one of the unintended consequences of the Italian state structure was to provide incentives por new political entrepreneurs. This chapter introduces the Italian institutional framework, the distinction between 'ordinary' and 'special' regions, and the recognition of *ethnicity* in the Italian Constitution. The creation of the 'ordinary' regions in Italy is considered as a precipitating condition for the revolt of the North (see Putnam, 1993; Kitschelt and McGann, 1995). However, the structure of incentives to claim recognition was provided by the existence of 'special' regions in Italy. The implementation of the 'ordinary' regions multiplied access points to the institutional system, providing a new avenue to claim the recognition of minority languages and generating new institutional grievances. This is the basis for new political entrepreneurs to demand regional 'specialty' across the Italian North. The chapter also explains the particular version of nationalism packaged by the new parties and its common roots: a combination of *ethnism*—with the emphasis on linguistic recognition—and the *Thirworldism* typical from the movements seeking autonomy in the 1970s, with the adoption of the political discourse of *internal colonialism* in European states.

The Ethno-Territorial Cleavage in the Italian Party System

Existing explanations of *ethno-territorial* politics in Europe cannot explain why *ethnicity* becomes an organising principle for political action in the absence of *ethnic* traits or why claims of economic *peripherality* emerge in *core* regions. Using the cases of the new parties claiming nationhood in the Northern Italian regions in the 1970s, the chapter shows the multiplication of demands for *ethnic* and *national* recognition. Underlying structural trends in *cores* and *peripheries* in European states, we still need to highlight the crucial role of political entrepreneurship and political opportunity structures in making new territorial identities politically salient.

The example-setting of the official *ethnic* minority provided the structure of incentives to claim *ethnic* recognition in the other regions of the Italian North. Putnam notes that the creation of the 'ordinary' regions in Northern Italy and the visibility of regional institutional efficiency in the North was behind the rise of regional political mobilisation in the Northern Italian regions (Putnam, 1993). However, this chapter shows that it was *not* the salience of the 'ordinary' regions, but the attempts to make the 'ordinary' into 'special' regions, the logic behind party formation in Piedmont, Lombardy and Veneto. The institutional recognition of the German-speaking population of Bolzano acted as an example-setting to claim *ethnic* recognition, not only in the 'special' regions with identified minorities (Val d'Aosta and Friuli-Venezia Giulia), but also in the 'ordinary' regions of Piedmont, Lombardy and Veneto. New political mobilisation introduced new categories of *nationhood*: the Piedmont, the Lombard and the Venetian *nations*. Rather than the *ethnic* potential in each region, what explains the rise of new claims of distinctiveness is the availability of *ethnicity* as a principle of legitimacy for the acquisition of rights in the Italian state.

Throughout the postwar period the Italian party system retained its structuring power. Other sources of identification—class and religion—supported the main cleavages in Italian politics. Over time, as Bartolini and Mair show, the stability of electoral alignments shifted from a domain of competition to one of identification (Bartolini and Mair, 1990). Italian politics were characterised by the stability of electoral alignments and the pervasive role of mass parties. During the 1980s the first signs of erosion of traditional alignments—as measured by decreasing party identification and increasing electoral volatility—offered new political opportunities in the Italian political system. However, it should be stressed that although there were significant signs of exhaustion, the Communist and Christian Democratic parties still represented the main political actors in the Italian political system. Fundamental transformations in the Italian society and the economy in the post-war period did not alter the stability of electoral alignments.

In the 1970s ethnicity and nationhood became part of the political discourse available in European democracies. I describe the process of party formation and show how the new parties de-constructed the Italian nation to essentialise the Lombard, Venetian and Piedmont nations. I look into the party platforms and the economic demands advanced by these parties. The chapter finally shows the strategies and the political opportunity structures during the 1980s.

The ethnic wave of political mobilisation in the late 1960s and 1970s made *ethnicity* a widely available category of practice in the public sphere in West European states. The de-colonisation process that took place in the 1960s transformed the international arena with the creation of new states in Africa and Asia. Self-determination—and *ethnicity* as the relevant criteria to grant it—became a powerful normative basis for claims for institutional recognition in European pluralist democracies. *Ethnicity* was the relevant criterium to claim recognition (by groups and movements) and to grant it (by states and international agencies). In the 1970s the politicisation of distinctiveness as *ethnic* was pervasive, to the point of making Milton Esman introduced its well-known collective volume as follows:

> so compelling are the normative claims of ethnic self-determination that nowhere in contemporary Europe have regional grievances been successfully politicized except where they enjoy an *ethnic* base (my emphasis, 1977, p. 377).

Thus, the European wave of political mobilisation for the recognition of territorial identities was *ethnic*. Pre-war regionalist and nationalist parties, in Catalan or Basque nationalism claimed *nationhood*, but *ethnism* and recognition of ethnic status defined the territorial identities emerging in the 1970s. *Ethnism* also differed from regionalism. In contrast to conservative, regional associations and parties for whom cultural distinctiveness is a historical legacy to be preserve, *ethnic* associations and parties claim upon cultural distinctiveness the granting of rights of self-determination and autonomy.

As an ideology, *ethnism* profoundly influenced the new movements and parties in Europe from the 1960s onwards.[1] The starting point for these new political actors was the *ethnic* element. For the ideologists of ethnism, the social and political organisation of national minorities was secondary. Ethnic minorities were all *ethnic* minorities although they differed in the *degree of consciousness* they exhibited (Salvi, 1975). In these views, ethnic mobilisation would follow an evolutionary trajectory, from ethnic and cultural distinctiveness to consciousness to political assertion (Sagredo de Ihartza, 1977).

In the 1950s, associations and organisations were created at the European level to expand the protection of the *ethnic* minorities, of and in, Europe. The Federal Union for European Nationalities was originally founded in 1950. The Union was open to all the democratic organisations for *ethnic* defense, aimed to coordinate the activities of national and linguistic minorities and adopt a chart for the rights and protection of minorities in Europe. In addition, the organisation dedicated its activities to groups 'who lacked international protection, to follow the evolution of the situation of minority groups and to call attention to European governments and the European Parliament over their situation' (Heraud, 1963: 283-284).[2] The journal of the association, *Europa Ethnica*, aimed to become the mouthpiece of national minorities in Europe.[3]

By the end of the 1960s and early 1970s, renewed interests in national and *ethnic* minorities followed these early organisational attempts. New international organisations, such *as L'Association Internationale des Langues et Cultures Menacèes* did not confine their activities to legal recognition and protection of minorities, but also actively sought the *revival* of minority languages and cultures in Europe. As the letter of intention to constitute the Association put it:

> We have the intention to proceed to the rescue of the languages and cultures (now when it is still time) and to favor their development and normalization. For that reason, we wish to gather in a common movement those who, a bit everywhere, bring forward the defense of their own language and own *ethnic* culture (Europa Ethica, 1\1964:82).

In the 1970s, the creation of CIEMEN (Centro Internazionale Escarré per le Minoranze Etniche e Nazionali) provided a forum for legitimation and contestation of the situation of *ethnic* minorities in Europe.[4] Under the direction of Aureli Argemí, the secretary of the bishop of Montserrat in Catalonia—who went into exile to Milan after the Franco regime expelled him from his public pronouncements in favor of Catalonia—CIEMEN became a forum that gather *ethnicists* around Europe, organise conferences and published a newsletter.

New Regional Political Mobilisation in Northern Italy: Background Conditions

After the Second World War, West European states underwent two fundamental changes that proved stable during the post-war period: the fixing of their territorial boundaries and the creation and consolidation of stable democratic regimes. The institutionalisation of *ethnicity* is a new development in post-war European politics. In the postwar period European states combined the signature of international agreements with Constitutional and legal provisions to recognise and protect *ethnic* groups, linguistic minorities and historical nationalities. After the war the Italian state had to address the question of the status and rights of the minorities within the country. The question involved the borders with Yugoslavia (the city of Trieste and the zone of Istria), Austria (the *irredentism* of the German-Speaking population of the province of Bolzano in the South-Tyrol) and France (the French-Speaking minority of Val d'Aosta). The new Italian democracy attempted to solve the problems of the territorial boundaries with the introduction of special provisions for these territories.

The post-war Italian Constitution introduced a two-tier regional system that distinguished between 'special' and 'ordinary' regions. Title V of the Italian Constitution established the organisation of the Italian state structure. Article 114 of the Italian Constitution states: 'The Republic is divided in regions, provinces and communes'. Article 116 of the Italian Constitution granted political autonomy to five special regions. Article 116 reads: 'To Sicily, Sardinia, Trentino-Alto Adige, Friuli-Venezia Giulia and Val d'Aosta are attributed particular forms and conditions of autonomy according to special statutes with constitutional laws'. The creation of 'ordinary' regions was justified on the grounds of political decentralisation and pluralism within the Italian state. The implementation of the 'special' regions—except for Friuli-Venezia Giulia—was immediately undertaken. However, the implementation of the 'ordinary' regions had a conflictual and interrupted history and was delayed for twenty years. After the war, the Christian Democratic party favored state decentralisation and the creation of the 'ordinary' regions. However, their implementation was paralysed by fear of Communist control of the *red* regions of Emilia-Romagna and Tuscany. Finally, the question of the regional governments was reproposed in the late 1960s. Legislation was enacted to implement the election of regional governments and the creation of the regions in the early 1970s (Gourevitch, 1979). The first regional governments were elected in 1970 and started to operate in 1972.[5]

Background: Ethnicity as an Institutionalised Category in Italy

In the Italian constitutional framework, 'specialty' was a single criterion to grant political autonomy to the five regions listed above. The classificatory system introduced by the Italian state established a basic distinction between 'ordinary' and 'special' regions. However, speciality for these five regions was defined according to different principles. The speciality of Trentino-Alto Adige was singled out on *ethnic* grounds. Already in 1946, before the Italian Constitution was written, the Italian and Austrian governments signed an international agreement for the equal rights and protection of the *ethnic* minority in the province of Bolzano, which became known as the De Gasperi-Gruber agreement. The first clause of the agreement reads:

German-Speaking inhabitants of the Bolzano province and of the neighbouring bilingual townships of the Trento province, will be assured of a complete equality of rights with the Italian-Speaking inhabitants within the framework of special provisions to safeguard the ethnical character and the cultural and economic development of the German-speaking element.[6]

The Constitutional Law of February 5\1948 contains the Special Statute for the Trentino-Alto Adige. Article 2 of the Special Statute establishes: 'In the region all citizens shall enjoy equal rights irrespective of the linguistic group to which they belong, and their respective *ethnic* and cultural characteristics shall be protected.'

The statutes for the other four 'special' regions did not contain provisions for the protection of *ethnic* minorities. The special statute for Val d'Aosta (*Legge Costituzionale della Regione Val d'Aosta*, February 1948\n.4) does not refer to linguistic or *ethnic* minorities. In its article 48, the statute only established that: 'the Italian and French languages are equal in Val d'Aosta' (Lenguereau, 1961).[7] Autonomy to Sicily and Sardinia was granted on geographical and political considerations (the emergence of separatist movements that failed to consolidate in the post-war period), but there was no mention of an *ethnic* element.

In 1963 the special statute of Friuli-Venezia Giulia (*Legge Costituzionale della Regione Friuli-Venezia Giulia*, January 1963.n1) was the last one to be adopted. Italian parliamentary debates on the special statute focused on two issues. First, debates addressed the question of the geographical boundaries of the new region—whether to create one or two separate regions (Friuli and Venezia-Giulia) or one region with two autonomous provinces (such as Trentino-Alto Adige), as well as the statute of the city of Trieste, which under the Paris Treaty was considered a free territory under international supervision (Ginsborg, 1990: 110).[8] Second, parliamentary debates focused on the proper criteria to specify the 'specialty' of the region. Finally, the special statute of 1963 neither recognised any special territorial conditions about the region nor introduced specific measures to protect its linguistic minorities (Agnelli, 1987; Bertolissi, 1987).

New Party Mobilisation in the Northern Regions: Background Conditions

The second *ethnic* wave in European party systems, involved in Italy the mobilisation of minorities in the 'special' regions of Val d'Aosta and Friuli-Venezia Giulia. These minorities also asserted their demands vis-à-vis the Italian state and demanded a similar institutional recognition to the one granted in the Statute of the Trentino-Alto Adige.

Assessing Ethnic Potential in the Italian North

Many scholars commonly agree with the statement that the Northern 'ordinary' regions of Piedmont, Lombardy and Veneto did not exhibit *ethnic* potential. Rather than regional cultures, Lombardy and Piedmont were characterised by the presence of a variety of local dialects and local traditions. Moreover, industrialisation processes and massive migratory flows to both regions in the post-war period made them a composite cultural reality. The lack of implementation of the 'ordinary' regions generated some movements demanding regional autonomy in the North during the 1950s. The *Movimento Autonomista Regione Piemonte was* born in 1952, and elected some local councilors in the city of Torino in the 1953 local elections. The movement died in 1956. Although the MARP had also expanded to the Lombard and Venetian regions, its presence there was even more marginal. In the 1950s there was also an autonomist movement in the province of Bergamo, Movimento Autonomista Bergamasco. This movement was, in fact, the first one to use the symbol of the warrior Alberto de Guissano, later used by Bossi's Lega Lombarda.

Despite the *naturalness* with which *ethnicity* as a criteria to identify minorities was commonly presented in Europe in the 1970s, many political debates on the 1960s and 1970s actually focused on which relevant markers, which cultures and collectivities were *ethnic*. These debates were not only about the boundaries of the collectivities, groups, or linguistic minorities, but also about their definition as *ethnic*. In the 1960s and 1970s, there is a proliferation of taxonomies on European *ethnic* and national minorities. These classificatory efforts also included the Italian *ethnic* minorities. Table 2.1 presents five alternative classifications of the Italian minorities during the 1970s.

Table 2.1 Italian Minorities: Competing Classification Criteria

Heraud (1)	AIDLCM (2)	Salvi (3)	Sagredo de Ihartza (4)	Pellegrini (5)
Ethnic Minorities	**Linguistic Minorities**	**Territorial-Linguistic Minorities**	**Ethnies** Sards	**National Minorities** Sud-
Valdostans	Albanians	Albanians	Harpitains	tyroleans
Rheto-	Catalans	Catalans	Piedmonts	Slovens
romans or	Croats	French	Friulians	Linguistic
Ladinians:	French	Greeks	Occitans	Minorities
Grisons	French-	Ladinians:	**Minorities**	Val
Dolomitans	provenzal	Dolomitiche	**from Other**	d'Aostans
Friulians	Friulians	Friulians	**States**	('Elected'
Slovens	Greeks	Occitans	Germans	Minority)
Sud-	Ladinians	Sardinians	Slovens	Ladinians
tyroleans	Occitans	Serbocroats	Greeks	(Bolzano)
Northern	Sardinian	Slovenes	Albanians	**Regional**
Italians	Slovenes	Germans		**Dialects**
Piedmonts	German			Ladino
Ligurians	Gypsies	**Forbidden**		Friuliano
Emilians		**Nations**		Sardo
Lombards		Sardinians		**Linguistic**
Non		Friulians		**Pockets**
Venetians				Albanians
Sardinians				Greeks
Sicilians				Franco-
Albanians				provenzal
Greeks				Occitan
				Serbocroats
				German
				Gypsies

Sources, my elaboration: 1. Heraud, 1963, 1992; 2. ADLCM, 1974; 3. Sergio Salvi, 1975; Sagredo de Ihartza, 1975; 5. Giovanni Battista Pellegrini, 1986

These taxonomies are different both in the selection of the criteria to define the minorities and the actual listing of the existing minorities within Italian borders. Some of the minorities were considered *ethnic* by most of the authors, others were contested. The taxonomies presented as given what was, instead, the result of an arbitrary classificatory process. For instance, the recognised *ethnic* minority of South Tyrol was not an *ethnie* nor a minority in Sagredo's work—it is part of the German *ethnie*—but was the *ethnic* minority *par excellence* in the rest of the authors. For Heraud the French-speaking minority in Val d'Aosta was an *ethnic* minority. Krutwig considered that this minority was not French-speaking nor a minority (it belongs to a broader Harpitania). Pellegrini considers that it is not a *natural* but *chosen* French-speaking minority, because they in fact speak a *patois* (Pellegrini, 1986). Moreover, the Ladinians of Trentino-Alto Adige are a recognised linguistic minority by the special statute of the region, but not the Ladinians in Friuli-Venezia Giulia. Pellegrini challenges altogether the assertion that Ladinians do speak a language, because he considers it as a dialect or variant of the Italian language. For Salvi and the Italian section of AIDLCM, Occitans should be considered an Italian linguistic minority. In contrast, for Heraud and Sagredo they are not (for the former Occitans are geographically concentrated in Southern France, for the latter they are an *invented* ethnie).

Veneto was always excluded from these classifications, although some authors stressed in the past the 'peculiarities' of the Veneto region (Evans, 1967). Peter Gourevitch states that in Italy: 'Regions that have *ethnic* potential include: the South, Sardinia … perharps the Venetia' (Gourevitch, 1979, p. 305). The Veneto region distinguished itself from the industrialised North in many respects. The Venetian dialect was, and is today, widely spoken in the region. According to Evans:

> Venetians distinguish themselves not only for the use of the language, but also in broader cultural terms from the rest of Italians. For Evans: "Veneto is a culturally and socially homogenous zone ... geographically, historically ... ethnically, to cross the Po, in a certain sense, means to change worlds, not only geographically but also in what relates to culture, to the very attitudes towards existence in its entirety" (1971, 9).

Table 2.2 The Use of Italian Regional Dialects (%)

	Family	Friends	Strangers
Veneto	52.7	42.3	17.2
Calabria	40.4	25.8	11.2
Sicilia	39.7	24.8	13.1
Basilicata	37.5	26.7	10.2
Molise	33.8	22.3	11.0
Campania	33.1	23.7	12.3
Abruzzo	26.4	20.0	9.8
Marche	24.2	18.7	8.2
Friuli V. Giulia	22.5	17.3	7.0
Puglia	22.2	13.2	5.6
Liguria	14.9	7.6	1.1
Lazio	11.1	7.0	3.5
Italia	23.6	16.6	6.8

Source: ISTAT, 1997: 2

Table 2.2 shows the percentage of the population in the Italian regions that use the dialect with family, friends and strangers. Still in the 1990s, the Venetian dialect was the most used in Italy.

The Veneto region had also a historical past of an independent administration. Venice was an autonomous republic until the region became part of the Austrian Empire. Thus the *ethnic* potential of Veneto vis-a-vis that of Piedmont and Lombardy was very different.

However, variations in the presence of objective or subjective traits in the different regions of Northern Italy did not determine different trayectories of political mobilisation in all three regions. In the three regions Veneto, Priedmont and Lombardy, new nationalist parties emerged. Also the timing of party formation was similar. In all the regions new parties claiming rights of political autonomy on the basis of ethnic and cultural distinctiveness emerged in the late 1970s and early 1980s.

Assessing Territorial Grievance Potential in the Italian North

The various regions of Northern Italy greatly differed among them. The 'special' regions of Friuli-Venezia Giulia, Trentino Alto-Adige and Val d'Aosta are very small and, in electoral terms, marginal in Italian politics. In contrast, Lombardy is the biggest region in size and population. Regional political mobilisation in Italy did not take place in the traditionally considered periphery, the Italian South, but in the *core* Northern regions. Piedmont and Lombardy should be considered particularly unfavorable sites for new political mobilisation (Gourevitch, 1978). Both regions were politically and economically central to the Italian state both in the process of state formation and in the post-war period. The Savoy monarchy in Piedmont but also and more broadly, Northern political elites, played a large role in the formation of the Italian state (Gramsci, 1951; Mack Smith, 1988). Table 2.3 identifies the 'cores' of the Italian state. The political and economic leadership in Italy was historically in the hands of Piedmont and Lombardy.

Table 2.3 Gourevitch's Location of Economic and Political Functions

Country	U.K.	Spain	France	Italy	Germany	Belgium
Political Leadership						
State-building	England	Castile	Ile de France	Piedmont	Prussia	Wallonia
Present	England	Castile	Ile de France	Piedmont Lombardy	Rhine Westphalia W. Prussia	Wallonia
Economic Leadership						
Industrialisation	England	Catalonia Basque Provinces	Ile de France North, Lyonnais	Piedmont Lombardy	Prussia Western	Wallonia
Present	England Scotland	Catalonia Basque provinces	Ile de France North Lyonnais	Piedmont Lombardy	Rhine-Westphalia	Flanders

Source: Gourevitch, 1978: 308

Second, both the Lombard and Piedmont regions belong to what is considered the economic core of Italy. Piedmont and Lombardy were, and are still today, the wealthiest regions in Italy and they include most of the industrial triangle of the Italian North.

In contrast, Veneto occupied a very different structural position within the Italian North, as part of a *Third Italy*. In Veneto, the pattern of industrialisation adapted, rather than removed, the main characteristics of the local society (Trigilia, 1987). Veneto exhibits some of the structural conditions for successful regional political mobilisation (Gourevitch, 1978; Diamanti, 1993). The Veneto region had a more economically peripheral position in the Italian state (Trigilia, 1987). During the last two decades, however, a process of diffused industrialisation transformed the region into an area of high economic growth, high productivity and an export-oriented economy. The local type of industrialisation adapted the elements of traditional agrarian societies to new economic scenarios without eroding the basis of the local society (Trigilia, 1987).

Table 2.4 Regional Industrialisation Rates (1971-1990)

	1971			1990	
N	*Region*	*Value*	*N*	*Region*	*Value*
1	Lombardia	179.26	1	Lombardia	156.46
2	Piemonte	167.87	2	Veneto	144.57
3	Emilia-	125.10	3	Piemonte	143.06
4	Toscana	124.45	4	Emilia-	131.22
5	Veneto	123.27	5	Marche	127.13
6	Valle d'Aosta	119.19	6	Toscana	114.26
7	Friuli-V.G.	118.45	7	Friuli-V.G.	102.24
8	Marche	101.50	8	Umbria	99.15
9	Trentino-A.A	95.8	9	Valle d'Aosta	94.25
10	Umbria	95.43	10	Trentino-A.A	93.40
	Italia	100.00		Italia	100.00

Source: Istat, 1972; 1991; Piattoni, 1997

In Veneto economic industrialisation was paralleled by the transformation of politics in the region. During the 1980s, the erosion of the Christian Democratic party in Veneto—which had a strong regional character shaped by its ties to the Church and the local society—became visible. The Venetian DC—considered the functional equivalent of an *ethnic* party—entered a period of crisis that undermined the role of Venetian elites within the DC

(Pansa, 1985). At the same time that the party weakened their clientelistic linkages within the region and the relationship between the party and the Church was slowly undermined by secularisation. In fact, some scholars have pointed to these factors in order to explain the early rise and success of Liga Veneta (Diamanti, 1993).

During the 1980s the geography of new territorial political mobilisation in Northern Italy showed a striking development. Veneto did experience a weak and negative trend in political mobilisation; Piedmont remained resistant to mobilisation efforts, and Lombardy became the site of successful political mobilisation. The different types of industrialisation patterns of Piedmont and Lombardy on the one hand, and Veneto, on the other, do not explain the political trajectories of regional mobilisation in these regions. In fact, it was in the region where structural factors were *less* favorable, Lombardy, where political mobilisation took off by the end of the 1980s.

In the past emphasis on structural socio-economic processes and functional links between *cores* and *peripheries* left the study of political mobilisation as a secondary question. In this light, politics 'translates' socio-economic changes in the political arena. In contrast, this chapter emphasises the role of political processes in two main ways. First, the *ethnic* element was not given but equally constructed upon the same basis in all the regions in the same period. Second, by the end of the 1980s Lombardy, rather than Veneto, gain political visibility as the source of new territorial conflict in Italian politics. Collective action problems and political opportunity structures shaped the trajectories of these new parties during the 1980s. The erosion of traditional cleavages provided the political opportunity to make new territorial identities the basis for shaping new electoral alignments. Although long-term structural trends and socio-economic change defined the framework in which these new political entrepreneurs operated, the timing and politicisation of the new categories of *ethnic* and national belonging made political processes a crucial variable to explain the trajectories of new political mobilisation.

For new political entrepreneurs, nationalism offered a principle to claim political autonomy and assert new rights. Thus, a territorial identity became an alternative principle to class and religion to explain political reality. This chapter shows how new political entrepreneurs organised on this principle to claim the recognition of the Piedmont, Lombardy and Venetian *nations*. The new parties constructed the *ethnic*, cultural and economic boundaries of their nations to *match* the administrative boundaries established by the Italian state for the 'ordinary' regions of the North. The new political parties deconstructed the category of the Italian state while essentialising the existence of the new Northern nations.

In the 1970s, *ethnism* was coupled with new radical views about the states and about the economic system.[9] The de-colonisation experience during the 1960s provided a new set of ideas about the position of territorial minorities vis-a-vis central governments.[10] '*Thirldworldism*' provided a new interpretation of political and economic events that explained *ethnic* oppression as a product of internal colonialism. What distinguished these political movements from previous regionalist interpretations was the shift towards radical, leftist and revolutionary ideas about economic development and 'national liberation'.

The Structure of Incentives for Political Mobilisation: Institutionalised Ethnicity as Example-Setting

In the first decades after the war, the conflict over the political status of the German-Speaking population of Bolzano—the South Tyrol question—received widespread international attention. The negotiations of the Austrian and Italian governments, the participation of United Nations in mediating the dispute, and the outburst of terrorism during the 1960s gave great visibility to the conflict. The German-speaking population in the province of Bolzano was granted political autonomy and special cultural and fiscal rights by the Italian state. However, regional political autonomy did not suppress political conflict in the region. The SVP (Sudtiroler Volkspartei) considered insufficient the provisions introduced in the special statute of the region and denounced their lack of implementation in the post-war period.

The conflict about the German-Speaking minority in the South-Tyrol involved the participation of the Austrian government and United Nations. The Austrian government sent a memorandum to the Italian government in 1956 denouncing the lack of implementation of the Paris Treaty. In its 1957 Congress, the Sudtiroler Volskpartei renewed its claims for Austrian help, denouncing the policies of the Italian government against effective regional autonomy and the *forced* migration of Italians into the region. In 1959, the party would create a major institutional crisis removing its representatives from the regional *giunta*.[11] The Italian government established the so-called 'Commission of the 19' to draft a new system of political autonomy for the region, known as *il pacchetto*. In its 1969 extraordinary congress, the SVP voted affirmatively for the adoption of the new statute. A new statute reducing the functions of the region in favor of the autonomous provinces of Bolzano and Trento was formally approved in January 1972 (Agostini, 1986).

For modernisation theorists, the situation of the German speaking minority of the South Tyrol represented the only *ethnic* conflict in Western Europe in the first two decades after the war (Esman, 1977). As Urwin put it:

Around 1960 the majority veredict of academia upon the violent and irredentist behavior of the German-Speaking population of the Alto Adige was probably that it was an atavistic intrusion into the placid water of Western politics: the prevailing belief was that nationalist agitation of this type was an anachronism in West Europe, the home of the nation-state (Urwin, 1983: 221).

It should be noted that the 'solution' of the *ethnic* conflict in the Italian border took place in the midst of the wave of ethno-territorial mobilisation across Europe. The compromised solution for the South-Tyrol in the early 1970s was considered *again* an anomaly with respect to European trends. As Peter Katzenstein put it:

Contemporary Western European politics has recently been marked by an astonishing revival of ethnic political conflict. States that in earlier centuries had faced their crisis of national integration and that only a decade ago were involved in a process of supranational integration are now confronted with ethnic conflict and disintegration at the sub-national level. South Tyrol is the only area where developments have moved in the opposite direction (Katzenstein, 1977: 287).

If the situation of the German-speaking population of Bolzano was considered a historical *anomaly*, in political terms it was considered a political *success*: linguistic rights, political autonomy, but also a special fiscal regime was devised for the region—substantial state subsidies were also provided for (Cinsedo, 1989).

The European wave of political mobilisation in the 1960s and 1970s involved groups, associations and parties in the Northern Italian regions. Two main elements shaped their mobilisation. First, and not surprisingly, claims of recognition were increasingly shaped by using ethnicity as the label for cultural distinctiveness. Ethnic status provided a principle of legitimacy sanctioned by the Italian state and the international system. *Ethnic* status defined the claims of the minorities in the special regions of Val d'Aosta and Friuli-Venezia Giulia (Salvi, 1975). The first region to become active on new *ethnic* claims and demands for collective rights was Friuli-Venezia Giulia. The approval of the statute of the special region in 1963 led to a re-organisation of political parties in the region and the creation of new parties and movements for the representation of the Slovenian and Friulian minorities in the region (Salvi, 1975). In turn, in Val d'Aosta the lack of *ethnic* recognition was blamed on the political class of the region which could not exert enough pressure on the Italian government. The lack of support of the French government was identified as the major reason for the lack of *ethnic* recognition (Cuaz Chatellier, 1971; Heraud, 1971).

New Political Mobilisation in Northern Italy

In the 1970s in the Northern Italian regions, traditional regional associations co-existed with new organisations that incorporated European currents on *ethnism* and denounced internal colonialism and the oppression of the Italian state. These *ethnic* movements and parties incorporated the discourse of colonialism and shaped their grievances as internal colonies of the Italian state. Table 2.5 summarizes the coexistence of 'old' and 'new' trends with the scattered evidence on the cultural associations and political groups which were active in the 1960s and 1970s in the Northern Italian regions.

Table 2.5 Regional Associations in the Northern Regions in the 1970s

REGIONS	CULTURAL ASSOCIATIONS Regional and Ethnic	POLITICAL GROUPS AND PARTIES
Val d'Aosta	French: Academie de St. Anselme Comite des Traditions Valdotaines La Societe de la Flore	Union Valdotaine Union Democratique Valdotaine Rassemblement Valdotain Unione Valdotaine Progressiste
	French-provencal: Escolo do Pou Centres des Etudes franco-provencals	HEL (Harpentaya Etnokrateka Libera) ALPA (Akson Liberaxon Peeple Alpee), P.P.H. (Partito Popolare Arpitano)
Piedmont	Occitanists: Escolo do Pou Coumboscuro Piedmontists: Compania dij Brande	Occitanists: MAO (Movimento Autonomista Occitano; UDAVO (Unione degli Autonomisti delle Valli Occitane). Piedmontists: Assion Piemontes, Assosiassion Liber Piemont
Trentino Alto-Adige	Bolzano: Sudtiroler Kulturinstitut Sudtiroler Kunstlerbund Trento:	Sudtiroler Volkspartei Partito Popolare Trentino Tirolese
Friuli-Venezia Giulia	Friulians: Societa Filologica Friuliana Scuole Libere Friuliane Int Furlan Slovenians: Slovenska prosveta Zveza slovenske Katliske prosvete	Movimento Friuli Movimento friuli Indipendente Slovenska Skupnost (Unione Slovena) Slovenska Levica (Sinistra Slovena)

Sources: Sergio Salvi, 1978; Sagredo de Ihartza, 1978

In the 1970s the diffusion of *ethnism* in Northern Italy is the product of a European wave of mobilisation. The publications of Sergio Salvi, new journals and pamphlets and the presence of political activists from other

European countries—Francois Fontan, founder of the Parti Nationaliste Occitaine, and Federico Krutvig—one of the ideologues of ETA—contributed to the diffusion of these new ideas in Northern Italy. In particular, the Northern regions of Piedmont and Val d'Aosta became the *recipients* of the new European currents.

Thus, ethnicits were present in the Northern Italian regions during the 1970s. In the late 1960s, the 'voluntary exile' of Francois Fontan, the founder of the *Parti Nationaliste Occitaine* led to the formation of a Movimento Autonomista Occitano in 1968 in Piedmont. According to Salvi, 'Fontan exported in the valleys the idea of an Occitan nation and linked the linguistic alienation of the Italian Occitans with their economic, social and cultural alienation' (Salvi, 1973, p. 171). Il MAO claimed the creation of a region with special statute for all the Occitan valleys in Piedmont.[12] The Journal *Assion Piemonteisa* launched in 1975 an appeal to create a League of the Alps— including Val d'Aosta, Piemonte and some provinces of Liguria. The declared objective was to gather autonomist movements with common goals 'for the defense of an *ethnie*, a language, the search for autonomy and the defense of an identity threat and oppressed by the centralised politics of the state' (Assion Piemonteisa, Anno VI 1975). Roberto Gremmo, one of the early activists in Piedmont and founder of the *Movimento Autonomista Rinascita Piemonteisa,* attempted (unsuccessfully) to organise groups in Lombardy and Veneto already in 1973.[13]

The emphasis on linguistic recognition of the regional languages represented a first step in the assertion of *ethnic* distinctiveness. Having a language as opposed to a dialect marked the dividing line between the recognition of a collectivity and its *ethnic* status. As Gremmo wrote:

> It has been often remarked (properly) that language is the synthetic index of nationhood, of a people, of an ethnie. It is therefore evident, how the valorization of the language means a first step towards a more general valorization of other features (cultural in a broader sense) which participate (or collaborate) in determining the specificities of a particular ethnic group (Gremmo, 1975, Assion Piemonteisa, Anno IV, Novembre, Dicembre 1975, "*In Difesa della Lingua. Indice Sintetico di Una Nazionalità*").

During the 1960s and 1970s new associations and groups in the Northern Italian regions demanded the recognition and protection of linguistic distinctiveness and minority languages within the borders of the Italian state. Some associations for the protection of regional cultures and languages and the promotion of poetry and theatre in the vernacular had a historical record back to the beginning of the century, such as the *Società Filologica Friuliana*. Others were newly born in the 1960s and 1970s, such as the Occitanist *Escolo do Pou* in Piedmont (Salvi, 1975).

The Italian section of the *Association Internationale des Langues et Cultures Menaceès* (AIDLCM) provided a framework for new activists to claim the official recognition of regional languages, as *languages* and not dialects.[14] The AIDLCM battled in the 1970s for the official recognition of linguistic minorities in Italy. The AIDLCM had as its main goal the creation of a legal framework to specify and protect linguistic minorities under article 6 of the Italian Constitution. The Italian Constitution establishes the protection of linguistic minorities although it does not specify which are the linguistic minorities in Italy.[15] Article 1 of the AIDLCM proposal was the following: 'According to article 6 of the Constitution, Albanians, Catalans, Croats, French, French-provencal, Friulians, Greeks, Ladinians, Occitans, Sardinians, Slovenes, Germans and Gypsies are linguistic minorities' (Europa Ethnica, 3\1974). The AIDLCM also requested the introduction of articles for the protection of linguistic minorities within the statutes of the new 'ordinary' regions of Piedmont, Molise, Basilicata and Calabria.[16]

Efforts to organise and mobilise on ethnic claims multiplied in the late 1970s with the first signs of erosion of traditional parties in the Northern regions. In 1977 a meeting of political parties and movements resulted in a federation of minorities of the Northern regions of Italy. The founding members of this federation were: Movimento Friuli (MF), Movimento Occitano-Provenzale (M.O.P.), Partito del Popolo Trentino Tirolese (P.P.T.T.), Slovenska Skupnost (S.Sk.), SudTiroler Volkspartei (S.V.P.) and Union Valdotaine (U.V.). As their program put it, these were 'autonomist parties which represent and aim to protect the Friulian, Ladinian, Occitan, Slovenian, German and Valdostan, ethnolinguistic communities'. The political goals of the federation were the 'development of the ethnic and linguistic characteristics of our own people and their cultural, economic and social interests within the framework of a political federalism in Europe' (Minoranze, 6-7: p. 57, CIENEM, 1977). In 1978, the creation in Piedmont of L'Unione Ossolana per l'Autonomia and the visibility the movement acquired at the local level brought about the solidarity of the autonomists in Piedmont.[17]

'Ordinary' into 'Special': New Party Mobilisation in the 1980s

The first European elections in 1979 marked a turning point in the development of movements and parties in the Northern Italian regions. As it is well-known, one of the leaders of Union Valdotaine, Bruno Salvadori, decided to put together a common list of autonomists to gain representation in the European parliament for the minorities of the Italian North. In 1979, Union

Valdotaine presented itself as a confederate union of parties and autonomist movements, federalist, regional forces and independents for a Europe of 'autonomies, progress and freedom'.[18] The list put together by Union Valdotaine incorporated groups and associations from all the regions in the North. The list included groups from the 'special' regions of Val d'Aosta, Trentino-Alto Adige and Friuli-Venezia Giulia (Union Valdotaine, Partito Popolare Trentino Tirolese, Union Slovena and Movimento Friuli). It also included for the first time, groups from the 'ordinary' regions of Veneto (from Liga Veneta), Piedmont (including candidates, Rinascita Piemontese, Movimento Autonomista Occitano, Coumboscuro (Movimento di Autonomia e Civiltà Provenzale Alpina), and Lombardy (Partito Federalista Europeo located in the province of Mantova).

The European elections of 1979 also provided the *stimulus* for some activists in the regions of Piedmont, Veneto and Lombardy to transform their associations into party organisations and compete in Italian elections for the recognition of their 'specialty' within the Italian state. Liga Veneta was officially born in 1980 as a political party. Gremmo's *Movimento Autonomista Rinascita Piemonteisa* operated on an informal basis until 1984 when the movement became *Union Piemonteisa*. Lega Lombarda began her activitivies in 1982 in the province of Varese.

Union Piemonteisa was created under the leadership of Roberto Gremmo.[19] In Piedmont, the first *ethnic* claims emerged with the Occitanist movement and Gremmo was initially linked to the Occitanist movement. Gremmo's political background was in the 1968 movement. He became a key propagator of European currents on ethnism during the 1970s in Piedmont. His efforts were concentrated on publications of party journals—he published a journal in solidarity with Catalonia—and the polemic against traditional parties. Early in the 1970s he tried to proselytise on the ethnic question in Veneto and Lombardy, as he put it 'with no success'. He controled first the Movimento Autonomista Piemontese and then founded Union Piemonteisa.

Liga Veneta is considered the mother of the leagues (*la madre di tutte le leghe*).[20] Liga Veneta was the first party to organise formally and also the first one to gain political visibility. After the experiment of the European elections of 1979, and the formal creation of the party in 1980, Liga Veneta already competed in the regional elections the same year.[21] The Venetian party emerged from the *Società Filologica Veneta*, born in 1978.

Lega Lombarda was launched in 1980-1981 for the first time as Lega Autonomista Lombarda. The origins of the first Lombard political group are in a journal published in 1981 by local politicians in the province of Como. Although Umberto Bossi was part of this group of activists, he was not formally responsible for its creation. There were at least two attempts to launch a Lombard party before Umberto Bossi. However, the project only took off under the leadership of Umberto Bossi and Lega Lombarda was formally constituted in 1984.[22] In contrast to Liga Veneta (which did not change its name during the 1980s), both the Piedmontese and Lombard parties went throught several changes. Lega Autonomista Lombarda became Lega Lumbarda from 1986 onwards, to change the name again to Lega Lombarda at the end of the decade.

The available institutional framework—the 'specialty' of the *ethnic* minority in the province of Bolzano—and its institutional recognition shaped the claims-making of these new political parties. Liga Veneta, Union Piemonteisa and Lega Lombarda claimed the recognition of *nations* whose territorial boundaries corresponded to the ordinary regions of Piedmont, Lombardy and Veneto. The claim of distinctiveness—we are different— provided the logic of political action. As an early document of Liga Veneta put it: 'We are neither Celts nor Slavs, neither Italians nor Germans, but Venetians, and it is our firm intention to continue to be so' (Liga Veneta, 1982). The new party formations in Piedmont, Veneto and Lombardy claimed the introduction of 'special' statutes for the ordinary regions for the acquisition of similar rights of fiscal and cultural autonomy as granted to the German Speaking population of the Trentino-Alto Adige.

National identity became the basic principle for political identification and organisation. As the first journal of Lombardia Autonomista included the following appeal in its first page:

> Lombards! It does not matter your age, your job, your political orientation, what matter is that you are—we are—all Lombards (Lombardia Autonomista Marzo, 1982).

The new parties in Lombardy, Veneto and Piedmont grounded their identity claims on their *ethnic* status: within Italy as *internal colonies*, within Europe as European *ethnic* minorities.

Their claim of distinctiveness was based on the *ethnic* and linguistic traits of the now Northern *nations*. In Veneto, the *Società Filologica Veneta*, created in 1978 under the example of the historical *Società Filologica Friuliana*, aimed to 'preserve the cultural legacy of Venetians and their language'. As the Declaration about the Unity of the Venetian Language elaborated by the Association put it:

> The *Società Filologica Veneta* aims to assert the vitality and unity of the pan-Venetian linguistic reality. The latter, developed upon cultural and ethnic bases solidly united, has maintained over 3000 years its own homogeneous and original identity, an undisclaimable patrimony of Venetians and Europe (*Società Filologica Veneta*, Amantia and Vendramini, 1994).

Likewise, the parties in Lombardy and Veneto made language the basic collective trait to recognise their cultural distinctiveness and the basis for the granting of collective rights for political autonomy. The parties claimed the protection and recognition of the Lombard, Piedmonts and Venetian *languages* in the Italian institutional framework.

This claim of distinctiveness involves a reinterpretation of historical processes by essentialising the nation and its origins in a distant past and by constructing the state as a modern artifact imposed on their nations. The Lombard, Piedmont and Venetian nations were presented as a-historical collectivities. As the Presentation of the program of Liga Veneta put it,

> For thousands of years Venetians have constituted a nation, that is, a people wholly defined on the basis of their own constant cultural, ethnic, social, moral, economic, linguistic (and many other) characteristics (Presentation and Program of Liga Veneta, 1982).

The existence of these nations and their ethnic distinctiveness is presented as natural, self-evident.[23] In the ideological elaboration of the parties in Piedmont, Veneto and Lombardy, past historical developments explained their present cultural distinctiveness. The Piedmont kingdom, the Venetian Republic and the coalition of Lombard cities gathered by Alberto di Giussano against the emperor Federico il Barbarossa in 1167—were legitimising historical precedents for their present *national* caims.

The parties contrasted their views on the essential, self-evident nature of the Piedmont, Venetian and Lombard nations with the modernity and artificiality of the Italian state. For instance, throughout the 1980s the parties contested the legitimacy of the plebiscite—a mockery in their views—that sanctioned the process of Italian unification and the heroes of Italian national unification. According to one of the members of Liga Veneta: 'in fact it is still to be demonstrated that the Venetian people ... were very anxious to be liberated by the Savoy' (Beggiatto, 1988). Or as Brodero and Gremmo put it: 'only a minority, sexually (men), social (the wealthy), and cultural (Italian) voted in the plebiscite' (Brodero and Gremmo, 1978, p. 21).

The Italian state is considered an active invader endangering the survival of their own cultures and exploiting their resources and economies: the Italian state imposed a process of cultural assimilation and uniformity within its territorial boundaries.[24] Regional leaders considered that a history of lost independence and oppression under the Italian states made the 'ordinary' regions internal colonies within the Italian state—'*Il nostro povero Piedmont, the most colonised of the colonies*' (Rinascita Piemontese, 1978). In these views, the colonialism and uniformity imposed by the Italian state *forced* a cultural assimilation of the Italian North with the South.[25]

Views on Europe played a crucial role in the definition of the emerging new territorial identities in Northern Italy. The Italian North as 'European' is contrasted with a 'foreign' Mediterranean culture. As one editorial of *Vento del Nord* put it:

We state, far from any foolish supremacy, that the European civility is the best which has appeared in the history of the world ... it has been the matrix of the best geniuses of humanity. We feel the 'pride' of being a European citizen, equal to those equals in the world, inferiors to nobody (Vento del Nord, November 1981: 1).

The parties claimed the recognition and protection of ethnic languages and cultures as European: 'We want everywhere the defense of local culture sedimented in centuries: languages, dialects, uses, customs, folklore and traditions as *European patrimony* to save no matter the cost' (my emphasis, *Vento del Nord*, 1981, p. 1).

These new parties brought to the fore both international norms and Italian Constitutional provisions to support their claims. Union Piemonteisa, Liga Veneta and Lega Lombarda claimed that the situation of their regions had to be reversed by the recognition of their right to self-government under an international system, which protected *ethnic* and national minorities. As Achille Tramarin, the first member of Liga Veneta in the Italian parliament, put it:

Today, every democrat, every anti-racist, every anti-colonialist must call a great principle of universal progress, that of consenting indigenous people an absolute priority in the job market, in housing, in credit, housing, education, in health services, in the direction of politics and economics. The Chart of the United Nations and the Helsinki treaty sanctioned the principle upon which every people must be *padrone* in its own land (*Un Censimento per Essere Italiani. La libertà dell'individuo deve essere preceduta dalla libertà del popolo*, Vento del Nord, 1981, p. 11).

Party Strategies and Political Opportunity Structures

The comparison of the trajectories of these parties during the 1980s provides a lesson to assess the extent to which political process shape the salience of new territorial identities. The strategies of the party leaders were similar. They appealed to voters by denouncing the Italian state, the Roman parties, the economic *exploitation* and peripherality of these regions within the Italian state. Yet the parties in Piedmont, Lombardy and Veneto followed very different electoral trajectories during the 1980s. In the European elections of 1989 and the local and regional elections of 1990, Lega Lombarda entered a cycle of electoral growth and political visibility, while Liga Veneta and Union Piemonteisa fell into oblivion.

The failure of the new parties in Piedmont and Veneto and the demise of alternative sources of territorial identification in the Northern Italian regions were fundamentally shaped by collective action problems. 'Entry costs' for these new parties were insurmountable. Factionalism hindered the ability of the party leaders to take advantage of existing political opportunities.

The political opportunity structure was slowly changing, showing some avenues for new parties. At the end of the 1970s the ·Christian Democratic party and its governmental allies had been in power during the entire post-war period, but the traditionally excluded Communist party had also, during the 1970s, become a governmental party.[26] The creation of a local anti-party platform *Lista per Trieste* or, as it was known, *il Melone* in the city of Trieste showed the electoral potential for protest politics against traditional parties in the late 1970s. The political revolt had its origins in a group of intellectuals and politicians who felt betrayed by the provisions included in the Treaty of Ossimo signed by the Italian and Yugoslavian governments in 1975 (Cecovini, 1985).[27] The list competed in local elections for the first time in 1978s, electing a new major on a ticket that claimed to defend the city from traditional parties.

Political change and electoral volatility were slowly growing in the three 'ordinary' regions The Communist party was particularly strong in the industrialised regions of Piedmont and Lombardy. The Communist party grew during the 1970s in these two regions. In Piedmont, the Communist party experienced a positive trend during the 1970s while the Christian Democratic party had entered a period of electoral decline since the early 1970s. The percentage of vote for 'other parties' in the general elections held in Piedmont during the 1980s went from 7.9% in 1979 to 15% in the general elections of 1987. In Lombardy, traditionaly the Christian Democratic party had a stronger position than in the Piedmont region. But by the end of the 1970s the DC also started a process of electoral decline in Lombardy. The Communist party in contrast, experienced in the 1970s a positive electoral trend, shiting from 23% in 1972 to 31% of the vote in the 1976 general eletions. However, during the 1980s both the Communist party and the Christian Democrats entered a period of decline. In Lombardy, like in Piedmont, the percentage of vote to 'other parties' went from 7.7% in 1979 to 12% in the general elections of 1987.

Unlike the Lombard and Piedmont regions, the Veneto had a specific pattern of electoral competition that distinguished the region throughout the entire post-war period. Veneto was the most Catholic and Christian

Democratic region of Italy until the 1980s. The DC, however, entered a period of electoral decline in 1979. DC vote in Veneto went from 50.1% to 43.4% of the vote. In Veneto, moreover, the Communist party was always a minor force and Communists in the region were isolated from the Catholic world (Riccamboni, 1992). The Communist party also experienced a period of electoral decline from 1979 to 1987. In Veneto, the percentage of vote for 'other parties' went up as well. In 1979 it was merely 6.4% but it doubled in 1987 (12.5%).

The different political opportunity structures in these regions have to be considered in explaining the trajectories of these parties during the 1980s. The opening of political space needs to be considered in light of party dynamics during the decade. The electoral trajectories of these parties increasingly diverged during the 1980s. The party in the Piedmont region was always in a marginal position—electing candidates to local and provincial governments but never to the Italian Parliament. The history of the party in Piedmont remained obscured and it never gained political visibility at the national level. In the 1985 regional elections, Union Piemonteisa did not obtain any seats to the regional council but Roberto Gremmo was elected to the provincial council in the city of Turin (Gremmo, 1992).

Liga Veneta represented the first success of Northern autonomism. In 1983, Liga Veneta obtained 4.2% of the votes in the Veneto region and elected one deputy and one senator to the Italian Parliament. The early success of Liga Veneta took place in the electoral strongholds of the Venetian DC. The attempts to couple identity with interests in the de-mobilised and industrialised areas of the small and medium-size firms, were, according to Diamanti, one of the underlying reasons behind the electoral success of Liga Veneta. Franco Rochetta, was elected in 1985 to the regional council in Veneto. However, by 1987 Liga Veneta had disappeared from the Italian parliament and was marginalised by the end of the decade.

In contrast, the weakest party in the early 1980s became the most successful new party of the First Italian Republic. Lega Lombarda entered for the first time the Italian parliament in 1987, electing one senator and one deputy. Until 1987, the Lombard party was practically non-existent. Like Union Piemonteisa, Lega Lombarda obtained a seat in the provincial council of the Varese province—the only provice in which the party presented its lists in 1985 and the birthplace of the party. In 1987 Lega Lombarda elected one senator and one deputy to the Italian parliament. Bossi, the secretary of the party, entered the Italian Senate—from then on he would be known as the *Senatur*—while the *fedelissimo* Leoni (one of Bossi's loyals) became the first representative of Lega Lombarda in the Italian Parliament.

Students of Lega Nord explain the electoral success of Lega Lombarda and the failure of its sister parties in Veneto and Piedmont on the basis of differences in programs and strategies between Lega Lombarda on the one hand, and Union Piemonteisa and Liga Veneta on the other. The political capabilities of Umberto Bossi are usually brought to the fore. For instance, Biorcio and Diani identified different logics of political action behind the new parties: the 'populist' nature of Lega Lombarda vis-a-vis the 'ethnic' nature of the parties in Piedmont and Veneto (Melucci and Diani, 1992; Biorcio, 1991; 1997). According to these authors, Lega Lombarda turned towards a broader anti-party populist platform (anti-tax, anti-party, anti-state rhetoric), whereas the parties in Veneto and Piedmont were *trapped* by their *ethnic* and cultural claims, which could only appeal to a minority of the electorate.

Although suggestive in light of later events, this explanation emphasises the political differences among the new regional parties, whereas what was rather striking were the similarities in their ideas, programs and strategies. First, the persistence of *ethnic* claims and language issues in Veneto and Piedmont vis-a-vis the disregard of *ethnic* issues by Lega Lombarda is usually brought to the fore to assert different party strategies. However, the evolution of *ethnicity* was similar for all the regional parties. The election posters of the parties combined since the beginning the Italian with the Piedmontese, Venetian and Lombard. The first local councilors elected in 1985 used the dialects in their first public interventions. Yet the significance of the dialect as a *symbolic* form of assertion was downplayed by all the party leaders—not only Bossi—during the decade, as they tried to appeal to a broader audience. In all of them—not only in the case of Lega Lombarda—the emphasis on cultural and linguistic content decreased during the decade. It is worth remembering that in the late 1980s Bossi was still playing the linguistic card. The strategic capacities and vision of Bossi as opposed to the *ethnic* minority appeals of the parties in Veneto and Piedmont is the official version packaged by Bossi himself in the early 1990s to discredit its old partners and explain his own success (Bossi, 1993).

Second, a comparison of party programs in the 1980s shows that they were almost identical. The first statute of Liga Veneta already included the main battlegrounds of the new parties during the 1980s. The other parties in Lombardy and Piedmont basically copied the statute and party program and included the same set of cultural political and economic demands. Claims for the re-assertion of cultures and languages were accompanied by the request of priority for Venetians, Lombards and Piedmonts in the assignment of jobs, housing, and welfare. The fiscal system of the Trentino Alto-Adige also provided an example to frame the fiscal demands advanced by these parties. Party programs included a request for the management of regional resources: 'the product of our work and taxes should be controlled and managed by Venetians, Piedmonts and Lombards'. Party programs also asked for the transformation of Italy into a federal state. 'Integral federalism', as Liga

Veneta called it, would provide a new 'social, economic and political model'. Third, all the new regionally-based political parties competed in elections during the 1980s incorporating a claim of *ethnic* and cultural distinctiveness, but also *fiscal* demands and the protest against traditional parties and the bureaucratic and inefficient Italian state. The anti-tax polemic, the attack against the central government, the South as the source of social and political corruption, also shaped the views and programs of Union Piemonteisa and Liga Veneta. One of the first posterboards of Liga Veneta in 1981 exemplifies the early importance of fiscal issues and taxation for all the new parties: Why do Venetians have to pay for the debts of Italians? (Manifesto, n.9, 1981). Protest against the central government and traditional parties (that neglected the interests of these regions in favor of the South) appeared in their programs and pamphlets. They all presented themselves as political alternatives to the corruption and lack of representation of traditional parties. All the party programs included the 'struggle against the *Mafiosa* and opportunistic mentality of the Roman government' and the degration of Lombardy, Veneto and Piedmont. The polemic against the South and their claims for the priority of Lombards, Venetians and Piedmonts for the assignments of jobs gained the parties the early accusations of racism that accompanied their appearance in the public sphere.[28] In short, all the party leaders behaved in an opportunistic way and their electoral strategies were similar.

The new political parties also exhibited striking similarities in their organisations. First, executive leadership was an accentuated feature since their origins. In an earlier period, Achille Tramarin in Veneto, Roberto Gremmo in Piedmont and Umberto Bossi in Lombardy became the leaders of the new parties. Later during the decade conflicts in Veneto and Piedmont divided the parties in splinter groups. The political leadership of Gremmo and Tramarin with Farassino and Rochetta and Marin, respectively. Second, they operated as small groups—they described themselves as *carbonari*—and dedicated their activities to proselytise and elaborate party manifestos and posters. The new parties were very weak organisations and lack resources to mobilise and compete in elections. Throughout the 1980s, the new regional parties relied mostly on voluntary participation to conduct their activities. Party journals and the production of pamphlets and graffitti across the regions represented the main component of party activities and financial commitments during the 1980s. The organisational expansion of the parties was very restricted during the decade. The new parties invested their resources in the publications of party journals and their distribution—at the local level—as well as reproducing in graffiti the party slogans (Diamanti, 1993). The presence of the party in Veneto was clearly visible by the graffiti and posters that reproduced the party messages.[29] Later in Lombardy the slogans of Lega Lombarda appeared everywhere in highways and walls.

Internal conflicts within Union Piemonteisa and Liga Veneta led to the creation of other parties with similar programs and objectives, and the presentation of competing *autonomist* lists in Piedmont and Veneto. The electoral prospects of the parties in Veneto and Piedmont were hindered by internal factors. Party factionalism weakened the emerging party organisations and prevented their consolidation. Both in Veneto and Piedmont, conflicts within Union Piemonteisa and Liga Veneta about party leadership of the parties ended in court disputes about the rights to use party labels and symbols. These conflicts were covered extensively by the local press and weakened the public image of the parties and their leaders. The confusion with the multiplication of regional electoral symbols added to their difficulties to gain parliamentary representation.

The first Congress of Union Piemonteisa took place in 1987. Conflicts during the 1980s over the Leninist leadership of its founder, Gremmo, led to the creation of a new party, Piedmont Autonomista. In 1987 the autonomist lists were divided between Union Piemonteisa and the new Piemont Autonomista of Farassino, a well-known folklore singer. The attempts of reconciliation between the two factions in 1988—orchestrated by Bossi— were short-lived. Piemont Autonomista retained the autonomist label while Gremmo attempted other political platforms.[30]

In Veneto similar conflicts took place. The problems that invested party leadership after 1983 also marked the electoral prospects of Liga Veneta. The early electoral success of Liga Veneta and the election of two representatives in 1983 were also accompanied by internal struggles among its founders over the control of the party and its leadership. On the basis of the party's statutes, one of the new elected representatives, Tramarin—at the time the party's general secretary—should have resigned from his position. His refusal led to a major political conflict within Liga Veneta that ended with a court decision that granted the name and symbols of the party to the group around Rochetta and Marin. The conflict led to the creation of a new party, Union del Popolo Veneto. In the 1987 elections, the party won 3% of the votes and remained without representation in the Italian parliament. Bossi took any opportunity to engage himself in controversies and insults that gave him visibility and by the 1989 European elections, Lega Lombarda became a massive electoral success. In the 1990 regional elections Lega Lombarda became the fourth party in Lombardy.

Conclusions

This chapter explained the incubation period of territorial political mobilisation in the Northern regions of Italy. In the early 1980s new political mobilisation took place in the absence of *ethnic* traits and in the *core* regions of Northern Italy. The regional economies provided very different potential for political mobilisation. The Veneto region, an ideal scenario for predicting a successful political mobilisation represents an outstanding example of the importance of political factors in the rise of new ethno-territorial cleavages. A positive electoral trend and the institutionalisation of the Venetian question in the Italian party system did not follow the early success of Liga Veneta in 1983. Instead, Lega Lombarda became an electoral success at the end of the 1980s. The new parties in Piedmont and Veneto were weakened by internal struggles that prevented their consolidation and made them a political failure. This chapter showed how the cases of political mobilisation in Piedmont, Veneto and Lombardy provide an outstanding opportunity to assess the impact of political processes in shaping the rise of new territorial conflict.

The chapter challenged the contemporary salience of the *necessary* condition established by theories on ethno-territorial mobilisation. Rather than considering the presence of pre-existing *ethnic* collectivities as a necessary condition for political mobilisation, we explored the presence of *ethnicity* as an institutionalised category. *Institutionalised ethnicity* provided a structure of incentives for political entrepreneurs to organise on the basis of the same principle. This chapter showed that in order to understand new *peripheral* nationalism in Europe, we need to consider how cultural differences are recognised and institutionalised in European pluralist democracies. The evidence presented in this chapter showed how the institutionalisation of ethnicity in the Italian Constitutional framework and the diffusion of *ethnism* in the 1970s, made *ethnicity* an available category in the public sphere.

The chapter showed the malleability of ethnicity and nationhood in the hands of political entrepreneurs as they define and construct cultural differences. The journals of the new parties de-constructed the category of the Italian nation and essentialised the existence of Venetian, Piedmont and Lombard nations oppressed under the Italian state. The rights of self-government on the basis of *ethnic* and cultural distinctiveness was coupled with demands to refashion existing fiscal and distributive arrangements within the Italian state. The parties showed striking similarities in their strategies, platforms and ideas. Political entrepreneurs fashioned an image of their regions as *national peripheries* of the Italian state to challenge existing distributive arrangements in Italy.

The different electoral trajectories of these regional parties during the 1980s do not explain why today the North and Padania have replaced the 'ordinary' regions as the category of *nationhood* advanced by Lega Nord. At the end of the 1980s a coalition of political parties turned into a single party platform under the leadership of Bossi, Lega Nord. In order to explain the creation of Lega Nord and the expansion of political mobilisation to the other regions of the North, the next chapter explains the cooperative strategies that led to the creation of Lega Nord. It will show how boundary-drawing politics in Northern Italy was radically transformed in the early 1990s. In the context of widespread electoral de-alignment with the symbolic removal of Communism as the main structuring force of political alignments in the Italian party system, the power of politics to refashion political conflict was yet to be seen. Neither Lombardy, nor Veneto nor Piedmont provided the territorial boundaries of political conflict. At the end of the 1980s, the new and regionally-based parties merged into a single party organisation under the leadership of Bossi. With other partners in the Ligury, Tuscany and Emilia-Romagna regions born in the 1980s, the new political actor no longer claimed political autonomy for Veneto, Piedmont or Lombardy, but political autonomy and self-government for a united Italian North.

Notes

[1] The points of reference for the new movements in Western Europe were: Francois Fontan, *Ethnisme. Vers Un Nationalisme Humaniste* (Bagnols: Librerie Occitaine, 1961), Guy Heraud, *L'Europe des Ethnies* (Paris: Presses d'Europe, 1963) and Federico Krutvig (under the name of Fernando Sarrailh de Ihartza), *Vasconia. Estudio Dialectico di una Nacionalidad* (1963). Heraud's book was considered the 'Bible' of *ethnonationalists*. For the importance of the distinction between *ethnie* and *nation* for Sagredo and the influence of *ethnism* in ETA ideology, see Gurutz Jauregui Bereciartu, *Ideología y Estrategia politica de ETA. Análisis de su Evolución entre 1959 y 1968* (Madrid: Siglo XXI Editores, 1981), Robert P. Clark, *The Basques Insurgents. ETA 1952-1980* (Madison: The University of Wisconsin Press, 1984). For an extremely critical view on Ihartza's *Vasconia*, see Gregorio Moran, *Los Espanoles que dejaron de serlo. Euskadi 1937-1981* (Madrid: Planeta, 1982), 284 and ss.

[2] According to article 2 of the statutes of the Federalist Union of Ethnic Communities in Europe: 'for ethnic community, we mean a community which is manifested for '*caracteres de base*' such as language, culture and own traditions'. Statute de L'Union Federaliste Des Communauteès Ethniques Europeéennes, *Europa Ethnica* 4\1967:189.

[3] Guy Heraud, Johann Wilhelm Mannhardt, Povl Skadegard and Theodor Veiter eds., *Europa Ethnica*. Virteljahresschrift fur Nationalitatenfragen. Mit offiziellen Mitteilungen der foderalistischen Union Europaischer Volksgruppen. Revue Trimestrelle des Questions Ethniques. Contenant aussi des Communiques officiels de l'Union Federaliste des Communautes Ethniques Europeennes. A Quarterly Review for Problems of Nationality. Containing Official News of the 'Federal Union of European Nationalities'. Wilhelm Braumuller (Wien, Stuttgart: Universitats Verlagsbuchhandlung, 1961).

[4] CIEMEN's first secretariat was in Milan. After the transition to democracy in Spain, the headquarters moved to Barcelona.

[5] A package of new regulations in 1975 (Law 382), and in 1977 the 616 decrees, effectively decentralised a set of functions into the hands of regional governments. For a description of the devolution process, see R. Putnam, *Making Democracy Work. Civic Traditions in Italy* (Princeton: Princeton University Press, 1993).

[6] The De Gasperi-Gruber Agreement on the Alto Adige (Rome: The Presidency of the

Council of Ministers, 1960), 14. The text of the agreement was inserted in the Peace Treaty, Annex IV: 'The Allied and Associated Powers have taken note of the provisions agreed upon by the Austrian and Italian Governments on September 5th 1946'.

[7] Title VI of the statute for the special region introduced some provisons for the use of the French language in schools and public administration.

[8] Zone A was under British and American supervision. In 1948, the United States, Great Britain and France promised the Italian government that the city of Trieste would return under Italian rule. M. Bertolissi, *La Regione Friuli-Venezia Giulia dalla Costituente allo Statuto*; A. Agnelli and S. Bartole eds., *La Regione Friuli-Venezia Giulia. Profilo Storico-Giuridico Tracciato in Occasione del 20 Anniversario dell'Istituzione della Regione* (Bologna: Il Mulino, 1987), 78-79. Different criteria to grant special statutes to the region were discussed in the Italian Parliament. On the one hand, some wanted to recognise the pluri-lingual character of the region and the presence of minorities—Slovenians and Ladinians. On the other hand, some stressed that speciality should be granted for strategic considerations, taking into account the international arena and the nature of the region as a *double* border with Yugoeslavia and the Communist regimes of Eastern Europe.

[9] The writings of Sagredo de Ihartza provided an ideological corpus to ETA. Fontan was the founder of the Parti Nationaliste Occitaine in 1959. Fontan, alongside with the Comitè Occitain des Etudes et D'Action (COEA) born in 1962 had attempted to relaunch the Occitanist movement in Southern France. For the evolution of the Occitanist organisations in these years and the relationship between Fontan's PNO and the C.O.E.A., see Robert Lafont, *La Revendication Occitane* (Paris: Flammarion, 1974), 268. In 1963 the movement ENBATA was born at the Congress of Itxassou. ENBATA was the Basque movement of Euskadi North, the Basque provinces in Southern France. The Congress of ENBATA was attended by representatitives of Occitans, Bretons, Quebecois and Flemish. The so-called Carta de Itssaxou influenced movements across Europe in this period. See, Sagredo di Ihartza, *Vasconie ou l'Europe Nouvelle* (1977). On the creation of ENBATA, see Jokin Apalategui, *Los Vascos de la Nación al Estado* (Zarauz: Elkar, 1979), 333.

[10] Leftism and the radicalisation of these movements went hand in hand in this period. From the Socialist and Federalist ENBATA to the revolutionary struggle of ETA and PNO, this period saw the coupling of left ideologies and ethnism. Krutwig's so-called *Thirworldism* greatly influenced ETA's introducing the idea of *internal colonies*. As Clark puts it: 'The tercermundistas believed Euzkadi was suffering from a colonial relationship, just as had Algeria or Vietnam under the French. In this case, the imperialist power, Spain, was closer to the colony and had penetrated its society and culture to a greater degree than in the other cases. But Euskadi was a Spanish colony all the same. The only way to liberate the Basques was to wage a war of national liberation, a revolutionary war that would target as enemies all non-Basques and all members of the Basque bourgeoisie who would not cooperate in the struggle.' R. Clark, *The Basques Insurgents: ETA 1952-1980* (Madison: The University of Wisconsin Press, 1984), 34.

[11] A resolution of the United Nations in October 31st 1960 called for direct negotiation between both countries (No. 1497 (XV). The Austrian government considered its negotiations with the Italian government unsatisfactory, and reintroduced again at United Nations the question of the German-speaking population of Bozen in July 1961.

[12] Brodero was a member of the Escolo do Pou, a cultural association created in 1961 for the promotion of the Occitan language. The association was active both in the Piedmont and Val d'Aosta regions. S. Salvi, *Le Lingue Tagliate. Storie delle Minoranze Linguistiche in Italia* (Milano: Rizzoli, 1978), 171.

[13] In a personal interview, Roberto Gremmo explained that in the late 1960s and early 1970s he didn't find anybody in Lombardy and in Veneto in his first attempts to mobilise in these

regions. In Veneto Gremmo met a worker with whom he launched a regional journal, *Veneto Libero*. Gremmo's original idea was to produce a journal 'a bit *ethnic* and a bit new left'. The journal died after the second issue.

[14] The Società Filologica Veneta belonged to the AIDLCM. Sergio Salvi also reports the creation of a section of the AIDLCM in Lombardy in 1975. This section of the AIDLCM (sezione Lombardia, Ticini e Grigioni) had the scope of: 'constituting a Lombard *microkone* valid in all the territories of the same dialect, and then, to propose it as the the constitutive nucleus of a 'Padanian' nationhood whose linguistic consciousness is just starting to breath. They talked about a Padanian ethnie or a Galic-Italian ethnie, excluding so far the *parlate Venete*'. S. Salvi, *Le Lingue Tagliate. Storie delle Minoranze Linguistiche in Italia* (Milano: Rizzoli, 1978), 9.

[15] Article 6 of the Italian Constitution does not specify which are the linguistic minorities in Italy. The article states that: 'The Republic protects with appropriate norms linguistic minorities.' Costituzione della Repubblica Italiana e Leggi sulla Corte Costituzionale (Rimini: Maggioli Editore, 1995).

[16] The proposal of the AIDLCM included protection in four ordinary regions: Piedmont (for German, French-Provencal, French or Occitan linguistic minorities); Molise (for the Albanese and Croat minorities); Basilicata (for the Albanese), and Calabria (for Greek and Albanese). *Europa Ethnica* 2\1971: 81-82. For the request in the Piedmont region, see A. Brodero and R. Gremmo, *L'Oppressione Culturale Italiana in Piemonte* (Ivrea: Editrice BS, 1978).

[17] Mobilisation took place at the local level. In the Piedmont region, *L'Unione Ossolana per l'Autonomia* was born in 1978. The UOPLA was an autonomist movement at the provincial level which claimed the autonomy of the Val d'Ossola in the province of Novara. At the beginning UOPLA was a trasversal movement to all political parties. Later it became an independent political movement. The rise of UOPA was not an isolated case. In the same period there were at least two other attempts to create autonomist movements at the local level. In the Veneto region, a new movement for the autonomy of the province of Belluno was created. In the Lombard region, Bossi launched in the province of Varese L'Unione Nord-Occidentale per i Laghi pre-Alpini. In his books Bossi changed the name of the movement to L'Unione Nord-Occidentale per l'Autonomia.

[18] The electoral program of the alliance included: first, a European parliament for the confederation of the ethnies and regions of Europe; second, the strengthening of regional autonomy and powers; third, the resolution of the problems of the border regions; fourth, the free use of minority languages and the local ethno-linguistic communities, fifth, the ownership of natural resources to manage regional economies; sixth, the creation of a managable society for the fight against 'consumerism and moral and physical pollution'; and seventh, the collaboration with the other elected minorites to the European parliament.

[19] There are no studies on the autonomist movements and parties in the Piedmont region. For a personal account of the creation of Union Piemonteisa and the conflicts that led to the creation of Piedmont Autonomista, see Roberto Gremmo, *Contro Roma. Storia, Idee e Programmi delle Leghe Autonomiste del Nord* (Aosta: Collana Il Grial, 1992).

[20] Ilvo Diamanti and Percy Allum, 'The Autonomous Leagues in the Veneto' in Carl Levy ed., *Italian Regionalism. History. Identity and Politics* (Oxford: Berg, 1996).

[21] Liga Veneta obtained 14,000 votes in these elections. For the early impact of Liga Veneta, see I. Diamanti, *La Lega* (Roma: Donzelli, 1993), 43.

[22] La 'Lega Autonomista Lombarda' was originally created by a small group of local politicians in the province of Como. This group was in contact with Roberto Gremmo in Piedmont. They launched a local newspaper *Vento del Nord*. In the newspaper appeared the first board of Lega Autonomista Lombarda The president was Renzo Schelfi. On the first

attempts to create a Lega Lombarda (without the presence of Bossi) see Roberto Gremmo, *Contro Roma. Storia, Idee e Programmi delle Leghe Autonomiste del Nord* (Aosta: Collana il Grial, 1992).

[23] As a document of Liga Veneta put it: 'The Veneto is, among the European nations, one of the most homogeneous and easiest to identify and define; one among the oldest. The Veneto is a nation that, with the passage of systems and states, has known how to keep over millennium more or less the same ethnic boundaries... a {nation} that has kept longer than any other in Europe continuity in its own self-government, even succeeding in avoiding Roman conquest' (Liga Veneta, 1982). A similar claim was also advanced in Piedmont. As Brodero and Gremmo stated: 'today three and a half million of Piedmonts, with precise *ethnic* characteristics, live in a smaller area than the presently defined Piedmont region' (A. Brodero and R. Gremmo, 'Piedmont, a Forbidden Nation' in *L'Oppressione Culturale Italiana in Piemonte* (Ivrea: BS Editrice, 1978).

[24] As Brodero and Gremmo put it: 'the hurry to make Italy, no matter the cost, led to fight everything that seemed too far away from the 'ideal' of levelling-off and uniformity from the Alps to Sicily .... From which we can explain the anti-Piedmont, imperial-colonialist, megalomanic and war-monger policy of the so-called 'Risorgimento''. A. Brodero and R. Gremmo, *L'Oppressione Culturale Italiana in Piemonte* (Ivrea: BS Editrice, 1978).

[25] For Brodero and Gremmo: 'We are for the 'Lombardità' in Lombardy, as much as for the 'Napoletanità' in Campania and the 'Sicilianità' in Palermo, and at the same time, we are against the sort of cultural colonialism that surged from decades, and that tends today, from the current center of powers, and in particular from the media, to make our country an entirely Southern region'. A. Brodero and R. Gremmo, *L'Oppressione Culturale Italiana in Piemonte* (Ivrea: BS Editrice, 1978).

[26] The regional elections of June 15, 1975 changed Italian political life. The Communist party emerged from these elections as the largest party in every major city of Italy (Rome, Turin, Milan, Venice, Florence, Naples, Bologna) and the largest party in 7 regions, 34 provinces and 26 province capitals. Beyond the three regions of the red belt (Umbria, Tuscany and Emilia-Romanga) the left also gained control of Liguria, the Marches, and Piedmont.

[27] The city of Trieste was part of zone A (a free terrritory under international supervision: *il Territorio Libero di Trieste*). Zone A was reversed to Italy by the allies. In 1954 the London Memorandum established by the Italian and Yugoeslavian governements recognised the separate administration of Zone A (Italy) and Zone B (Yugoeslavia, distributed between Croatia and Slovenia). The treaty of Ossimo between Italy and Yugoeslavia formally recognised Zone B (Istria) as part of Yugoeslavia. The treaty established the creation of a Zona Franca Industriale di Confine (Zfic) which aimed to relaunch the economy of the city. The creation of the Zfic was a bitterly contested issue. Manlio Cecovini, *Trieste Ribelle. La Lista del Melone. Un Insegnamento da Meditare* (Milano: Libero Scambio, 1985), 9-11.

[28] For the first coverage of the Northern autonomists in the Italian press, see for Liga Veneta, *Il Gazzetino di Venezia*; for Lega Lombarda, *Arrivano I Barbari. La Lega Nel racconto di quotidiani e periodici 1985-1993* (Milano: Rizzoli, 1993); for Union Piemonteisa, see R. Gremmo, *Contro Roma. Storia, Idee e Programmi delle Leghe Autonomiste del Nord* (Aosta: Collana il Grial, 1992).

[29] Examples of these slogans include: 'Fuori I Romani dal Veneto', 'il Veneto ai Veneti', 'Roma Kankaro d'Italia'. I. Diamanti, *La Lega* (Roma: Donzelli, 1993), 50.

[30] Gremmo created the Liga Alpino-Padana and the Lega Contro la Droga e l'Immigrazione Clandestina. R. Gremmo, *Contro Roma. Storia, Idee e Programmi delle Leghe Autonomiste del Nord* (Aosta: Collana il Grial, 1992).

3 Manufacturing a United North

Why and how was the Italian north reshaped as a political unit, a new *peripheral* nation in Europe? In the early 1990s the rise of political mobilisation in Northern Italy, was considered the *activation* of the old territorial cleavage between North and South in the Italian party system. As Sani put it: 'the results of the 1992 elections marked the activation in Italian politics of a territorial cleavage adding and partially replacing, the traditional cleavages in Italy' (Sani, 1992, p. 560). The *Southern question* has informed our perceptions of the development of Italian state, polity and economy. In contrast, this chapter explains the construction of the *Northern question* in Italian politics.

In his well-known book on the new regional governments in Italy, Putnam writes: 'for at least ten centuries, the North and South have followed have followed constrasting approaches to the dilemmas of collective action that afflict all societies' (Putnam, 1993, p. 181). The negative aspects of territorial dualism are described by Sniderman as follows: 'the animus of the North against the South is deeply rooted in Italy's history. But it is a part of the past that is a part of the present. The contempt of the North for the South forms a thread woven through Italian politics and it is tied as tightly to the clash of contemporary politics as to the cleavages of history' (Sniderman et al., 2000, p. 84). In the post-war period, state efforts in the form of *intervento straordinario* sought to create a self-sustaining economy in the backward South. Nevertheless, the economic gap between North and South 'survived' all state efforts of industrialisation during the postwar period (Trigilia, 1992).

Thus, and in light of territorial disparities between North and South in Italy, the rise of political mobilisation in Northern Italy seems commonsensical. The rise and success of political mobilisation in the North, could be explained an angry response to major state redistributive efforts towards a *Sud assistito*. To some, the increasing globalisation of national economies and the process of European integration weakened the fragile basis of the Italian state (Mingione, 1993).

However, territorial dualism cannot explain the timing and the type of political mobilisation. This chapter focuses on understanding these two questions. First, territorial dualism cannot account for the timing of the revolt of the North. Structural explanations of the rise and success of Lega Nord emphasise long-term trends in the Italian economy. Why the North would revolt now as opposed to ten years earlier remains unexplained. Moreover, there is no empirical evidence to support the view of a growing gap between North and South in the 1990s. Second, the political manipulation of territorial dualism can explain the rise of distributional conflict in light of economic disparities between North and South. However, why were regional interests packaged with claims of nationhood and cultural distinctiveness? Why claims of nationhood and self-government as opposed to a mere tax revolt or a neoliberal party in the North?

In contrast to structural explanations for the salience of territorial dualism and *cleavage displacement* in contemporary Italy politics, this chapter argues that the rise of the Northern question was a *contingent* event, and focuses on how party mobilisation constructed a *new* definition of territorial dualism in Italy. This chapter highlights the timing and sequence of mobilisation to explain the rise of the Northern question in the Italian political system. It also explains the political process by which the Northern question was constructed in Italy: the determinants of party formation and the political opportunity structures that shaped the early electoral success of Lega Nord. It argues that the packaging of the North as a single economic and social unit was the *outcome,* and not the pre-existing condition, of political mobilisation.

The chapter brings evidence to show how the North became a new idea to organise and a new principle of political action. I emphasise the importance of Umberto Bossi's political leadership. However, unlike explanations that emphasise *charismatic* leadership, I put party leadership within the context of the ideas and strategies that led to the creation of Lega Nord. The creation of Lega Nord is explained as the product of the cooperative strategies of the parties in the 'ordinary' regions of Northern Italy seeking the recognition of the Northern Italian regions as *nations.* I show how the timing and sequence of political choices of these political entrepreneurs, as they understood the changes taken place in the Italian party system, matter to explain the rise of the Northern question. I highlight the importance of past political choices, as the new actors adjusted their behavior in light of the information they had at their disposal.

The success of Lega Nord is explained within the context of the demise of the Communist 'threat' and its impact in the stability of electoral alignments. Throughout the 1980s the lack of governmental alternatives to DC governments and public dissatisfaction with traditional parties led to renewed criticisms against Italian *partitocrazia*. Electoral volatility in the Northern regions increasingly grew, but during the 1980s there was a fundamental continuity in the main lines of conflict in the Italian party system (Mannheimer, 1991). However, by the turn of the decade, an exogenous shock (the collapse of Communism in Eastern Europe) marked a critical juncture in the Italian party system. It eroded the basis of the main political division in the Italian party system, that of Christian Democrats and Communists. The acceleration of de-alignment with the symbolic end of the Cold War and the refounding of the Italian Communist party had a snowball effect in eroding party alignments and bringing political visiblity to new claims.

The outcome of this political processes was the manufacturing of Padania, the construction of the North of Italy as a homogenous political, cultural and economic unit. The new cleavage was the product of political entrepreneurship that coupled identity and interests—the 'heart and the pocket' in the words of one of the leaders of Lega Nord—to construct a new political conflict. Political mobilisation in Northern Italy shows how the new party elites can use the principle of legitimacy embedded in nationalism to package new identities and interest to redraw the territorial and redistributive boundaries within Europe. The coupling of identities and interests in new mobilisation hits at the core of distributive conflicts in Europe. The legitimacy embedded in nationalism allows new political entrepreneurs to contest the redistributive policies of the state. Mobilisation is not only about claiming rights of political and economic autonomy, but also about avoiding fiscal obligations vis-a-vis the state.

Paradoxically, the political exploitation of the North-South territorial cleavage in Italy exposed that differences *within* Northern Italy were more important to explain the electoral success of Lega Nord. Regional economies, and not a united North, were on of the main political novelties of the 1990s in Italy. Moreover, the differential erosion of traditional electoral alignments in Northern Italy defined the strategic scenario available for the party leadership. Already in 1992, Italian elections signaled the limits of the geographical penetration of Lega Nord. Widespread electoral de-alignment in the North of Italy was combined with the electoral stability in the Communist regions. The Communist territorial subculture in the center-North regions left only marginal avenues for the expansion of Lega Nord. However, the erosion of the Christian Democrats and the Socialist party in the North was the fertile ground to expand their electoral base.

The geography of electoral success also changed. From a party located in Lombardy expanding into metropolitan areas in 1993, Lega Nord evolved into a party confined to the small localities of the peripheries of the industrial North and the Northern provinces located in Veneto and Eastern Lombardy. While the center of attention in the early 1990s was the revolt of Lombardy, the Veneto region replaced Lombardy with the 'miracle' of the North-East. In the past, the Italian North was characterised by profound differences in electoral alignments. The geography of electoral support for Lega Nord showed great disparities within the Northern regions. In fact, the electoral support for Lega Nord has been shifting from the 'protesting' Lombardy to the 'miracle' of the North-Est.

Virtuous cycles of mobilisation bring about self-reinforcing patterns and political inertia. In the early 1990s, the stakes of electoral competition were higher than in the previous decade. Lega Nord was not only the most successful new political actor in the Northern regions, but also brought about a cycle of mobilisation that undermined alternative claims of territorial distinctiveness (the ordinary regions) from the electoral arena. I emphasise the importance of the centralisation of party alternatives before the fall of the Berlin wall and the symbolic removal of the Communist *threat* in the Italian party system. The time horizons of political choices matter as party leaders in Veneto—today one of the most *autonomist* areas in Northern Italy—pondered about the consequences of the political choices that led them into a political pact for the unity of the North. For the party leaders that signed the agreement that created Lega Nord, it was a win-win strategy for all. Only when the disparities in the electoral support for Lega Nord across the Northern regions became more visible during the 1990s did they realise of the political costs of past choices. As the electoral success of Lega Nord in Veneto and the costs of Bossi's party centralisation became apparent, Venetian politicians attempted to break away. The pact gave legal ownership of Liga Veneta and its symbol to Lega Nord, but more importantly, shaped the boundaries of territorial conflict in Italian politics as *the Northern question*. Considerations of political opportunity then (the information available at the time and the uncertainties about their electoral prospects) and today (the crowding in of the electoral market) make, in their views, mobilisation on the basis of the 'ordinary' regions of the North no longer a feasible option. This was, in fact, the political lesson of the 1990s.

Background: Territorial Dualism in Italy

A variety of scholars have emphasised the profound social, economic and cultural differences between North and South since Italian unification and how these differences deeply marked the development of the Italian state, its economy and political institutions (Banfield, 1958; Putnam, 1993; Gramsci, 1951). The gap between North and South became a founding element of the Italian state and shaped its development. A diffused view of Italy holds that North and South in Italy *are* different.

The structural differences between North and South have been explored at three different levels: economic, cultural and political. In economic terms, the disparities between North and South were already visible at the time of Italian unification. The North industrialised and the South remained a backward agricultural society. Moreover, the structural differences between North and South in Italy proved resilient. Despite state industrialisation efforts in the post-war period, the rate of industrialisation of the South remained stabilised around 25% of the economic activities since the 1960s (Trigilia, 1992).

Different 'cultures' between North and South are also brought to the fore to explain why the Italian regions are so different. An academic tradition that started with Banfield's study of a Southern village linked Southern 'backwardness' with cultural differences in the form of *amoral familism* (Banfield, 1958). In the same tradition, cultural differences between North and South have been recently studied by Robert Putnam. Putnam argues that in the North a civic and participatory culture prevails, while in the South dominates a hierarchical, individualist and passive one. For Putnam, these two cultures determine and explain not only differences in the institutional performance of the Italian regions, but also different economic trajectories of North and South (Putnam, 1993).

North and South are also treated as different political systems. In many accounts, the South is the source of the pathological characteristics of Italian politics: corruption and clientelism and Mafia. The political differences of the South vis-á-vis the North relate to two different questions. First, the relationship between voters and parties in the South was established on the parties's ability to 'deliver the goods', and hold clienteles in the distribution of state resources. Second, the very sense of statehood is at stake in the South. The Mafia, Camorra and related phenomena challenged the very existence and legtimacy of state institutions.

The socio-economic gap between North and South, however, was never *translated* into the Italian party system. According to Lipset and Rokkan, and despite the lack of cultural or national homogeneity in Italy, the pattern of formation of the Italian state prevented the formation of a territorial cleavage in the Italian party system. The sequence of cleavages in the formation of the Italian party system accounted for the key absence of a territorial cleavage. For Lipset and Rokkan,

> In Italy the thrust of national mobilization came from the economically advanced North ... the impoverished provinces to the South and on the islands resisted the new administrators as alien usurpers but did not develop parties of regional resistance. In contrast to the development in Spain, the territorial conflict within Italy found *no direct expression* in the party system (Lipset and Rokkan, 1967, p. 43).

The erosion of traditional cleavages in the Italian party system offered opportunities for *cleavage displacement*. The territorial dualism explanation suggests that the traditional North-South socio-economic disparities in Italy are the main source for the success of Lega Nord. Scholary research on the sources and persistence of North and South in Italy provides considerable *ammunition* to consider the rise of political mobilisation in Northern Italy commonsensical. The image of the inevitability of a political conflict between North and South in Italian politics is, however, misleading.

Cleavage Displacement: North and South: A Growing Divide?

During the 1980s the economic gap between North and South was allegedly accelerating and constraining the sustainability of the Northern economy. One view sustains that the economic gap between North and South has been growing. As Putnam writes in his well-known, *Making Democracy Work. Civic Traditions in Modern Italy*:

> Throughout the twentieth century the North-South gap has grown relentlessly, despite swings in world conditions (war and peace, the Great Depression and the postwar boom), fundamental constitutional changes (monarchy, Fascism, and parliamentary democracy) and great changes in economic policy (the fascist attempt at autarky, European integration, and, not least, a massive program of public investments in the *Mezzogiorno* over the last forty years) (1993, p. 158).

In many views, the North-South divide is *not* new, but it is *no* longer sustainable. Mingione argues that globalisation implies the 'fading away of the socio-economic basis of the nation-state' (Mingione, 1993, p. 315). The Italian translation of global economic processes would be manifested by the political revolt of the North. As Mingione puts it: 'the increasing electoral success of the localistic leagues in the North reflects structural tensions and the crisis of the dual social integration system of hegemony in Italy' (Mingione, 1993, pp. 317-318).

In the postwar period Italian governments engaged in a major effort to develop the South. Under the form of *intervento straordinario*, subsidies for the industrial and infrastructural development of the Southern economy were channeled by an *ad hoc* state agency, *la Cassa per il Mezzogiorno*. The increasing burden of the South in state public expenditures could not be sustained. Trigilia estimates that in the second half of the 1980s, while the percentage of public expenditures in the South was 35%, the fiscal contributions from the South amounted to only 18% of the total (Trigilia, 1992, p. 61). By 1990, 19.7% of the population in the South was unemployed, compared to 6.5% in the North (Trigilia, 1992, p. 41). Table 1 shows the evolution of Italian public deficit and public debt since 1970. The dramatic increase of both, especially at the turn of the 1990s, sent an alarm about the burden of the Italian state.

Consumption and Growth: the Gap between North and South

Macroeconomic indicators and the fiscal performance of the Italian state deteriorated during the 1980s. The image of the South as a burden to the Italian state was also suggested by the performance of pubic debt and public deficit in Italy.

Table 3.1 Italian Public Debt and Deficit (1970-1992) (% GDP)

	Public Deficit	Public Debt
1970	3.7	38.0
1975	11.6	57.6
1980	8.5	57.7
1981	11.4	59.9
1982	11.3	64.9
1983	10.6	70.0
1984	11.6	75.2
1985	12.6	82.3
1986	11.6	86.3
1987	11.0	90.5
1988	10.7	92.6
1989	9.9	95.6
1990	10.9	97.8
1991	10.2	101.4
1992	9.5	108.0

Source: Vincent della Sala, 1997: 23

The rise of Lega Nord is easily interpreted as the revolt of the wealthy North against the mismanagement of public resources and the economic burden of the South. Some scholars even argue that the South and Southern interests had also *colonised* the Italian state apparatus. As Tom Gallagher writes: 'By the end of the 1980s the North was coming to resemble an advanced economic periphery in a state directed from and staffed by personnel drawn from the South' (Gallagher, 1992, p. 472).

Economic factors provide the background to understand the rise of Lega Nord. Territorial dualism has marked the political and economic development of the Italian state. Still today socio-economic indicators show a wide disparity between North and South. The gap between North and South remains characteristic despite the efforts of Italian governments to create the basis for self-propelling economic development in the South (Trigilia, 1992). Economic differences between North and South retain their visibility. Average income in the South, despite its growth over the post-war period, has remained slightly over half the average income in the North. While all the regions of the South are classified under the European Commission framework as underdeveloped regions eligible for objective 1 of the European Community structural funds, the North remains one of the most developed economies in the entire European Union.

However, structural explanations about the *activation* of a territorial cleavage do not offer an explanation of the timing of political mobilisation and the nature of the claims.

Background Conditions and the Northern Question

The image of a growing gap between North and South is misleading. The comparative analysis of the decade 1981-1991 shows that the South did not win nor lose with regard to the national average. GDP per capita remained stabilised as 67.7% of the national average (Instituto Tagliacarne, 1993).

Table 3.2 shows the persistence of economic differences between North and South in the period after 1965.

Table 3.2 The Gap between North and South (1965-1987)

	1965		1970-73		1974-84		1985-87	
Areas	*Income*	*GDP*	*Income*	*GDP*	*Income*	*GDP*	*Income*	*GDP*
North-Center	114.2	119.4	111.8	116.8	110.8	117.1	113.2	117.7
South	74.9	65.8	77.6	68.9	79.5	68.7	76.7	68.7
Italy	100.0	100.0	100.0	100.0	100.0	100.0	100.0	100.0

Source: Wolleb and Wolleb, 1990: 43

The time-lag between economic grievances and the rise of the party is left unexplained. As Mingione has put it: 'it took twenty years for people in the North to *realise* the failure of national integration' (Mingione, 1993, pp. 316-317). Public expenditures in the South, while pervasive, were less significant than most accounts tell. The Southern economy grew faster than the Northern one in the early 1990s, mostly due to agricultural production (Instituto Tagliacarne, 1993). In absolute terms public expenditures per capita in the North exceeded expenditures in the South. According to Trigilia estimates, at the end of the 1980s and with a population representing 36.5% of the Italian total, the South received 34.7% of public expenditures (Trigilia, 1992, p. 56). Trigilia also shows the real dimensions of extraordinary intervention in the South. Between 1951-1988, the Italian state spent a total of 185 milliardi in the *Cassa per il Mezzogiorno*. The growth of public expenditures peaked in the 1970s and entered since then a decreasing trend. In terms of Italian GDP, *intervento straordinario* accounted from a maximum of 0.91% to 0.46% in the years 1987-1989 (Trigilia, 1987, p. 59).

While the *colonisation* of the state by Southern politicians and Southern interests has become a *commonsensical* statement about the Italian political system—widely publicised by Lega Nord—evidence to support this claim is scant. During the post-war period there was a stable pattern of proportional representation on territorial basis in Italian governments, both in terms of ministers and sub-secretaries (Mannheimer and Calise, 1981; Todesco, 1994).[1] Moreover, the composition of the national executive of the Christian Democratic party, which according to widespread views was held captured by Southern politicians, shows that politicians from the North were over-represented in the party executive and their share grew steadily during the 1970s and 1980s.[2] Finally, in the 1980s the main change in the Italian party system was the role played by the *Partito Socialista Italiano*. Its leader Bettino Craxi gave a new visibility to the North, representing a *modernised* and efficient Italy with a Milanese outlook (Rampini, 1994). While there is no doubt that governmental parties, in particular the DC, were losing votes in the North during the 1980s, and the Italian state was facing major problems with the escalation of public debt, we cannot conclude that the North had become an *advanced economic periphery* in Italy.

The economic disparities between North and South are established on the assumption that North and South are homogeneous units. The image of the North and South as economic and culturally homogeneous units, however, neglects the profound differences *within* North and South. First, scholars emphasise the differences in the economic structure within the North-West and North-East (Trigilia, 1987, 1994; Bagnasco, 1977). Second, recent studies on the Southern economy, in particular the research conducted by Piattoni, also show the internal differentiation within the South and the different trajectories of regional economies within it. As Piattoni, has put it: 'insistence on the supposedly deep-seated social and cultural differences between North and South fossilizes the debate around the wrong conceptual categories and fosters a sense of false impotence' (Piattoni, 1996, p. 307).

Thus, structural differences between the Northern and the Southern economies are in light of many scholars, less important than the crucial economic differences *within* North and South. Since the 1970s students of Italian economy have argued that the rise of *Third Italy* has broken with the traditional polarity between North and South.

These explanations cannot account for the packing of the economic interests of the North with the logic of political action of Lega Nord. Why identity and claims to nationhood as opposed to a mere tax revolt or a neo-liberal party territorially based in Northern Italy? Lega Nord claims redistribution on the grounds of a common Northern identity and the cultural homogeneity of the North vis-à-vis the South. Internal differentiation in cultural patterns between North and South can also be brought to the front. First, there are widespread differences in the cultures within the North. Scholarly research since the 1960s identified two different territorial subcultures in the North: the Catholic subculture characterised by the hegemonic role of the DC and the red subculture by the prevalent role of the Communist party in the red regions. In political terms, clientelism and corruption were widespread in the South, but *also* in the North. It is worth highlighting that the corruption scandals that plagued the Italian political system during the 1990s were mainly focused on widespread political corruption in the *Northern* cities. Moreover, the role of the Christian Democrats in Veneto and their clientelistic machine resembles many of the analysis of Southern clientelism (Pansa, 1980).

The characterisation of North and South as different units provides stereotypical images about Italy. In fact, stereotypes about Southerners are common in the North. Prejudices against Southerners—*terroni*—and anti-Southern sentiments are widespread in Northern Italy. However, these stereotypes do not explain the rise and success of Lega Nord. First, social prejudices against Southerners were as prevalent in the past as they are today. Migration flows in the post-war period made these prejudices particularly salient in the 1960s and 1970s when many migrants from the Italian South moved to the industrialised Northern cities. Second, stereotypes of Southerners were as widespread in the Northern industrial areas as in other localities of the North-Center and North-East. Kertzer's study of the neighborhoods in the periphery of Bologna found that the *only* thing that the Catholic and Communist worlds shared in the 1970s was their prejudices against Southerners (Kertzer, 1978). In the red regions, however, the electoral growth of Lega Nord has been very marginal. During my fieldwork in Northern Italy I had many opportunities to experience first hand how widespread are prejudices against Southerners in the North. However, it also opened up the multiple stereotypes and prejudices that circulate, not only about the Southerners, but also about Venetians (*terroni del Nord*), and provincials from Varese and Bergamo, to name just a few.

Views on the inevitability of North-South conflict and the activation of a pre-exiting territorial cleavage in the Italian state obscured the contingent history and the political process by which the idea of the North as a homogeneous economic, social and cultural unit was launched and the conditions under which it gained political salience. As I will explain later, however, social scientific discourses and prejudices and stereotypes are important in order to explain how the new party, Lega Nord, defined a new territorial identity of the North. The definition of territorial conflict, as the *Northern question* was self-reinforcing. Once packaged by Lega Nord, the definition of territorial conflict was very difficult to reverse, locking political actors into a trajectory of political change.

The Exogenous Shock: The Italian Party System in Disarray

The opposition between Christian Democrats and Communists provided an image of profound electoral stability in Italian politics throughout the entire post-war period. However, since the 1970s the erosion of Italian political system was analysed at three distinctive levels. First, the crisis was signaled by the erosion of mass parties and mass organisations that dominated the first two decades of the post-war period. Second, electoral de-alignment and increasing instablity of voting patterns initiated during the 1970s. Third, increasing public dissatisfaction with political parties was reinforced by the dynamics of unstable and multi-party governments in Italy.

While the 1980s were marked by fundamental continuity in electoral alignments, the role of party organisations had been profoundly transformed by economic and social change in the previous two decades. The crisis of representation of Italian parties is a common theme during the 1980s. The ideal type of mass parties characterised by the organisational encapsulation of society in collateral organisations, mass membership and the parties' capacity to mobilise underscores many analyses of the Italian Communist Party and the Democrazia Cristiana in the first decades of the post-war period. The emergence of *partitocracy* or the 'oligipolistic' management of the political market changed the role of political parties as their functions increasingly shifted from societal encapsulation and mobilisation, to parties' penetration and management of the state apparatus and public sector. In many West European countries, the economic crises of the 1970s were to trigger a major reconfiguration of social and political coalitions. In contrast, the Italian party system remained trapped in the old system of alliances that blocked the political system and prevented political change (Pasquino, 1987, 1992). Two main features of the Italian party system exacerbated the crisis of representation of party politics in Italy: coalition government and the penetration of state institutions and the public sector. The possiblity of alternation in government during the 1980s looked as remote as with the previous *pactum ad excludendum* against the PCI.

However, during the 1980s there was a fundamental electoral and political continuity in Italian politics. The *compromesso storico* and the Turin strike in 1980s marked a turning point in the turmoil history of post-war Italian politics. The decade of the 1980s is, from the point of view of social and political mobilisation, a watershed. The leadership exercised by Bettino Craxi in the Italian governments from 1983 onwards brought about renewed efforts for modernisation and institutional reform. By all accounts, the 1980s represents a demobilised period in the political history of Italian parties and social actors.

Lega Nord was born at a moment when not only the mobilisation capacities of the Italian traditional parties was greatly diminished, but also public dissatisfaction with political parties—a classical feature of Italian political culture—was increasing (Almond and Verba, 1958; Manheimer, 1991). In 1989 the fall of the Berlin Wall and the collapse of the Eastern European Communist regimes removed the main cleavage that had structured Italian politics in the post-war period and had excluded the Italian Communist Party from Italian governments during the entire period. The symbolic demise of Communism had a snowball effect in traditional electoral alignments.

The key to understand the sequence of political change is thus, an exogenous shock: the fall of the Berlin Wall and the demise of the Communist regimes in Eastern Europe. The impact of these changes on the strongest Communist party of Western Europe cannot be overemphasised. On the one hand, events in Eastern Europe led to an internal debate within the Italian Communist party that involved its ideological and programmatic transformation. The history of the Italian Communist party ended in 1991. The divisions within the party leadership led to the refounding of the party as PDS, *Partito Democratico della Sinistra*, and a splinter group, *Rifondazione Communista* (Ignazi 1992). On the other hand, the end of the Communist threat removed the political key to Christian Democrat's unity and cohesiveness. More importantly, the removal of Communism as the dividing line in Italian politics had very different impacts in traditional electoral alignments in Northern Italy. Electoral alignments showed patterns of change but also profound continuity. The impact, however, was mostly felt in the governmental DC. It weakened the internally heterogenous DC, and left the party without identity resources (Follini, 1982; Galli, 1993).

Moreover, scandals of political corruption followed the external shock on the Italian party system. The corruption scandals, known as *Tangentopoli*, began with the arrest of the Milanese Socialist Mario Chiesa in February 1992. The Milanese judges uncovered a system of bribes from business to political parties. As Waters has pointed out, the scandals highlighted how parties exploited their clientelistic relationship wtih economic groups and the scale of corruption in the system (Waters, 1994). Although the scandals first targeted Socialist politicians, politicians from all the governmental parties were investigated. In addition to the Tantentopoli affair, in 1993 the judiciary also investigated the relationship of the DC leadership—including Giulio Andreotti, Antonio Gaba, Paolo Cirino and Alfredo Vito—with the Naples Mafia (Waters, 1994; p. 172).

The differential erosion of traditional cleavages in Northern Italy provided distinctive opportunities and constraints for Lega Nord's leadership. to make the territorial identity of the North a new political alternative in the Italian party system. While the red regions maintained patterns of fundamental stability, electoral alignments in the North showed sharp changes. The crisis of the DC in the North provided opportunities for Lega Nord to define new conflict and shape new electoral alignments.

Cooperation and the Creation of Lega Nord: *L'unità fa la Forza*

During the 1980s 'entry barriers' in the Italian political system constrained the ability of the new parties in the regions of Piedmont, Lombardy and Veneto to make territorial identities an attractive idea in the electoral arena. After almost a decade of mobilisation efforts, they were marginal political actors. Lega Nord was created upon a set of regionalist parties that emerged in the early 1980s in the Lombardy, Veneto and Piedmont regions. The new parties competed in the electoral arena and mobilised on the claim of recognition of different territorial identities—the Northern ordinary regions—*colonised* and *oppressed* by the Italian state. During the 1980s the parties attempted—quite unsuccessfully—to gain representation at the local, regional and national level. Lega Nord is the result of an electoral coalition of regionalist parties that evolved into a single centralised party under the leadership of Bossi. The new party was officially launched in 1991.

The dynamics of collective action among party leaders during the 1980s explains the rise of the *Northern question* as the relevant dimension of territorial conflict. The political choices made by the party leaders in the ordinary regions of Northern Italy during the 1980s led from coordination of party programs to centralisation of party alternatives, and finally ended in the creation of a united Lega Nord under the leadership of Umberto Bossi. In 1989, the party leaders adjusted their behavior in light of the information available at the time. Lega Lombarda had entered a positive trajectory in 1987 while party organisations in Piedmont and Veneto could not take off in the electoral arena.

The new parties created in the 'ordinary' regions of Northern Italy had, as last chapter showed, similar programs. In Italy they aimed at the recognition of the 'ordinary' regions of the North as 'special' regions. At the European level their goals aimed at the creation of a federalist Europe, a Europe of *ethnies* and peoples. This European ideal was shared by all the parties and reflected the influence of the European federalist movement. Federalism in Europe—*Ethnic* federalism as envisaged by Heraud—provided a set of new ideas about reconfiguring borders in a united Europe (Heraud, 1963, 1971). These ideas were introduced by the Partito Federalista Europeo of Mantova, an earlier political ally of these parties.[3]

Cooperation among the party leaders of Union Piemonteisa, Lega Lombarda and Liga Veneta—Gremmo, Bossi and Rochetta—involved three aspects. First, their cooperation was about sharing ideas and party programs. Second, their cooperation also led to sharing resources, such as the publications of the party journals and frequent money loans. Third, their cooperation also involved electoral alliances in European and local elections.

Their collaboration was shaped by the common understanding that these new *nations* were united as Northern and European. As Northerners, they shared a common culture and historical legacy. The pre-existing Piedmont, Venetian and Lombard nations were considered part of a supra-national Northern reality: they were different among themselves, but equal within the North of Italy. According to Gremmo, the founder of Union Piemonteisa:

> supra-national cultural realities undoubtedly exist in the world: for instance, Egipticians are a nation despite they belong to the greater Arab world. The same applies to the Alpine Arc, where peoples, minorities, different nationalities with precise characteristics (which are undisclaimable and qualifying) recognize themselves united ... by a common civility which has its own roots in a millenarian origin, very different from that of the (Mediterranean) peoples of the peninsula. The *Padania* is the *logical* continuation of this discourse ... (*Vento del Nord*, 1981, p.13).

Cooperation among the regional parties took place not only because of the commonalities in their political projects but also for strategic reasons. The electoral symbol became the most valuable strategic resource in the hands of the new regional parties during the 1980s. According to the Italian legislation on elections, new parties had to collect a certain amount of signatures to be allowed to present their lists and compete in elections. Parliamentary representation, however, waived this legal requirement. In European elections, the larger size of the electoral districts provided an incentive to cooperate and present common electoral lists. One of the solutions to 'entry costs' in electoral competition was to cooperate by presenting common lists in elections. As last chapter explained, the first European elections in 1979 marked a turning point in the development of new political parties in the Northern Italian regions. One of the leaders of Union Valdotaine, Bruno Salvadori, decided to put together a common list of autonomists to gain representation in the European parliament. In 1979, Union Valdotaine presents itself as a confederate union of parties and autonomist movements, federalist, regional forces and independents for a Europe of 'autonomies, progress and freedom'.[4]

During the 1980s electoral symbols were often exchanged and borrowed to compete in elections. In the European elections of 1979, 1984 and 1989, the electoral coalitions were supported by the symbols of the parties with parliamentary representation at that time: Union Valdotaine (1979), Liga Veneta (1984) and Lega Lombarda (1989). This practice was also used for local and general Italian elections. Lega Lombarda and Union Piemonteisa borrowed the symbol of *Lista per Trieste* in the general elections of 1983. Lega Lombarda and Union Piemonteisa also borrowed the electoral symbol of Liga Veneta in the local and regional elections of 1985. Thus, whoever had parliamentary representation, also had leverage to negotiate and define both the political goals of the coalition and its constituting members.

In the early 1980s the new parties in the regions of the North created a federation for the cooperation of autonomist parties after the first alliance in the 1979 European elections. In 1981, the parties had a meeting in Nancy to work towards a European federation of Federalists and Autonomists (including Partito Federalista Europeo, Moviment D'Autonomia e Arnassita Piemonteisa, Lega Lombarda, Liga Veneta e Movimento Friuli (*Vento del Nord*, n.2, Gremmo, 1981).[5]

The regional parties ran together for the European elections of 1984 and 1989. In the European elections of 1984, the federation and electoral alliance was presented under the electoral symbol of Liga Veneta. The parties reached an agreement in the city of Verona (Veneto) to present a single list to the European Elections of 1984. The electoral coalition, the Union for a

Federalist Europe included *Partito Federalista Europeo, Movimento Autonomista Rinascita Piemontese, Lega Autonomista Lombarda, Liga Veneta and Partito Popolare Trentino Tirolese per l'Unita Europea.* Lombardia Autonomista describes it as 'an alliance of Padanian-Alpinian people against traditional parties' (Lombardia Autonomista 17, 1984). The Document formalising the Alliance states: 'the new alliance aims to become the nucleus for the construction of a great federalist political force as an alternative to traditional parties' (Lombardia Autonomista. N. 17 Gennaio 1984).[6]

In contrast, in the European elections of 1989, the alliance was presented under the electoral symbol of Lega Lombarda. The electoral alliance for the European elections of 1989 was made on April 20, 1989. This time the electoral alliance was defined as an 'alliance of autonomist, ethnic and federalist movements for the representation of the regions of Northern Italy' (Lombardia Autonomista, 1989). The parties participating on the electoral coalition also changed. The movements participating in the alliance were Lega Lombarda, Liga Veneta, Piemont Autonomista, and three new parties— Union Ligure, Alleanza Toscana, Lega Emilia-Romagna. Table 3 lists the three alliances for the European elections of 1979, 1984 and 1989 with the different partners involved in each of them.

Table 3.3 Electoral Alliances and European Elections

1979 Union Valdotaine's Federation	1984 Unione per l'Europa Federalista	1989 Alleanza Nord
• Union Valdotaine • Liga Veneta • Rinascita Piemontese • Movimento Autonomista Occitano • Partito popolare Trentino Tirolese • Coumboscuro (Movimento di autonomia e Civilta Provenzale Alpina) • Union Slovena • Movimento Friuli • Partito Federalista Europeo	• Partito Federalista Europeo • Movimento Autonomista Rinascita Piemontese • Lega Autonomista Lombarda • Liga Veneta • Partito Popolare Trentino Tirolese per l'Unita Europea	• Lega Lombarda • Liga Veneta • Movimento Autonomista Piemontese • Union Ligure • Alleanza Toscana • Lega Emilia-Romagna

The European elections of 1989 represented an electoral success for the autonomist parties. The alliance obtained two seats in the European parliament.[7] Italian newspapers and academics began to pay attention to Bossi and Lega Lombarda. Umberto Bossi, became the main political novelty in Italian politics (Mannheimer, 1991; Biorcio, 1991, 1997). In fact, the electoral results were an electoral success of Lega Lombarda in the Lombard region, since the results of the electoral alliance outside Lombardy were marginal (Diamanti, 1993).

Alleanza Nord, originally devised as a confederation of autonomist parties, was also a program for a closer collaboration among the parties. Article 1 of the statute of the electoral alliance declared:

> The creation of the Northern Alliance establishes the reciprocal information, solidarity and collaboration of the autonomists, ethnic and federalist movements historically representatives of the Padanian-Alpinian regions and peoples and of those closer in terms of culture, traditions, and vocation, in order to elaborate a common political line at the supra-regional and European level (from the Statutes of Alleanza Nord, Piemont Autonomista, April 1989, p. 1).

The alliance also involved the formalisation of the political practices developed during the 1980s: a political project to consolidate one party and one list in each single region—trying to integrate local movements into regional ones and eliminate competition over the territory—and a policy of non-intervention in party internal matters. In fact, all had violated the policy of non-intervention in the internal affairs of their allies during the 1980s. As last chapter explained, political factionalism characterised the development of these new parties during the 1980s. The division of autonomist lists in Veneto and Piedmont allowed Bossi to take advantage of those divisions to improve its party's position within the coalition. Conflicts between competing lists in Piedmont and Veneto provided Bossi with the opportunity to negotiate among the factions and further strengthened its political leverage. In 1984, Bossi mediated the disputes between Tramarin and Rochetta in the Veneto region. In 1987 and 1988, Bossi dealt with the competing factions in Piedmont, those of Gremmo and Farassino. He greatly benefited from the divisions among his allies.

Parliamentary representation in 1987 gave Bossi the possibility to choose partners for the electoral alliance in 1989. The leader of Lega Lombarda put a lot of pressure on his allies to unify the party alternatives. In turn, the other parties had incentives to stay within a broader coalition to improve their chances of getting parliamentary representation. From 1984 to 1989, the partners of the alliance changed. Of the original regional parties participating in the electoral alliance of 1984, only Lega Lombarda and Liga Veneta remained within the electoral pact that formed the basis of Lega Nord. In 1989, the electoral alliance was formed by Lega Lombarda, Liga Veneta and the Farassino faction in Piedmont on the one hand, and three other parties, Union Tuscana, Lega Emilia-Romagnola and Union Ligure. The group in Ligura was born as a fiscal protest. They contacted Lega Lombarda's secretary. In Tuscany, the Fragassi family—father and son—coordinated a political group. In Emilia, in contrast, the emerging organisation was the product of the initiatives of the provincial secretary of Lega Lombarda in Cremona who created the first *cell* in the city of Parma.

After the electoral success in the European elections of 1989 Bossi launched the proposal to create a unified party. The organisational secretary of Lega Lombarda at the time explained the events:

> There were two moments for us, before and after 1989. We had the meetings in which Bossi explained that unity makes for strength. First we made an electoral agreement, non-political, to request regional autonomy. Then we created a federalist movement, all together against Roman centralism (Patelli, Milano 1996).

The creation of a united Lega Nord was sanctioned in December 1989. The agreement among the party leaders took place in the Lombard city of Bergamo and was originally intended as a confederation of political parties. The agreement was to remain inactive for a period of two years in order to 'get used to the idea' (Gobbo, Venezia 1996). Lega Nord was fully launched as a political party only in its first congress in 1991.[8]

In the transition from autonomist parties to a united Lega Nord the party leaders had initially sought coordination rather than centralisation. Lega Nord would have served as an umbrella to run national and European elections, while the regional organisations would have the control over regional and local elections. However, what was devised as a confederation evolved into single centralised party under Bossi's command. Lega Nord acquired legal ownership of the symbols and labels of all parties. The efforts of Liga Veneta leaders, the couple Rochetta and Marin, to make an agreement that would reflect an *equal status* for the Venetians within the party organisation failed. As Rochetta put it:

> We negotiated for months, we wanted an agremeent among equal partners. Marin became the first president of Lega Nord ... (Venezia, 1996).

Thus, the process of party formation reflected the power relations within the nationalist 'sector'. Lega Nord was the product of negotiations between the party leaders, but fundamentally reflected the hegemony of Lega Lombarda. The agreement was, in fact, the starting point for Bossi to eliminate all the competition over the territory. The starting point for the strategies of the party leadership is summarised in the ten commandments of the party ideologue in the early 1990s, Gianfranco Miglio. He strongly recommended to make Lombardy the nucleus of a Padanian Lega. Number 7 of Miglio's commandments stressed the importance of making Lega Lombarda the core of a Northern-Padanian one:

> without the Padania (Piemonte, Lombardia, Veneto, Liguria and Emilia Romagna), Lombardy by itself wouldn't win this fight, and without the success of Lega lombarda and its persistence, Padania will never take off (Miglio, 1994: 17-20).

The transition from independent regionally-based political parties into a united Lega Nord involved the transformation of marginal autonomous organisations into party administrative divisions—*national* secretaries—within a single centralised party. Lega Nord became a coalition of 'unity in diversity'. The first statute of Lega Nord was approved in the first federal Congress of the party in 1991. Article 3 of the first statute established that Lega Nord has legal ownership over the labels Liga Veneta, Lega Lombarda, Piemont Autonomista, Union Ligure, Alleanza Toscana-Lega Toscana-Movimento per la Toscana, Lega Emilio-Romagnola (article 3 Statute). Liga Veneta (which became Lega Nord-Liga Veneta) was the only one, together with Bossi's Lega Lombarda, to retain the right to use the old party symbol in local and regional elections. This passage has large implications for the trayectory of territorial mobilisation in Northern Italy. In the early 1990s the quest for unity was considered the only road towards electoral success:

> Bossi's merit was in leaving behind localism. For instance, in Spain there is no relationship between Basque separatists and other separatists ... that weakens autonomism. We are today the strongest autonomist movement in Europe. By creating Lega Nord we avoided fragmentation and the temptation of each of us working for its region. With the Alleanza Nord we made an electoral agreement and then slowly the autonomist movements understood that unity brings strength (Speroni, Busto Arsizio, 1996).

The timing and sequence of these political choices explain the peculiar trajectory of territorial conflict in Italian politics. The centralisation of the party supply and organisation preceded the collapse of traditional parties and the transformation of the main dimensions of political conflict in the Italian party system. By looking at the sequence of mobilisation, we understand the rise of the 'North' as the relevant dimension of electoral competition, as well as the impact of the differential erosion of traditional cleavages in the North.

The choices made by the leaders of the parties during the 1980s are here reconsidered in light of subsequent events in the 1990s. The leadership and elite of Lega Nord considered the explanation for creation of the single party as self-evident. They see the creation of Lega Nord as the possibility of going together against their common enemies—the state and the Italian traditional parties—without eliminating the roots of their *national* distinctiveness. As one member of Lega Nord in Veneto stated: 'One single region by itself cannot struggle against the state. We already have a hard time fighting as a North, imagine one single region!'.

The timing and sequence of the choices that centralised the autonomists at the end of the 1980s profoundly modified the politics of territorial conflict in Northern Italy. The goal of the party leadership became the transformation of the Italian state with the introduction of a new institutional system to represent the North. This goal was defined in the party statutes as the creation of a federal state in Italy. Article 1 of the statutes of the party establishes:

> The federalist and transnational political movement Lega Nord (later indicated as Movement, Federation or Lega Nord Italia Federale) aims at the peaceful transformation of the Italian state into a modern federal state through democratic and electoral means [...] to fulfill the aspirations of self-government of the peoples united under the Italian state, taking into account the need for a social

development linked to the ethno-linguistic cultural, historical and economic characteristics of these peoples, aiming at an effective and mutual parity and a peaceful collaboration with all the European peoples and the world (Statute of Lega Nord).[9]

In addition to demands for a new state structure in Italy, Lega Nord introduced a new party platform known as *liberismo federalista*. Lega Nord's moved the distribution of economic resources as the core of its territorial claims.[10] Although this *liberismo federalista* became the official party ideology, party elites were more united by its opposition to the other Italian parties than by the cohesiveness of their policies and their purposive goals. The use and distribution of economic resources was claimed not on the grounds of a neoliberal agenda of 'more or less state' but as a matter of political rights, questioning the whole edifice of the Italian state. Lega Nord did not claim the reduction of the tax burden *per se*, but the claim was made on the basis of the political rights of the North. One of the founders of Lega Nord refused the consideration of Lega Nord as a neoliberal party, rejecting this characterisation of the party (Leoni, Varese, 1996). The dismantled of the role of the state targets more the political practices that support clientelismo and *assistenzialismo* in the South and less public intervention to fight unemployment (Lega Nord 1992 Party Program).

Lega Nord's coupled the 'heart and the pocket', identity and interests to redraw the territorial boundaries within the Italian state. Lega became the second party in Lombardy and acquired political visibility as the new phenomenon in Italian politics. Giorgio Bocca, the influential journalist, published the same year a book that recognised the protest of Lega Nord in the official mainstraim as part of political debates (Bocca, 1990). Ruzza and Schimidtke analysed the convergence between the Italian newspapers and the issues politicised by Lega Nord in these years around the issues of political corruption, inefficient political system, waste of public resources and inadequate state services (Ruzza and Schmidtke, 1993).[11]

The *Northern question* gained visibility with the politicisation of three main issues: political corruption and anti-party and anti-state rhetoric, taxes and economic resources, and the presence of migrants from the South and Northern Africa in the North of Italy. However, the symbolic construction of a united North gave the party its political identity and 'brand' recognition. Whether in the form of federalism within the Italian state, or later secession and independence for Padania within a united Europe, Lega Nord has always claimed that 'the North is different' and must be institutionally recognised as such. In a profoundly changed European environment, this new politics is about the redefinition of the boundaries between state, market and society.

Rather than neo-liberals, in fact this is the politics of *welfare chauvinism*—the term is used by Kitschelt and McGann, 1995 (see Tarchi, 1998).

From a United North into *Padania*

The transformation of the political parties claiming nationhood for the 'ordinary' regions of Northern Italy into a united Lega Nord under the leadership of Bossi led some scholars to conclude that nationalism was no longer the founding principle of the new party. However, a territorial identity remained for the party leadership the legitimising basis of their politics. The basic claim—we are different, we want to be treated differently—did not changed with the creation of a single party. Neither changed the coupling of identity with the economic rights of the North. However, as the claim to a territorial identity moved from regional *nations* to a united North, the categories of belonging and nationhood, its geographical boundaries and the markers of cultural distinctiveness were reshaped anew. The transformation of the regional parties into Lega Nord led to new territorial boundaries and new views on cultural sameness and diversity to incorporate all the peoples of the North.

In the fabrication of the North as a homogenous economic, cultural and political unity, Lega Nord combined two main elements that informed the discursive practices of Lega Nord's leaders and the party ideological production: social scientific discourse, and European integration. Lega Nord grounded the claim of institutional recognition of the distinctiveness of Northern Italy as Padania, a nation, a multi-national reality, a 'civic' culture, a macro-European region. The party leadership made the categories of belonging malleable and in the making. During the 1990s asserting a distinctive territorial identity of the North for party leaders, organisers and supporters encompased a variety of views on the content of cultural distinctiveness, collective belonging and the relevant differences that make the North 'a' people. Some claim the cultural basis of their identity, while others stress the fundamental socio-economic nature of their homogeneity. As one of my interviewees described this malleability: 'We still need to define where Padania reaches but different socio-economic processes and different identities do exist in the North.' The first statute of the party did not specify the territorial boundaries of the North, the subsequent ones limited Padania.[12]

Lega Nord introduced a new language of differences, a new way of defining political conflict upon territorial basis. The basic claim is the existence of a North as an homogeneous people: 'we are a people with the same socio-economic fabric'. Lega Nord also shaped a new territorial identity that encoded a set of new ideas about territorial boundaries. Lega Nord's leadership fabricated the North as an homogeneous unit with common attributes and interests. The sameness of Northerners is represented as natural and self-evident. Languages, cultures and *ethnies* are part of the content of identity—the legacy of the origins of the party—and they are invoked to legitimise differences.

However, the party leader rejected *ethnicity* as the single criteria for territorial distinctiveness. In the early 1990s, Bossi rejected the exclusiveness of the *ethnic* identities of the Northerners to define the peoples of the North: 'Not for us. Not in the developed West. The cement can't be only *ethnic*. It must be also economic' (Lega Nord, February 3, 1993, p. 1).

This evolution of the identity politics of Lega Nord is usually highlighted (Biorcio, 1991, 1997). As a member who was directly involved in the creation of Lega Nord with Bossi put it:

> We moved from an ethnic-cultural discourse to a socio-economic one. The Padania is a people and has a similar socio-economic fabric. Though we point to a socio-economic logic ... we do have the cultural element (Ronchi, Milano, 1996).

Less common in academic writing is the recognition that cultural essentialism is at work, although the markers of cultural distinctiveness have shifted from *ethnic* and linguistic traits to *civic* and economic ones. The internal sameness of the North is essentialised as the culture of the North. In the views of the party, the productivity and wealth of the North are a manifestation of pre-existing cultural differences: a culture of hard work, entrepreneurship and autonomy. Bossi defined the new cultural distinctiveness for the North as follows:

> the isolation of every single region is not feasible because we face a powerful opponent, the national state (lo stato nazionale). The European culture, bring forward by Lega, has entered into collission with a centralist and anti-democratic culture of a great part of the country ... In order to make our culture the winner, we absolutely need to avoid falling into the traps of micronationalism, into the battle for the local language. These are the things which will come about by themselves in a second stage, they are the natural consequence of the changed balance of political power (Lega Nord, May 28, 1993).

In addition, social-scientific discourse was used to modernise the very idea of cultural distinctiveness. The new claim of distinctiveness involves the essentialisation of *civicness*: the idea of a civic North which is essentialised in 'democratic, participatory and well-governed' and in its productive hard-working people. 'Civicness' becomes a new marker of belonging to the nation.[13] The new nation is no longer the Northern nation, but Padania.

> Padania is the North of Italy which has a civic tradition in the communes. Our project is based on our territory and civic traditions. Our inheritance are the comunes with their elected powers. This is our political *gene*, the sense of autonomy and freedom. This sense remains in our cities and in our spirit (my emphasis).

In this reformulation of the Northern question, current economic processes simply accentuate and manifest the resiliance of cultural differences. As an article on *Quaderni Padani* put it:

> in Padania the level of internationalization of the economy is more profound than in the South and progress rapidly. This process is in Padania, not only the result of a renewed dynamism in the new European and world economic climate, but also of conditions linked to identity, geographical position, the economic and social fabric ... (Corti, 1995).

The claim of distinctiveness is based on their commonalties as Northerners and Europeans. As one of the early founders of the Lega in Lombardy introduced himself: 'I am a European who lives in Padania'.

Lega Nord claims the Northern economic rights on the basis of cultural distinctiveness and nationhood. As an article in a journal linked to Lega Nord, *Quaderni Padani* put it,

> Economical and social factors, especially in relation to European integration and the processes of internationalization of the economy, play today a determinant role in the process of taking national conciousness by the padanian-alpinian people ... a hundred and thirty years of centralized hood and nationalist rhetoric did not yet serve to construct an identity and a unity for which there were no basis: at most they were able to hide part of the cultural diversity under a veil of conformistic levelling. Today the veil is being torn precisely by the socio-economic differences (Corti, 1995, p. 15).[14]

The fabrication of a united North incorporated also a diverse and *multicultural* North. Sameness within the North also encompasses diversity. Lega politicians from Lombardy, Veneto and Piedmont assert the differences within the North but downplay their political relevance. Lega Nord is, from this point of view, a plural reality composed by the differences among the regions which are recognised and institutionalised in the party organisation. A representative of Lega summarised the elements to understand unity and diversity: 'the North is homogeneous and dishomogeneous from the rest of Italy. The are differences between Piedmont, Lombardy and Veneto but they are small. The differences between us and the rest of the country are, however, *fundamental* differences' (my emphasis).

As one representative put it: 'federalism is part of our culture, in our tradition of small states and local governments'. For the party leadership, the existing Italian regional governments are a by-product of the centralised Italian state and existing regional autonomy in Italy is a *mockery*. Lega Nord refuses the possibility of advancing political autonomy by reinforcing existing regions. The idea of federalism provides a common front against the centralist state.

What matters for the party leadership is the recognition of the North as a single and distinctive political unit. As one member in the regional council in Lombardy put it: 'We want federalism ...but for one part of the country'. In the early 1990s Lega Nord advanced a very peculiar federalism based on the cultural homogeneity of three cantons within Italy. According to Gianfranco Miglio, professor of Constitutional Law and the party 'ideologue' at the time, a future federal Italy had to be grounded in history. Miglio writes in his Model of a Federal Constitution:

> It should be immediately mentioned that the birth of a federal system in Italy can only take place *starting from the present Regions* (in original), keeping and combining their identities in different ways, and above all engaging the same people, honorary and bureaucratic, that managed them so far ... Whatever the rearrangements, the Federations's Cantons must be formed by the fifteen ordinary Regions—already normally grouped—for statistical and geo'economic purposes (but also on the basis of daily speech) in three large areas: The PO Valley (Liguria, Piedmont, Lombardy, Veneto, Emilia Romagna), Central Italy (Tuscany, Umbria, Latium, Marche) and Southern Italy (Abruzzo, Molise, Puglia, Campania, Basilicata, Calabria). Each of these constituent entities is in fact united by an undeniable historical-cultural homogeneity (Miglio, 1994, p. 9).

The fabrication of Northern homogeneity as a cultural and social unit is the basis to request this type of federalism. In the early 1990s, and at the same time that the Northern question is being reshaped and reformulated, political change in Italian North is starting to undermine the central claim of the Lega Nord movement.

Undoing Northern Unity: the Differential Erosion of Traditional Cleavages

Lega Nord entered a virtuous cycle of electoral success with two aspects. First, the first wave of expansion showed the increasing availablility of voters for traditional parties to shift and vote for Lega Nord (Natale, 1991; Diamanti, 1993). Second, Lega Nord was also successful expanding the geography of electoral support from Lombardy to the other regions of the North (Diamanti, 1993). In 1989 the impact of the erosion of the major divisions that structured the Italian party system during the post-war period provided a favorable opportunity structure for the reconfiguration of electoral alignments in the Italian party system. The weakening of the DC created a vacuum to bring about new ideas. Lega Nord's advanced the territory as an alternative politics to class and religious divisions and against traditional parties in Italy. The 'marriage' of *leghismo* with Catholics and the working class was repeatedly announced by Lega Nord's leadership: religious and class identifications were 'over' (interview with Leoni, Lega Nord, organo ufficiale della Lega Nord, 1992, December 4th). In the early 1990s Bossi's efforts were dedicated to make Lega Nord the natural heir of the Christian Democratic party in the north. According to Bossi, 'Lega Nord is the new party of Catholics. The DC is dead and buried' (Lega Nord, organo ufficiale della Lega Nord, 1993, July 7th).

The strategy behind the creation of Lega Nord was to expand the electoral geography of Bossi's electoral success in Lombardy to the other regions of the North. 1990 marked the take off of Lega Nord in the Italian party system. In 1990, with the borrowed symbol of Lega Lombarda, and in 1992, already with the symbol of Lega Nord, the party leadership tested its ability to make the North a political reality outside Lombardy.

The local elections of 1990 confirmed the political breakthrough of Lega Nord in the Lombard region. After its success in the 1989 European elections, The party also began to expand its electoral geography from Lombardy to the other regions of the North (Diamanti, 1993). By 1992, Lega Nord was making significant inroads in Veneto. The first electoral test for a united Lega Nord took place in the 1992 Italian general elections. The outcome of the 1992 Italian elections redefined the electoral map of Italy (Sani, 1992). Table 4 shows the four Italies identified by Sani in the early 1990s.

Table 3.4 Sani's Four Italies: The Italian Party System in Disarray (%)

	Padania	Etruria	South-1	South2	Italy
DC	26.6	21.7	34.5	47.2	31.0
PDS-RC	17.0	39.9	19.5	16.1	22.2
PSI	12.3	12.6	15.1	15.2	13.5
Lega Nord	18.4	4.5	0.6	0.3	7.6
Laics	8.8	8.9	12.3	10.0	9.9
MSI	4.1	4.4	7.6	5.4	5.4
Concentration					
DC +PDS	39.0	53.0	50.0	59.0	48.0
DC+PDS+PSI	51.0	65.0	65.0	75.0	61.0
DC 87-92	-8.9	-3.5	-1.9	+0.2	-4.3
PCI87-92	-6.0	-4.0	-5.4	-5.8	-5.3
PSI 87-92	-2.7	0.3	+1.3	+2.2	-0.3
Volatility	0.22	0.09	0.12	0.10	0.15

Source: Sani, 1992: 561

The erosion of traditional parties in the North was profoundly visibile in the Northern regions. Electoral volatility was the highest of all the Italian regions. Lega Nord obtained 18.4% of the vote in the Padania identified by Sani. Lega Nord became the second party in terms of votes in the North, after the Christian Democrats. The latter, in turn, were invested by a profound crisis and obtained their lowest percentage of vote in the post-war period in the North.

The geography of electoral support for Lega Nord within the North, however, began to exhibit widespread differences. Lega Nord was extremely successful in the territorial areas of the old Catholic subculture where the DC had played an hegemonic role in the post-war period. In contrast, the electoral inroads in the areas controled by the Communist party—the red regions—were marginal.

Some scholars find the causes for the political success of Lega Nord in the *economia diffusa* of the Northern territorial economies (Trigilia, 1994, 1996; Gobetti, 1996: 2). Lega Nord's success cut in half Terza Italia. Lega Nord was most successful in the areas of the Catholic subculture—the East provinces of Lombardy and Veneto—whereas its presence in the areas of the Communist subculture—Tuscany, Emilia-Romagna—was politically marginal. The strongholds of the DC or the areas known as the Catholic territorial subculture suffered the impact of the external shock of removing the Communist threat. Veneto, the core of the white subculture, was the most affected region in Northern Italy by the erosion of traditional electoral alignments.

In Veneto, according to Diamanti and Riccamboni, the *religious cleavage* was able to resume the other cleavages, fundamentally the territorial one (Diamanti and Riccamboni, 1992, p. 7). The DC relied on the Church for the production of values. The DC enjoyed exclusive cultural legitimacy as the result of its association with the Catholic Chuch (Stern, 1971, p. 176). From the association with the Catholic Church derived the relative organisational weakness of Christian Democrats in these areas. Christian democratic rule in these areas shaped specific patterns of politics, and political participation, as well as a mis-trust of the state.[15]

The concept of subcultures coined in Almond and Verba's Civic Culture was further developed by Italian scholars to describe the societal and political networks, the type of politics and the main characteristics of Communist and Christian democratic politics at the local level (Galli, 1967; Pizzorno, 1966). The development of mass party organisations encapsulated Communist and Catholic subcultures in political, but also *geographically*, separated camps: both subcultures were territorial. The Catholic subculture included Tri-Veneto and the Communist subculture included Tuscany, Emilia-Romagna and the Marches. The two subcultures were segmented from the dominant elite culture and became 'institutionalised traditions' during the post-war period.[16] The political subcultures were closed systems that provide a wholeness of social and political life.

The political subcultures also defined a form of local political dominance: the parties enjoyed monopolistic political legitimacy (Stern, 1971). Both Communist and Catholic subcultures were characterised by a high capacity to aggregate and mediate interests at the local level. Trigilia treats both territorial subcultures as: 'local political systems through which not only a particular identity is reproduced, but also interests are mediated locally' (Trigilia, 1986, p. 131). It was the Church that provided the legitimacy to Christian Democrat politicians and the state and not vice versa (Diamanti and Riccamboni, 1992; Riccamboni, 1997; Messina, 1997).

In contrast, the Comunist territorial subculture, although suffering from these changes, showed more continuity in electoral aligments and proved a political barrier to the strategies of Lega Nord. Although scholars treated Third Italy as a single political and economic model of regulation characterised by the presence of territorial subcultures, the differential erosion of the political subcultures and traditional electoral alignments provided completely different scenarios for new territorial conflict.

The emergence of Third Italy and its economic success as a distinctive model undermined the main elements of territorial subcultural politics (Trigilia, 1986). The process of industrialisation fundamentally transformed some of the traditional elements of the subcultural areas. Some features of the local society and the subcultures provided a favorable environment for the spread of the small and medium size firms. At the same time, industrialisation eroded the closure of the subcultures. However, despite the commonalities in the white and red subcultures identified by scholars, fundamental differences existed in the type of political atittudes and participation in each of them.[17]

The processes of industrialisation and secularisation in the Catholic subculture undermined the hegemonic position of the DC. The transformation of politics in the Catholic areas involved changes in the role of the Church and the DC in these areas. Secularisation eroded the centrality of the Church in these communities. This erosion manifested itself in the uncoupling of the ties between religion and politics. On the one hand, the Church takes increasingly on a more autonomous and independent role vis-á-vis the governmental party. Vatican II and the weakening of the anti-communist policy puts the Church in a more independent position vis-á-vis political parties. On the other hand, the erosion of the Catholic subculture also shapes a new DC's policy in these areas. The party will reinforce the uncoupling of the ties by becoming more autonomous from the Church and its associational network. The active policy pursued by the *Dorotei* (the main DC current in these areas) will be to 'deliver the goods', promoting clientelistic ties and the party as the main agency to mediate interests between center and periphery, securing the ties between local and national politics. The erosion of the Catholic subculture in the North is identified as a major factor in explaining the electoral success of Lega Nord.

In the 1980s the primacy of Veneto as the DC stronghold was undermined by the electoral growth of the Christian Democrats in the South. Molise and Basilicata became the regional strongholds of the DC. Table 5 shows the dominant position the DC held in Veneto over the entire post war period.

Table 3.5 The Italian Regions and DC Vote

	1948		1963		1976		1983		1987		1992
Veneto	60.5	Veneto	52.7	Veneto	51.3	Molise	55.5	Molise	57.3	Molise	46.5
Friuli	57.0	Abruzzi	45.4	Molise	50.7	Basilicata	46.0	Basilicata	46.1	Basilicata	38.2
Abruzzi	53.7	Calabria	43.9	Basilicata	44.5	Veneto	42.5	Veneto	43.5	Abruzzi	38.0
Lombardia	52.5	Puglia	43.2	Abruzzi	44.2	Abruzzi	42.1	Abruzzi	42.2	Campania	32.4
Lazio	51.7	Friuli	42.6	Friuli	42.3	Sicilia	37.9	Sicilia	38.8	Calabria	32.4
Sardegna	51.2	Basilicata	42.5	Sicilia	42.2	Calabria	36.8	Calabria	37.0	Veneto	31.5
Trentino	50.4	Sardegna	42.5	Puglia	41.7	Puglia	36.3	Puglia	37.9		

Source: Diamanti and Riccamboni, 1992: 40

The erosion of traditional electoral alignments is here linked to the timing and sequence of political mobilisation. The situation of the DC in Veneto was characterised by its fundamental political stability, even at the end of the 1980s. In 1983—the success of Liga Veneta provoked the same type of arguments about the causes of the erosion of the DC and the rise of *leghismo* in Veneto (see for example Diamanti, 1993). Yet in 1987 the DC had improved its electoral results compared ot previous elections in the region. Political *inertia* sustained the stability of the Christian Democrats in the North. The transformation of the Christian Democrats in the North deteriorated the stability of electoral alignments in the 'white' zones and provided increasing opportunities to define new political space. Yet it is only *after* the critical juncture of 1989 that the position of the DC in these areas became really at risk. The strongholds of the DC in the Catholic territorial subculture suffered the impact of this external shock. Veneto, the core of the white subculture, was the most affected regions in Northern Italy by the erosion of traditional alignments. Veneto became, from 1992 onwards, one of the most *autonomist* regions in Northern Italy. Table 6 shows the percentage of votes to 'other parties' (that is new parties) in the crucial Italian elections of 1992.

Table 3.6 1992 Votes to 'Other Lists' by Region

Region	%Vote other parties
Veneto	34.1
Lombardy	27.6
Piedmont	24.9
Friuli Venezia Giulia	23.5
Trentino Alto-Adige	22.8

Source: Diamanti and Riccamboni, 1992: 175

For Diamanti and Riccamboni, the success of political autonomism in Veneto is obscured by the presence of other autonomists lists. Overall, and including the votes for Lega Nord and other minor parties, in the 1992 elections the autonomist vote was 25.5% of the total vote (Diamanti and Riccamboni, 1992, p. 174).

Electoral support for Lega Nord in the general elections of 1994 departed from 1992 in significant ways. As Diamanti has pointed out, the presence of Lega Nord in metropolitan areas and in many provinces of the North greatly diminished with the competition of Forza Italia. The electoral results brought about a geographical *dualism* in electoral alignments within the North. Metropolitan areas and the old industrial North deserted Lega Nord while the provinces of the periphery in Veneto and Eastern Lombardy became the electoral stronghold of the party. This geographical dualism in electoral support undermines the long-term goals of Lega Nord—the construction of an independent North. For one of the Lombard members of Lega Nord's parliamentary group:

> Venetians are different. There is a true autonomism in Veneto. They have a cultural and economic identity since they were less exposed to migration. There the leghista are all Christian Democrats. They have their interests in mind. They do not care about Padania, they only want autonomy for Veneto. I challenge you to put all these together. It is very risky ... Bossi fears that a dualism will be born. The Venetian autonomism is not secessionist ... Electorally, there is a Venetian hegemony, but they do not have the control over the party (Marano, Varese 1996).

The Role of Political Choices in the Rise of the Northern Question

In 1992, the creation of Lega Nord was a win-win strategy for all parties involved. Bosssi lead the revolt of the North but the other autonomists were also gaining political representation too. However, the virtue of the choices that created Lega Nord was later questioned in light of two crucial questions. First, in the late 1980s the organisational and expansionary efforts of Bossi's Lega Lombarda separated the former from its sister parties in Veneto and Piedmont.[18] Initially, a *primus inter pares*, Bossi struggled to eliminate regional leaders of Lega outside Lombardy, its earlier allies and founders of Lega Nord to assert his control over the organisation. From the political marginalisation of Roberto Gremmo in Piedmont in 1987 to the expulsion of Franco Rochetta and Marilena Marin in Veneto in 1995, Bossi has sought to eliminate any alternative sources of leadership within the organisation. During the 1990s, the same type of internal dynamics prevailed within the united Lega Nord.

In addition, the electoral *dualism* between Veneto and Lombardy in the electoral support for Lega Nord increased in every election during the 1990s. The choices of the leaders of the parties in Veneto were the product of the circumstances and information they had in 1989. A small event—the signature of a forgotten pact between the leaders of the parties in 1989—had large consequences for the trajectory of territorial conflict in Northern Italy. An interview with Franco Rochetta, the leader of Liga Veneta who signed the pact with Bossi in 1989 showed the extent to which political choices matter and they are very difficult to reverse. Lega Nord acquired legal ownership of the symbols and labels of Liga Veneta. The conditions under which the pact was signed in 1989 reflected the power relations within the autonomist sector at that time. For the ex-leader of Liga Veneto, Franco Rochetta,

> We were the first ones and precisely because of that we had the worst time. We wanted to create a movement for the reawekening and rinascita paralleled to the one in Catalonia a hundred years ago, abled to unite the identities and the interests, that's what we wanted to do. In the administrative elections of 1990 and 1991 Bossi was attacking Liga Veneta, saying that we were worried with folklorist battles over the dialects. This is Bossi's technique, it is not true, but all the newpapers repeated his words. We didn't make a battle for the language. Veneto is a nation like Catalonia, and we were always federalists. what could we do? We didn't have other alternative than going together ... Today Liga Veneta does not exist anymore. What exists is the Venetian section of Lega Nord (Venezia, 1996).

The first and only deputy of Liga Veneta in the Italian Parliament,

Achille Tramarin, today no longer involved in politics, after remembering the experiences of Liga Veneta, Union del Popolo Veneto and Moviment Autonomista Veneto answered to the question of why today there is no a Venetian party in the region commented:

> Both the new electoral law and the ruthless war of Bossi against all. There is not political space, today everything is occupied by Lega Nord (Tramarin, Padova, 1996).

The virtous cycle of political mobilisation that marked the trajectory of Lega Nord in the early 1990s also undermined alternative definitions of territorial conflict in the North. Strategic considerations on past, present and future opportunities in the political arena and the political inertia created by the Northern question are the key to explain the structuring of the territorial question in Northern Italy. Alternative political projects—the splinters of the original regional parties failed in their attempts to gain visibility. During the last decade, many leaders in Lombardy, Veneto and Piedmont left the organisation. They explained in personal interviews that exit from Lega Nord does not pay in political terms. As the leaders of the parties in Veneto and Piedmont (both the originals and splinters) claim, the electoral success of Lega Nord and the introduction of a new electoral system, a hybrid electoral system that makes it extremely difficult to organise political alternatives to Lega Nord's 'hegemony' in the definition of territorial conflict and in the nationalist or autonomist 'sector' in the North of Italy.

Conclusions

This chapter examined traditional or classical definitions of territorial dualism in Italy as the source of the activation of a territorial cleavage in Italian politics. Structural approaches that explain the North and South as 'different', cannot explain the timing of mobilisation, and the definition of the Northern question on the basis of cultural differences and claims of nationhood. Instead, this chapter showed the political process that led to party formation and the rise of the Northern question as a *contingent* outcome. The political opportunities offered by a critical juncture in the Italian party system—the fall of the Berlin wall and the demise of the Comunist threat in Italy led to the political choices for a united Lega Nord.

These choices modified the ideas, goals and strategies of territorial mobilisation in Northern Italy. The dynamics of collective action shaped the cooperative strategies between the leaders of new parties in the ordinary regions of the North. The electoral alliances between the parties became the platform for a single centralised party under the leadership of Umberto Bossi. The centralisation of all the parties preceded a major critical juncture in the Italian party system: the fall of the Berlin wall and the symbolic demise of Communism as an structuring force in the Italian party system.

While the party in Veneto struggled unsucessfully during the 1980s to make the territory a relevant dimension for political action, in 1992, the core of the white subculture, Veneto, was the vanguard of a political earthquake in the North of Italy. However, the choices in 1989 shaped a common fate and a single strategy for the entire North. Lega Nord acquired legal ownership of all the labels and symbols of the autonomist parties.

The rise of the *Northern question* in the Italian political system was a contingent event. This event was later interpreted, however, as an inevitable outcome on three accounts. First, Bossi rewrote the history of political mobilisation in Northern Italy as of his own making. However, there were many political actors involved in the making of Lega Nord. Second, Lega Nord rewrote the history of the transition from the First to the Second Italian republic as made by Lega Nord's opposition against traditional parties. Third, Lega Nord rewrote the history of the North and Padania as a self-evident cultural and economic unit, and an inevitable outcome of people's awareness of the territorial disparities between North and South in Italy.

Lega Nord advanced a new territorial identity that turned 'excluded' national minorities in Northern Italy seeking European protection into actively 'excluding' Europeans rejecting the presence of migrants from Africa and Eastern Europe and the so-called Mediterranean South. The markers of national identity changed significantly with the passage from the regional parties into a united Lega Nord. Initially cultural distinctiveness was *ethnic* and linguistic. The North is essentialised as a 'better culture' because of its civicness, productivity and wealth.

In some scholarly writing, the electoral success of Lega Nord was more about de-structuring of political cleavages, electoral de-alignment and protest against traditional parties than about re-alignment and the formation of new cleavages (Constabile, 1991; Pasquino, 1995). Lega Nord's success therefore, would be an outstanding example of protest politics. Cycles of protest, as Tarrow points out, favor challengers but also undermine the ability of new comers to consolidate their position in the political system (Tarrow, 1994).

All scholars emphasise the importance of public dissatisfaction and the weakening of traditional electoral alignments in the electoral success of Lega Nord (Mannheim, 1991; Biorcio, 1991; Sani, 1992). Lega Nord became the main beneficiary of the corruption scandals that plagued Italy in 1992. However, during the 1990s a fundamental transformation of the Italian party system radically modified the strategic scenario for Lega Nord. The very cycle of protest and judicial investigations of political corruption eliminated Italian traditional parties and demolished the already weakened political class of the First Italian Republic. A new party system with new electoral rules and new parties emerged. The visibility of the North-South question relied on the continuous mobilisation efforts of the party leadership and was a function of Bossi's ability to generate political controversies. As it will be developed in chapter 6, the ability of Lega Nord to expand its electoral base within the North shows significant variation during the 1990s. The party leadership faced with the reconfiguration of the Italian party system since 1994, crucial strategic dilemmas that compromised, in their words, their very political survival.

Notes

[1] See Mauro Calise and Renato Mannheimer 'I Governi Misurati', *Il Mulino* 4\81, anno XXX numero 276. Data covers the period 1948-1978. See also Claudio Todesco, Governanti in Carriera. Ministri e Sottosegretari Italiani delle Prime Dieci Legislature. Tesi di Laura. Universita degli Studi di Milano. Facolta di Scienze Politche. 1994.

[2] In the period between 1973-1986, the percentage of those born in the North of Italy in the Christian Democrat national executive was 38.2% (as opposed to 26.6% for the Center and 35% for the South). Moreover, the time series shows that from 1973 to 1986 the % of those born in the North rose from 33.3% to 45.2% . Data from Luigi Manconi, 'Due Tempi, due Ritmi. La direzione Democristiana, 1973-1986'. *Polis*. Anno III, No 1. Aprile 1989.

[3] The Federal Union of European Nationalities endorsed these views. The European federalist movement had its Italian section (Partito Federalista Europeo) in the city of Mantova in Lombardy. Il Partito Federalista Europeo was an ally of the first autonomist movements in the early 1980s.

[4] The program included: 1. A European parliament for the confederation of the ethnies and regions of Europe. 2. Regional autonomy and powers. 3. Solving the problems of border regions. 4. Free use of the languages of minorities and the local ethno-linguistic communities. 5. Ownership of natural resources and power to program and manage the economy. 6. A managable society for the individual fighting against consumerism and moral and physical pollution; 7. aclose collaboration with the other elected within the automist sector in other countries.

[5] Again in 1982, in a Conference organized by UOPA, there was an agreement towards 'an activation of a 'Federazione Autonomista Alpino Padana". The agreement was taken by Lega Autonomista Lombarda, Liga Veneta, M.A.R.P. (Movimento Autonomista Rinascita Piemontesa) and U.O.P.A. (Unione Ossolona per l'Autonomia) (Lombardia Autonomista. n.2. 1982).

[6] After the elections, in November 1984, a meeting of the representatives of the parties coordinated a 'common action' for the regional elections of the following year and stressed the improtance of, the need for the Union to better structure its political efforts and organization as a movement for the assertion of the Federal Autonomista, Ethnic and European ideals (*Autonomie Valdotaine*, n.17, 1984). In June 1985, the meeting of the

Steering Committee took place in Verona and confirmed the collaboration between the parties. In the fall of 1985, a Conference of Federalists and Autonomists takes place in Turin, which conclusions stress again the need for a federalist political force to create a Europe of Regions and Peoples (L'Unione Piemonteisa, n.16, 1985).

[7] The alliance obtained a total of 636,546 votes in the European elections.

[8] The transformation of the territorial boundaries of the new political project is also covered by the changes in the names of the party journal. Still in 1992 the name was Lombardia Autonomista. Constitutente della Federazione Politica Lega Nord. In October 1992 the journal is first released as Republica del Nord. Italia Federale: Nord-Centro-Sud. Organo Ufficiale della Lega Nord but by the end of the year, the journal's name get established as Lega Nord. Italia Federale: Nord-Centro-Sud. Organo Ufficiale della Lega Nord. Since September 1996, the journal is called Lega Nord. Padania Indipendente. Organo Ufficiale della Lega Nord.

[9] The statutes aproved in the Second and third Federal congresses (February 6, 1994 and March 5, 1995) include the same article 1. The first statute however, defined Lega as a federalist political movement without any reference to transnationality.

[10] According to the 1992 party program and in contrast to absolute liberalism—'founded on money and consumption—liberismo federalista implies the harmonization of productive activities with societal needs and societies moral and material values' (Lega Nord, 1991 Party program) ... The liberismo federalista becames 'a principle, a method, and a system' (Lega Nord 1992 Party Program).

[11] Carlo E. Ruzza and Oliver Schmidtke 'Roots of Success of the Lega Lombarda', *West European Politics*, Vol. 16, April 1993 Number 2: 1-23.

[12] If we take the national secretaries of the party as the regions included in the North, they are the following: Alto-Adige-Sudtirol, Emilia, Friuli, Liguria, Lombardia, Marche, Piemonte, Romagna, Toscana, Trentino, Trieste, Umbria, Valle d'Aosta and Veneto.

[13] Some Lega members mentioned Putnam's Lega work Making Democracy Work. Civic Traditions in Modern Italy as a prove of the 'cultural' differences and division between North and South. On the interpenetration of nationalist discourse with social-scientific discourse see Handler, The politics of Culture.

[14] Michele Corti, Padania Italia, Quale 'Questione Nazionale?', Quaderni Padani, Anno 1, n.2, Autunno 1995. p.15.

[15] Thus, Stern, interviewing local Dc politicians in two local communities in Veneto, found that the only value they shared in common was anti-communism. In contrast to Communist strongholds in which political struggle was fought by 'expanding the politically active public, the DC never had to struggle to establish cultural legitimacy in their northeastern strongholds' (Stern 1975, p. 64).

[16] According to Trigilia the crucial element for the consolidation of the territorial subcultural mobilisation is the conflictual relationship with the national state. Both Communist and Christian democrats in these areas mediated the relationship of people with the state. This conflictual relationship with the national state reinforced local identities through opposition vis-á-vis the center (Trigilia 1986, p. 128).

[17] Trigilia recognises some differences between the Catholic and Communist subcultures. First, there are differences in the main features of political identificacion. (p. 129). Second, the role of politics in the Catholic subculture is traditional, 'politics must guarantee and sustain the autonomy of civil society, rather than intervene in society to modify it' (p. 129). Whereas in the communist subculture the role of politics was crucial and the party occupied the central position in the regulation of the local society, it was not a political party, but the

Catholic Church and its collateral organisations to perform this role in the Catholic subculture (Trigilia 1986, p.129).

[18] The first Congress of Lega Lombarda took place in 1989. According to the numbers provided by the organisation in the first national congress of Lega Lombarda, Lega had 18,000 members (iscritti), 118 soci ordinari, 9 soci fondatori, and 8 provincial sections (Contorno, 1990, p. 83). At the turn of the decade, the political and administrative organization of the party included 13 employees and provincial sections across the Lombard region.

4 Lega Nord and the Political Construction of *Otherness*

The last chapter explained the political construction of a united North and the ways in which 'culture' entered into the categorical remaking of Northerners as 'Padanians'. In this chapter, in contrast, the focus is on the political construction of *otherness*. In studying anti-migrant mobilisation during the 1990s, two peculiarities of the Italian political scenario must be highlighted. First, and in contrast to other European countries such as Germany, the Netherlands or Belgium, the wave of migration towards Italy in the 1990s had no precedent in the post-war period. When the first migrants appeared in the late 1980s, it was a new social phenomenon. Instead of debates about citizenship of social and political integration of second-generation *gastarbaiders*—typical of other European countries during the same period—the politicisation of the question of migration in Italy is mainly shaped around the control of migration flows and new arrivals, and only secondarily about migrants' integration in Italian society. Moreover, in other European countries such as France, Germany or the Netherlands, migration is characterised by the presence of migrants from a few countries—such as Morocco and Turkey—but in Italy migration waves involved migrants from a variety of countries and continents: Africa, Eastern Europe and the refugees from the wars that destroyed the ex-Yugoeslavian federation. Second, in the post-war period migration flows were directed from South to North *within* Italy. The politicisation of the North-South question is also a crucial question in the creation and reproduction of *otherness* by Lega Nord. Thus, the question to investigate is if, and how, Lega Nord packaged both categories of migrants under the same cultural construction.

The question of new migration in Italy during the 1990s was further characterised by two main factors. First, although migration was a new social phenomenon, perceptions about the presence of migrants suffered significant changes over a short period of time. During the last decade, the Italian media and institutional actors played an important role in an emerging and dominant perception and consensus over the 'problem' of new migration and its 'solutions' (Maneri, 1997). Second, in contrast to other European party systems were one political party has exercised a 'monopoly' of anti-migration issues, the Italian scenario was shaped by the partial overlapping of Alleanza Nazionale and Lega Nord in early political mobilisation against migrants.

In this chapter three main questions are explored. What kind of party mobilisation against migrants is involved? Are there similarities in the representation of Southerners and new migrants? Is the anti-migrant program and ideology of Lega Nord different from other European parties of the new radical or populist right? This chapter focuses on defining and explaining the main features of Lega Nord as an anti-migrant party. It analyses both party mobilisation and party ideology as autonomous spheres in the political construction of *otherness*. This chapter explains the political construction of otherness by looking both at party mobilisation (to characterise the type of political action, the specification of target groups and the style of mobilisation) and party ideology (definition and main characteristics of the question of migration and otherness in party identity). In this chapter we focus on the discurse and representation of migrants through the production and statements of Lega Nord's leadership and party representatives.

Issue-attention cycles allow us to distinguish periods that characterised different strategic scenarios for the regulation of migration in Italy during the 1990s to situate the changing relevance of anti-migrant rhetoric in the politics of Lega Nord. Accusations of *racism* marked the trajectory of Lega Nord, yet the label of racism had a changing meaning over time. This chapter investigates continuity and change in the ways in which *old* and *new* migrants were represented. The portrait of migrants is linked to images of *purity* and *pollution*. Mario Borghezio, the well-known party representative in charge of organising anti-migrant mobilisation repeatedly demanded during the 1990s to the minister of Public Health the HIV a test for new migrants 'to avoid the danger of contagion' (*Il Corriere della Sera*, March 28, 1997). The chapter also explains the ways in which the categories of *ethnicity* and *race* were used in party mobilisation and party ideology. It explains a *reversal* of labels, as the use of *ethnicity* shifted from its reference to Southerners in the 1980s, to acquire an specific meaning in the definition of new migrants in the 1990s.

The main features of the ideological elaboration of Lega Nord as a fully-fledged system of thought against the *other* are also explained. By the end of the 1990s Lega Nord's denunciations of the presence and effects of migrants could be easily matched with other European parties not only in the representation of the *other* as a *criminal* element disrupting the social order in European societies, but also in the adoption of *cultural differentialism* as the explicit party ideology.

Since the early 1980s there was a search for the ideological legitimation of prejudice to provide a new definition of the Southern problem. In the 1980s the result was a definition of North-South differences in Italy on *ethnic* grounds. In contrast, in the 1990s the *ethnic* label was applied to new migrants. In turn, the North-South question became one of a *reversed internal colonialism* within Italy. Although the label *ethnic* is no longer used in party production and public statements about the South, collective markers remained *cultural* and pressed similarities into Southerners and new migrants—always defined as non-European.

What kind of evidence is relevant here? Party electoral programmes are an starting point. However, they do not say anything about the relative importance of migration both in party mobilisation and party ideology. For instance, in the first electoral program of a united Lega Nord in 1992, migration appears only as point 11 in a 12-point program. Nor can we assess the relative importance of the question of migrants within the party agenda by looking at the publications of Lega Nord's. For example, in 1995 in a document of the Lega Nord's group in the Italian Senate entitled 'Ten Proposals for Freedom', the last proposal discussed in the document is a project to regulate the presence of foreigners, *extracomunitari*, and to specify qualitative and quantitative requirements for new migrants to exclude those who had previously been condemned for criminal acts (*Le Ragioni della Lega. Federalismo e Liberismo contro l'Assitenzialismo del Polo. Lega Nord: 10 proposte per la Libertá. Gruppo Lega Nord, Senato della Repubblica,* 1995). Although the question of migration does not systematically occupy a relevant place in many party documents and electoral programs, it figures prominently in the statements of party leaders and representatives, in the actions taken by party activists and in the elaboration of the party ideology.

Lega Nord and the Question of Migration

The starting point is the generic classification of Lega Nord as an anti-migrant party. Party programs have always included the control of migration flows. However, beyond establishing that migration is one of the issues politicised by Lega Nord, there is little agreement on the relevance and main characteristics of party mobilisation and ideology. Debates about the determinants for the rise and success of Lega Nord during the 1990s evolved around three main issues. First, scholars have contrasting views about the relative importance of anti-migration rhetoric in the party identity. Some authors stress the importance of mobilisation against migrants in the very formation of Lega Nord (Biorcio, 1991; 1997). Moreover, for some scholars: 'the hostility against *extracomunitari* migrants (and until 1989 also anti-Southern migrants), is the fundamental mark of Lega Nord's identity and its public discurse; the refusal of alternative identities is a central element of the party subculture' (Balbo and Manconi, 1992: 85). Others, in contrast, do not consider the question of migration as one among several in party mobilisation and focus, instead, on the representation of local interests and the center-periphery cleavage (Diamanti, 1993; 1995). Second, scholars have also contrasting views about the relative importance of anti-migration mobilisation in the electoral success for Lega Nord and the extent to which Lega Nord's voters choose the party because of its attitudes against migrants. Whereas authors such as Biorcio emphasised this aspect in explaining the electoral success of Lega Nord, others linked electoral success either to political protest against the central government (Diamanti, 1993), or the moderation of demands in the party leadership with the emphasis on political autonomy from the central state and the Italian tax system (Kitschelt, 1995). Third, there are also contrasting views about the relative importance of anti-migrant rhetoric in the case of new migrants vis-à-vis the expression of prejudices and the negative portrait of Southerners. Biorcio finds out a 'substitution effect' in party mobilisation by which the rhetoric against new migrants replaced an earlier focus on anti-Southerner mobilisation (Biorcio, 1991, 1997).

Old and New Migrants

Sniderman's study on *ethnic* and *racial* prejudice in Italy (Sniderman et al., 1995) showed high levels of 'hostility' and prejudice against Southern Italians.

> to sketch the familiar historical portrait of Southern Italians as painted by their Northern compatriots, they lack—indeed take pride in lacking—essential qualities of character: honesty, independence, the willingness to work (Sniderman et al., 2000, p. 13).

The persistence of the divide between North and South in Italy allow to consider the expression of prejudice against Southerners 'commonsensical'. This is a common theme during the 1990s, as scholars mentioned that Lega Nord expressed socially diffused—and therefore 'given' prejudices against Southerners. As Sneiderman et al. point out,

> from its national formation, Northern Italians have shown a formidable measure of prejudice toward Southern Italians, we say prejudice, but not in the classical sense. There was *never* a presumption of biological inferiority, of an inherent and gross lack of intelligence or ability ... (Sniderman et al., 2000, p. 13)

Sniderman's argument is not accurate on two accounts. First, we must situate stereotypes and prejudices in its specific historical articulation. In Italian history there were ways to characterise the South in which collective markers acquired a *biological* dimension. This is not an academic nuance, but a historical fact. Antonio Gramsci in his 'Southern question'—to use a well-known example—a manuscript written in the late 1920s wrote:

> It is well known how this ideology has been diffused in a capilar form from those propagandist of the bourgeoisie to the Northern masses: the South is the

lead (palla di piombo) that prevents more rapid advancement of the civic development of Italy; *the Southerners are biologically the inferior beings*, semi-barbaric or full barbars, because of their natural destiny; if the South is backward, the responsability is not from the capitalist system or any other historical reason, but of the nature that has made the Southerners lazy, incapable, criminals and barbars, this view only tamed with the explosion purely individualistic of great geniuses, that are like palm trees in an arid and sterile dessert. The Socialist party was the main vehicle of this bourgeois ideology spread in the Northern proletariat ... (1951: pp. 13-14).

Thus, we can historically traced the presence of the portrait of Southerners with biological trait. Moreover, as Gramsci clearly put it, specific actors and institutions in the North—such as schools, newspapers and political parties—were involved in the process of production and reproduction of prejudices against Southerners (see also Kertzer, 1978). Second, and more importantly, the presence or absence of a biological element in the portrait of Southerners needs to be put in perspective in light of the uses of 'culture' as a quasi-biological attribute. This chapter shows the reworking of old stereotypes in a contemporary definition of cultural *distance* between North and South.

The results of the survey conducted by Sniderman et al show the presence of negative attitudes towards migrants regardless of their origins or the color of their skins. Thus, Sniderman concludes that *racism* is not part of public opinion in Italy: both East Europeans and Africans were equally regarded and evaluated as outsiders (Sniderman et al., 2000, p. 53). The comparison made by Sniderman et al. also yields surprising results because new migrants were viewed more favorably than Southerners (Sniderman et al., 2000, p. 85). For the authors, this finding shows that the status of *outsider*—defining a basic *interchangeability* of outgroups in Italy—is the relevant marker to define what here is treated as the construction of *otherness*. How is the interchangeability of groups constructed? Maneri's study also finds out that *race* has scarce relevance in the Italian media, given the characteristics of the Italian colonial past and the marginal location of racial categories in Italian socio-political culture. However, Maneri stresses that, if *extracomunitari* are not yet a racialised group in Italian society, the discourses around them are already *racialising* (Maneri, 1997).

To study the role played by political parties does not imply the negation of their social diffusion, resilience and pervasiveness. As one member of Lega Nord summarised it: 'Here we do not like Southerners. Bossi has not invented those sentiments' (Fassa, Varese, 1996). Yet for an external observer, one of the most striking developments in Italian politics during the 1990s was *not* the public expression and articulation of long-standing prejudices against Southerners, but the extent to which stereotypes circulated in the media and in the political arena, reproducing, reinforcing and reshaping anew, a public definition of territorial dualism in Italy.

In the early 1990s Balbo and Manconni stated that there was not in the Italian political system a political actor who fit the framework of 'an entrepreneur of racism', although they identify two political parties which they consider as 'organisations of intollerance': Lega Nord and Movimento Sociale Italiano (Balbo and Manconi, 1992: 82). There is certainly an affinity between Lega Nord and Alleanza Nazionale in the treatment of the migrant question and a basic overlapping in the styles of mobilisation against migrants. This overlapping is clearly visible at the local level with the first mobilisations against migrants on issues of safety and social order. This overlapping is also clear in the negative attitudes against migrants hold by Lega Nord and Allenza Nazionale voters. There is also a similarity in policy proposals. The are also differences on the politicisation of migration between LN and AN that go beyond the issue of the communities of reference (Padania or Italy). The most anti-migrant party in the Italian party system is Lega Nord. Certainly it is also the party with the most 'spoiled identity': the moderation of AN leadership in the transition of the old MSI into a post-fascist period, and the language of 'difference' used by the latter is in sharp contrast with the language of insults that became so characteristic of Lega Nord's leadership.

If mobilisation against Southerners was considered commonsensical by many Italian scholars—the expression of a diffused and shared *anti-meridionalismo* in the North of Italy—Lega Nord was considered a truly *political entrepreneur* in the early politisation of the question of new migration in Italy. Is there a substitution of the anti-migrant rhetoric from *anti-meridionali* to *extracomunitari*? Is Lega Nord's political discourse different in assessing the 'differences' between the two 'groups'? Rather than downplaying the anti-Southern rhetoric as a latent variable in the Italian political system and its almost taken-for-granted quality in party mobilisation, here two issues are highlighted. First, this chapter aims to show that there was no substitution effect in party mobilisation, from an anti-Southern rhetoric to an anti-migrant rhetoric. Both alternated and overlapped during the 1990s. Second, and more importantly, the ways in which party discourses constructed 'otherness' systematically linked the representation of Southerners and new migrants.

Continuity in Lega Nord's political campaigns against migrants can be established in the treatment of migration as a question of criminality and in the representation of waves of clandestine migrants as an invasion and a threat to social order. Maneri suggests that the articulation of ideology in the Italian media produced a criminalising discourse that appears both commonsensical and consensual, reflecting a fundamental consensus between social and political forces (Maneri, 1997).

The categorical remaking of the Italian population introduced by Lega Nord made a simple division. As one of the members of Lega Nord interviewed for this study put it: 'there are two Italies, one is African and the other European'. Hence, the conclusion that, as one regional councilor of Lega Nord put it: 'Italy has been constructed upon a mistake. For the last thousand years there has been a Celtic-Germanic culture and a Greek-Latin one'. *Otherness* is constructed upon the differences between two cultures, one Mediterranean-African, the other European.

Prejudices and common stereotypes of Southerners molded their views of Northern cultural distinctiveness. Lega politicians consider the South a different cultural unit. The *familiarity* of Lega Nord's statements with the stereotypes about Southerners is best illustrated by the statements gathered in an interviewed conducted in 1996 with, one of the 'moderates' of Lega Nord's group in the Italian parliament:

> For us, those who aren't able to succeed are those who don't want to. There is a better culture in the North and the proof is that they come here without being forced to do so ... Imagine if economic activities would collapse in the North ... only to maintain a bunch of parasites, to treat as *signori* those who don't do anything for a living, who don't produce anything ... Instead, here in the North mentality and will are the same (Conti Milano, 1996).

In Lega Nord's propaganda the presence of migrants is represented as a cultural cum economic clash, who in the views of the party leadership endanger the social fabric of the North. As one of the most outspoken party leaders against immigration put it: 'Since the very beignning we were against immigration because it is a dangerous phenomena which risk to disintegrate the social fabric. We are unprepared to deal with immigration and the latter has a violent impact upon us. We need to regulated these flows, and introduce more severe norms and solve this problem with the expulsion of undocumented immigrants' (Borghezio, Torino, 1996).

In addition to the constrast between Africa and Europe, the treatment and representation of Southerners and *others* in the political discourses of Lega Nord presents similarities on two accounts. First, both Southerners and new migrants are potentially and *de facto*, represented as criminals. The speeches and statements by Umberto Bossi are characterised by a language of insults. For the leader of Lega Nord, the Southerners are: 'Worms and Mafiosi, robbers and criminals ... brought to our land because we were distracted' (Parlamento del Nord, 1996). The first mobilisation undertaken by all the first regionally-based political parties during the 1980s was against the *soggiorno obbligato*, that is the compulsory residence of Mafia-related persons in the North of Italy. Southerners and *Mafiosi* are in the political statements of Lega

Nord's politicians, fundamentally identical categories. In these views, the new migrants are also criminals.

Second, in both cases party propaganda represents collective differences as cultural, but also, in both cases, culture is turned into a *quasi-biological* and physical attribute of individuals or groups. For example, the statements of Mario Borghezio—the leader behind the creation of the *Ronde Padane*—about the presence of Albanians in Northern cities: 'Albanians should return home, each must deal with their own garbage. If the *Ronde Padane* see Mafiosi faces, they will remove them violently' (*Il Corriere della Sera*, 26-4-97).

Next section provides the background to understand the new question of migration in Italy during the 1990s and Lega Nord's anti-migrant mobilisation.

Italy and Migration in the 1990s

Italian political and institutional actors and the media adopted during the 1990s the label *extracomunitario* to define new migrants. The term—unique to the Italian context and with no parallels in other European countries—refers both to new migrants as a general category, and to migrants from countries other than those belonging to the current European Union (Balbo and Manconi, 1992: 59).

As mentioned above, the flow of migrants into Italy during the 1990s was a new social phenomenon. In less than a decade the absolute number of migrants (legal residents) in Italy went from 573,258 in 1993 to 1,126,628 in 1999 (Istat, 1999, p. 364). In 1999, migrants represented 2% of the population in Italy. This percentage is still relatively low in comparative perspective. In other European countries the percentage of migrants relative to the population is much higher, such as in Germany (8.9%), France (6.35%), Belgium (8.9%) or the Netherlands (4.3%) (Ismu, 1999).

In contrast to other European countries, the pattern of migration into Italy—described by the ISTAT as *diffused migration*—is further characterised two main factors. First, the fragmentation of the migrant population from the point of view of *ethnic groupings* is typical from Italy and differs from other patterns in European states (Istat, 1999, p. 354). The biggest migrant community is formed by migrants from Moroccan origin, followed by Ex-Yugoeslavia and Albania. Migrants from Eastern Europe represent 25% of the total migrant population. The presence of migrants from China and The Philippines, Sri Lanka, India, Brasil and Peru is also significant (Istat, 1999, pp. 354-355). Table 4.1 shows the evolution of the distribution of migrant resident permits in Italy by continent and country of origins during the 1990s.

Table 4.1   **Resident Permits Granted by Continent and Country of Origin**

	1992	1997	1998
Continents and Countries			
Europe	206.656	369.737	382.924
European Union	100.404	128.123	135.207
Central Europe	86.471	220.691	226.387
Albania	24.886	66.608	72.551
ex-Yugoeslavia	26.727	74.761	73.492
Poland	12.139	23.163	22.938
Romania	8.250	26.894	28.796
Africa	227.531	301.305	310.748
Northern Africa	147.954	191.005	200.007
Mrocco	83.292	115.026	122.230
Tunisia	41.547	40.002	41.439
West Africa	50.265	76.285	76.934
Senegal	24.194	31.543	32.037
Asia	116.941	182.475	192.864
Central-South Asia	34.702	64.117	69.108
India	9.918	10.058	20.494
Sri Lanka	12.114	23.652	24.841
East Asia	63.793	102.658	107.796
China	15.505	31.615	35.310
Philippines	36.316	56.209	57.312
America	94.298	129.625	133.461
Central America	50.073	82.349	86.456
Brasil	10.953	15.505	16.193
Colombia	4.379	7.023	7.105
Dominican R.	3.681	9.012	9.588
Peru	5.022	21.934	22.996
Total	648.935	986.020	1.022.896

Source: Istat, Rapporto Annuale, 1998: p. 356

Second, and not surprisingly, the presence of migrants in the North of Italy is higher (52.7%) than in the Center (29.9%) and the South (17.4%) (data 1998, Istat, 1999: 8). In a classification of the presence of migrants in regional aggregates, North-West represented 32.9% of the migrant population, compared to 21.0% in the North-East, 29% in the center and only 9.9% and 6.6% in the South and the Islands (Istat, 1999: p. 365). A ranking of the Italian provinces in terms of the percentage of migrants in the population, shows that 9 out of 15 provinces with the highest migrant population were Northern provinces (Istat, 1999: 365).

In the early 1990s the transformation of the media discourse about migrants took place in Italy. It marked the emergence of a public and dominant consensus on the question of migration (Maneri, 1997). Research on the construction of *extracomunitari* in the Italian media found out a crucial passage between a discourse about migration around the 1980s—as a danger of racism *in* Italian society—to a new phase that started in 1992 in which a radically different discourse became dominant—migration as criminality and a threat *to* Italian society (Maneri, 1997). Thus, the early 1990s can be established as the crucial *entry point* of a new dynamic legitimising and feeding mobilisation against migrants.[1] From the beginning the debate is centered around the control of migration flows.

This general shift towards an analysis of migration as a problem also had implications for the politics of Lega Nord. The party leadership found a new scenario where their basic arguments about the 'problem' of migration were shared by other social and political actors. Party mobilisation and the visibility of the question of migration in Italian politics is linked to the changing legal and institutional framework: it is around the passing of decrees and laws during the decade (1991, 1995 and 1997) that the position of the Italian political parties was fixed.

Maneri's research shows that both classical racism and cultural differentialism play a marginal role in the collective imagination of the Italian public. Lega Nord's portrait of Southerners and new migrants as *criminals* in party mobilisation was later accompanied by the incorporation of *cultural differentialism* as a legitimising argument to derive the incompatibility of groups. If Lega Nord shares with the dominant Italian discourse an emphasis on the presence of new migrants in Italy as a problem of criminality, Lega Nord differs from other Italian actors in the use of the categories of *race* and *ethnicity* and in the use cultural differentialism as an explicit ideology over group differences. Next section explains the ways in which *race* and *ethnicity* appeared in party mobilisation during the 1990s.

Party Mobilisation against Migrants during the 1990s

Party mobilisation against migrants introduced a broadening definition of migrants as potential criminals. The distinction between undocumented and documented migrants in light of Lega Nord is: 'a mere hypocrital tool from the state to disguise the fact that most of documented migrants are such thanks to the continuous *sanatorie* of the different governments during the 1990s' (Enti Locali, 1998, p. 4). The focus on *clandestine* migrants instead of in the broader category of *extracomunitari* is also a partial answer to distinguish Lega Nord's position from other political parties. The language of *otherness* used by Lega Nord shifted during the decade from statements against migrants 'from the Thirld World', to *extracomunitari*, to use *clandestini* (clandestines) as a generic label for migrants in Italy. Considerations of public order in the regulation of migration flows were incorporated by other Italian political parties in their programs. Lega Nord explained migration flows in the north of Italy as a result of Roman centralism and conspiration theory. In 1990 with the passage of the *Legge Martelli*, the propaganda of Lega Nord equated 'migration from the Thirld World' to fascism and consider the passage of the decree a 'coup d'etat' (*Il Corriere della Sera*, 17-11-95).

The question of anti-migrant party mobilisation is explored along two dimensions. First, there are different periods in party mobilisation—that help to explain the relative dominance or marginality of the debate about migration during the 1990s. In this sense it is useful to specify *issue-attention cycles*—institutional and related to the passing of legal measures and the evolution of the arrival of migrants in Italy—which also marked the position of Lega Nord on debates about migration. Throughout the decade, these issue-attention cycles implied an increasing definition of the regulatory framework for migrants and an expansion of restrictive measures to control migrant flows. Second, a distinction between local and national politics is introduced to show continuity and change in party mobilisation in the 1990s. Whereas at the local level, the image of Lega Nord shows a basic continuity in the way party local sections and party representatives mobilised against the presence of migrants as a *threat* to their communities, at the national level the presence or absence of the question of migration during the 1990s was related to the larger political and institutional context. At the state-level, the question of migration did not have the same relevance in 1990, in 1994—when Lega entered the Berlusconi government—in 1995, when Lega fought for political visibility in a fundamentally different political scenario, or in 1997 when the new law for the regulation of migration was passed in the Italian parliament.

Issue-Attention Cycles

Three distinctive periods marked the political and institutional definition of the regulatory framework for migrants during the 1990s in Italy. First, the passing of the first law on migration, the *Legge Martelli* led to Lega Nord's well-known campaign against a decree that for the party leadership allowed *l'immigrazione clandestina* (clandestine immigration). The second turning point is party mobilisation against the *Decreto Dini* in November 1995. Dini's caretaker government included measures to please Bossi's party to pass in turn the budget for the following year. The Italian left clearly took this political opportunity to redefine Lega Nord's as a 'racist' party excluding any possibility of political agreement. Third, the passing of the law 40 in 1997 introduced a new legal framework to define the status of migrants. The position of Lega Nord's representatives clearly overlap with the one taken by AN and Forza Italia—the main difference being that Lega Nord's representatives did not vote in the Italian parliament for or against the law (Zucchini, 1998).

In each of these cycles in the regulation of migration, the political actors involved and the strategic context in which Lega Nord pursued its anti-migration agenda were different. The position of Lega Nord against the *Legge Martelli* gave the party a new political visibility and marked the rise of Bossi—and later Bossi's Lega Nord—into the public arena. The party requested a referendum to change the law as well as the expulsion of undcoumented migrants. This priority was clear to all. According to the statements of the national secretary of Lega Nord in Lombardy, Roberto Calderoli, 'our policy is to expel illegal migrants from here and to create *centri d'accoglienza* for the others' (*Il Corriere della Sera*, 6-10-1995).

From 1992 onwards Lega Nord leadership aimed to present a moderate image. Broader institutional change in Italy became the main focus of attention. The 1991-1994 period is characterised by the breakdown of the traditional Italian political system and the disappearance of traditional parties in the midst of corruption scandals. The agenda of institutional change became a priority for old and new political actors. Not surprisingly and as mentioned earlier, only point 11 in the 12 point-program of Lega Nord's mildy requested: 'a rigorous control of immigration to avoid risking the social and economic fabric of the country and a real cooperation with Third World countries' (Lega Nord, 1992 electoral program).

Between the passing of the *Legge Martelli* and the *Decreto Dini* in 1995, not only there was a new Italian party system, but also a new common sense emerged in the definition of migration as a problem (Maneri, 1997). Lega Nord leadership used the *Decreto Dini* as a springboard to clearly distanced themselves from both the government and left political parties. In 1995, Lega Nord intensified its campaign against clandestine migrants. The position of Italian political parties on migration had also changed. On the one hand, left-wing parties were also advocating new measures to control migration flows—to the point and not to forget, that there were talks between representatives of Lega Nord and the *Progressisti* in this period. On the other hand, the Dini government passed a decree that fundamentally included the main demands of Lega Nord, who, in exchange for the introduction of measures to control migration flows, voted for the budget. In 1995 the potential agreement between the left and Lega Nord included the regulation of those undocumented immigrants already working in Italy. Lega Nord claimed that unemployed immigrants should be expelled from Italy.[2] The independentist faction within Lega Nord proposed the creation of a 'national civic guard' to police migrants and Borghezio suggested to provide the police with special ammunition to fight undocumented immigrants.

Lega Nord's request of expulsion for all undocumented migrants made the agreement with the left more difficult. The pressures against the government and the threat to block the budget, led Dini to pass a new decree for the regulation of migrants: those convicted of drug trafficking, the management of prostitution and other criminal acts were to be expelled from the country (*Il Corriere della Sera*, 10-11-1995; *Il Corriere della Sera*, 19-11-1995: 3). Il Corriere, 20-11-1995: 1). The Italian left and the Greens criticised the decree, but also Berlusconi manifested his opposition to mass expulsions. In turn Bossi publicly contested two issues about the new decree: another regularisation campaign and the absence of an specific crime for *illegal* migration, which remained legally defined as an administrative, and not criminal, issue (*Il Corriere della Sera*, 18-11-1995: 3).

After the 1996 elections, the presence of a left-wing government and the renewal of an anti-system stand by Lega Nord led to party radicalisaton. In 1997 the radicalisation of the party position of migration is clearly seen in the the constitution of a new group—the association for 'civic' protection *Ronde Padane*—with the goal 'to be active over the territory for the prevention and defense of citizens threatened in their safety, property and identity' (*Il Corriere della Sera*, 25-3-1997). The *Ronde Padane* were to police the streets of the main cities—Milan and Torino—against the presence of migrants. The last period of party mobilisation must be analysed within the context of the partial marginalisation of Lega Nord in Italian politics. As research conducted by Zucchini on the passage of the new law on migration in the Italian parliament, the negotiations between different actors and parties made possible the emergence of a new political consensus to regulate the field of migration. The position of Lega Nord in the debates can be summarised as follows: against voting rights for migrants, against the introduction of discrimination as a crime, their preference for the introduction of illegality or irregularity as a crime, their opposition to residence permits with guarantees, their opposition to residence permits for those looking for employment, and their preference for a larger role of local governments in the implementation of migration policies (see Zucchini, 1998).

Lega Nord's trayectory is marked by accusations of *racism*. In order to understand how the issue of racism entered Italian political debates, the changing meaning of the label *racism* must be explained. By the early 1990s

Lega Nord had acquired in Italy a record on racism on two accounts. The first accusations of racism against Lega Nord focused on racism against Southerners. Already in 1985 accusations of racism against the autonomist parties in the Northern ordinary regions were based on their demands to give priority to the population of the Northern regions vis-à-vis migrants from Southern Italy. As the basis of their demands, the parties claim their right to control the territory and their resources (*comandare a casa propria*).

Accusations of racism also allowed the party leadership to gain visibility and media attention in their efforts to generate controversies. This function must be taken into account to explain how racism as a political tool was also used by Lega Nord. Rather than passive recipients of these accusations, the party leadership of Lega Nord made those accusations a political tool in the confrontation with other political parties and in their characterisation of the Italian state.[3] Lega Lombarda's propaganda was promoting by the end of the 1980s the view that the Italian state was *racist*, claiming that 'Mafia and racism' should go back to the South. Lega Lombarda campaigned also at the local level against the presence of migrants from the Third World—black migrants—and the passing of the *Legge Martelli*. The party leadership puts the emphasis on the fact that 'We are not racist' (*Noi non siamo razzisti*). As Borghezio put it: 'Lega is profoundly antiracist, but people are fed up with spending money for solidarity, people want order and legality' (*Il Corriere della Sera*, 19-11-1995: 3). Bossi stated the goals of Lega Nord as the need to introduce a quota systems for new arrivals in Italy—so to guarantee work and housing for all migrants—and the need at the same time to provide for measures to immediate expel those undocumented migrants involved in criminal activities in Italy (*L'Indipendente*, 14-9-1995: 3).

In 1995 some representatives of Lega Nord provided new ground for renewed accusations of racism. Two members of Lega Nord became specially well-known as the representatives of a more radical political wing: Mario Borghezio and Erminio Boso. From 1995 onwards they were very active within the so-called independentist faction of Lega Nord, but they were also the party hard-liners on the question of migration. First, both used in public statements physical traits to refer to migrants. For Boso:

> The white Italian race is progresivelly extinguising and the black race occupies its place. If we disappeared we will be overflow by black people (*Il Corriere della Sera*, 14/11/95).

Boso's proposal to take the footprints of migrants with a criminal record achieved wide coverage in the Italian press. As Boso put it: 'Beyond fingerprints, one should also index the feet of *extracomunitari* in Italy. Only by the feet can one trace the particular marks of each tribe' (*Il Corriere della*

Sera, 28/10/95).

Second, the statements of Borghezio and Boso were highly controversial and contested by Italian politicians from right and left, but also within the parliamentary group of Lega Nord. Other Lega Nord's representatives had to make statements to the press clarifying their own position on migration. For the senator Tabladini:

> to avoid the immediate response that we are racist, I say right away that Albanians, Slaves and Moroccans—who had somatic features like ours—and not black people, are those who comit the worst crimes like drug trafficking and prostitution (*Il Corriere della Sera*, 11-11-95).

Third, the Italian left used these statements to reject any future cooperation with Lega Nord. Cossutta stated: 'Lega is racist. We cannot make agreements with a racist party' (*Il Corriere della Sera*, 17-11-1995: 1). And the leader of the *Ulivo* at the time, Romano Prodi, this was also a turning point in political relationships with Lega Nord. As he put it: 'There is a gulf between us and Lega. The last positions taken by Lega Nord against migrants have produced a bottomless trench between us' (*Il Corriere della Sera*, 14-11-1995:5).

Local Politics: Grassroots Mobilisation and Target Groups

One of the ways to explore continuity in the politics of Lega Nord against migrants is the involvement of local politicians and local party sections in mobilisation against migrants. Grass roots mobilisation at the local level gave some of the members of Lega Nord a distinctive profile within the party organisation. In 1990 *i comitati di quartiere* emerged as a social response against the insecurity in Italian cities, such as Bologna, Milano and Torino. They were active at the local level and, although in principle independent from political parties, both Alleanza Nazionale and Lega Nord's tried to build political networks with the *comitati*. In fact, the *comitati* served as a springboard for political careers in both AN and Lega Nord (Maneri, 1997). Both Lega Nord and Alleanza Nazionale competed at the local level to gain the political support of the *comitati* in Northern cities.

Lega Nord's local party sections typically issued *volantini* (pamphlets) to protest against the presence of migrants in the neighborhoods and against the creation of *centri d'acoglienza*. After the political phase that brought Lega Nord into the Italian government with Forza Italia and Alleanza Nord in 1994, the party launched its own version of grass-roots mobilisation. The green shirts—a special security guard introduced in the spring of 1996—demonstrated against the presence of migrants under the slogan *Padania e' nazione e il resto e' Meridione* (*Il Corriere della Sera*, 9-6-1996). Nineteen ninety seven was also marked by renewed efforts to mobilise at the local level.

Despite a basic continuity in the anti-migrant agenda of Lega Nord, there were internal conflicts about the mis-matching of local and national levels in the party strategic outlook during the 1990s. Whereas the governmental experience at the national level in 1994 was short-lived, Lega Nord's representatives performed an institutional role at the local level while the party elite played the opposition at the national level. For example, in the city of Milan led by Marco Formentini, a prominent member of Lega Nord, the city council adopted measures for the *centri d'accoglienza* while Umberto Bossi publicly opposed the negotiations between the parties and requested, instead, the expulsion of migrants from Italy (*Il Corriere della Sera*, 26-9-1995). The radicalisation of the party elite in 1996 and 1997 over the issue of independence and secession of the Italian state also involved a radicalisation of political statements about migrants. In the local elections of 1997, some members of the party elite focused on campaigning against Albanians. The ex-president of the Italian parliament, Irene Pivetti, suggested to 'throw Albanian criminals into the see' (*Il Corriere della Sera*, 29-3-1997: 7).

Grassroots mobilisation against migrants during the 1990s targeted a variety of groups. Although Bossi's Lega Lombarda gained political visibility in 1990 with its campaigning against black migrants, political mobilisation it had an *ad hoc* nature. In 1990 the propaganda of Lega Nord stated that *Portare i neri da noi e' Schiavismo* (Bringing black people here is slavery). In 1990 Lega Lombarda campaigned against the center for refugees and migrants in the city with the motto that 'The first Harlem of Milan' was born.

Yet mobilisation at the local level also involved on-going campaigns against the presence of gypsies—for example, *No ai campi nomadi* or the alleged claim that Rom gypsies profited from the special funds attributed by the Prodi government to Albanian refugees (*Le Ragioni della Padania*, Lega Nord, 1996: 11). In addition to black migrants and Rom, Lega Nord's representatives publicly campaigned against migrants from Albania, which were targeted for their alleged criminal activities. In 1997 the electoral campaign for local elections was played out in many Northern cities around the question of migration. Both Lega Nord and Alleanza Nazionale campaigned against the presence of Albanians in Italy. The mayor of Milan Formentini declared that 'he would not allow the invasion of Albanians into Milan and that he would try every possible measure to free the city from their presence' (*Il Corriere della Sera*, 20-3-1997: 31). Giancarlo Pagliarini, one of Lega Nord's ex-ministers in the Berlusconi government, put it clearly: one vote for Formentini, one less Albanian in Milan (*Il Corriere della Sera*, 30-3-1997: 31).

If party mobilisation was characterised by the use of different migrant groups and by the definition of the problem of migration as one of criminality and social order, the ideological evolution of Lega Nord during the 1990s defined the party position on migration around the cultural incompatibility of groups. More specifically, Lega Nord adopted, as other political parties in Europe a new *cultural differentialism.*

Party Ideology: 'The Threat of Multiracial Societies'

The Italian situation has specific characteristics both in the social conditions of migration—the novelty of the process and the difficulties in characterising systematically migrant groups given the multiplicity of origins—and in the political scenario—a large political consensus about the problems and solutions of migration and the enlargement of the discourse of social order to most political parties. As it was shown above, Lega Nord's mobilisation during the 1990s had an *ad hoc* nature, focusing on campaigning against migrants—gypsies, Albanians or North-Africans—reflecting the social characteristics of migration flows into Italy.

In contrast, party ideology introduced and developed a main distinction between Europeans and non-Europeans. The categories of *race* and *ethnicity* had scarce relevance in Italian debates about new migration, as we saw above (Manneri, 1997; Sniderman et al., 2000). However, *ethnicity* and *race* were used explicitly by Lega Nord in the definition and characterisation of groups. The *ethnic* profile of the first autonomist parties in Northern Italy is considered by scholars an electoral failure (Biorcio, 1991; Diamanti, 1993; Melucci and Diani, 1992). Our interest here is not in the public success of the labels, but on their use and function. In a 1988 propaganda issued by Bossi's Lega Lombarda, for example, the *ethnic* problem in Italy was defined as follows:

> A centralized state is not in fact the state of all citizens but it is a state which is controlled by the *ethnic* majority of a country, which for us is that of the Southerners. In the present situation in Italy it is sufficient for a party represented in the whole of the territory of the state to become automatically a party with a Southerner hegemony and thus, a party driven to favor unilateral privileges that discriminate unfairly against the Cisalpine populations. A completely different question is the problem of black migrants because they are not an ethnic majority and therefore, they cannot become hegemonic. If ever they will provoke serious problems of social dissgregration, but certainly not fundamental problems of hegemony and freedom (Lega Lombarda, 1988).

Thus, territorial dualism in Italy was defined on *ethnic* grounds. In an interview with Bossi the year that propaganda against the *extracommunitari* was launched by Lega Lombarda, he declared:

> Q: Are you worried about black migrants?
>
> Bossi: No, that is a false problem. I think black people are nice. They cannot hegemonize us. In contrast, the Southerners can, because they have the state in their hands (*Il Manifesto*, May 21, 1988).

In 1989 and along the same lines, Lega Lombarda/Alleanza Nord propaganda equated *apartheid* with centralism in Italy, the presence of a 'state racism' in Italy generating *ethnic* and *racial* oppression (according to Lega Nord's leader, the ethnic or racial majority was the 'one in charge of the state', that is the Southerners).

The comparison between black migrants and Southerners was shaped by the idea that the *real problem* was the presence of Southerners in the North, and not the new arrival of black migrants. Comparisons between the two groups also became the subject of jokes by the party leader. As reported in an Italian newspaper in 1992, Bossi:

> Q: If a Lombard is on top of a tower with a black men and a Southerner, who would the Lombard push first?
>
> A: The Southerner. Why? Because first goes the obligation, and second, the pleasure (Gianni Fragonara, *Il Corriere della Sera*, April 19, 1992).

The use of the labels, race and ethnicity, changed in the early 1990s. The label *ethnic* became the category to define new migration. Instead, *cultural* differences between Northerners and Southerners entered party statements and speeches, without the *ethnic* label, to distinguish the 'two Italies'. As Bossi put it:

> there is no doubt that in Italy two different cultures are confronted, they are diffused in the country without precise geographical boundaries but with primacy of one over the other. A European culture, entrepreneurial, open and risk-oriented, fundamentally liberal and a Southern culture—*levantina e assistenzialista*—entrenched in the bureaucracy and the *ceti parassitari*, depending on the state and its guarantees, close to the Mafia logic ... out and against the rules of tolerance, democracy and efficiency, *this is not a conflict between macroregions or etnies, it is the conflict between two cultures* (my emphasis) (Bossi, 1993: 206-207).

By the late 1990s, however, the language of *ethnicity* had re-entered Lega

Nord's propaganda about new migration flows. Migration from outside European countries is identified as a problem for its potential in creating *ethnic* conflict:

> Those who oppose immigration from outside the European community are people who do not despise their own ancestors, their own language. They are proud of their own *ethnic* community without, however, considering themselves superior to others. They accept differences, prefer their own people to members of their ethnic groups without rejecting cooperation between them (Enti Locali, 1998).

Thus, the label ethnicity came back in party propaganda to describe not only the *other* but also *us*. As the same document of the party stated: 'by dint of the will to uproot sistematically and unilaterally every feeling of *ethnic* belonging, aren't we risking the accumulation of a latent aggressiveness?' (Enti Locali, 1998: p. 15). At the end of the 1990s, and in the name of the defense of 'our own people', the *ethnic* element is reintroduced by Lega Nord in the distinction between us and the other:

> facing the ridicule accusations of racism that are thrown against the patriots who fight against the destruction of their own people, we need to confirm the sacred right of our people to maintain and defend their own ethno-cultural and religious identity (Enti Locali, 1998, p. 4).

In Lega Nord's propaganda, the coming of a *multiracial* society is the contemporary threat in European societies:

> the multiracial model is the essence of American society. In contrast, Europe has never been multiracial. Athough in her millenaria history there have been internal migration and letting in of racially different components, nevertheless the European ethnies have mantained a basic homogeneity and a reciprocal affinity that derives from their common indoEuropean origin (Enti Locali, 1998: 22)

The instrumental uses of the label *ethnicity* and its changing political meaning should be explained for two main reasons. First, the use of the label ethnicity in the 1990s in political debates about migrants involves a *reversal* of representations. In the 1980s the characterisation of the *other* was a function of the *ethnic* hegemony of the Southerns in party leadership's statements and propaganda. In contrast, the *ethnic* label appears in the late 1990s increasingly linked to the presence of new migrants, to portrait both new migrant's groups in Italian society and the *ethnic* Padanian culture.

Second, although the labels were reversed over the two decades, their essentialising role remains the same and thus, 'culture'—whether *ethnic* or *civic* in the changing language of Lega Nord—naturalises collective differences, represented as intrinsic and natural markers to define individuals. The affinity between the use of cultural or racial markers as *natural* is the defining element. Precisely the exchange of labels between the two groups illustrates the contemporary malleability and applicability of *cultural differentialism*.

In search of a legitmising framework, cultural differentialism provides Lega Nord with a theoretical justification of prejudices. Cultural distance is also brought to legitimise the portrait of Southerners. Some scholars noticed already in the early 1990s a cultural differentialism in Lega Nord (Biorcio, 1991). Yet although some recurrent themes appeared in the statements and documents from Lega Nord since the early 1990s, it is only during the 1990s that we can explicity refer to the articulation of party ideology as a systematic view of group differences. This increasing sofistication of party ideological production is not unique to Lega Nord. Evidence from other new anti-migrant parties, such as the Flemish Vlaams Blok, also shows increasing ideological sophistication over time (Swyngedouw, 1997).

The rejection of a *multiracial* society in Italy was already present in Lega Nord since the early 1990s, but their integration into a coherent whole was a process completed over the decade. This representation of cultural differences has become familiar in Europe: one of a 'clash of civilizations' between a tolerant Europe and the threat represented by the Arab world. For Bossi:

> Lega defends marginal cultures, the small peoples with their traditional patrimony that must not be frozen, but kept alive respecting the roots that are the essence of humanity. This tolerant vision is essentially European, and as such must be asserted today more than ever, vis-à-vis the diffusion of the cultures of intollerance and integralism sustained by an imperialist and macronationalistic logic. The Islam, on the one hand, and American colonization on the other, threatened the great European culture that has in Padania a stronghold and in the South an advance post (Bossi, 1993: 205).

Lega Nord's ideology incorporated the same elements of extreme-right parties in other European party systems. Moreover, the identification of common themes in party ideology and their similarities with other European political parties is not related to the social and political conditions of the question of migration in Italy. These common themes are the following: demographic arguments about the extinction of the European society; the anti-globalisation view that refuses the transformation of societies in multi-cultural states, the explicit adoption of a *differentialist* view that characterises migrants' integration in host societies as impossible because of cultural *incompatibility*, and the identification of migrants as competitors for scarce resources.

In party propaganda, pseudo-scientific arguments about demographic change are a starting point to assess the dangers of migration as part of a larger process that involves the extinction of European societies. Lega Nord's propaganda holds that Europe has a problem in the Mediterranean as all the area—from the Magreb to Turkey—represents a *threat* on two grounds: religion and the lack of pluralistic systems. It is on the evolution of birth rates that Lega's propaganda places the extinction of the European civilisation and warns about: 'an unstoppable process and march towards extinction, is hidden by the migration wave that our country is suffering' (Enti Locali, 1998: 9). The propaganda of Lega Nord emphasises the protection of the family unit and the promotion of the traditional role of women and as a tool to increase birth rates. The problem is explained as one of values and mentality because 'selfish material considerations' create an environment that does not encourage the family as the 'basic unity' in Western society.

Lega Nord is against the development of *multiracial* societies as the prospective outcome of globalisation and contemporary imperialism. The United States and France are considered examples of inter-racial conflicts and violence. The *multiracial* society envisioned by Lega Nord 'eliminates cultural references and collective identities and represents 'another step in individuals' alienation' (Enti Locali, 1998). Lega Nord's propaganda asserts that public opinion is instintively against 'mass and other than European' migration. In Lega Nord's perspective, the racist *threat* is not in Western societies but in the destructive processes involved in the coming of multiracial societies.

For Lega Nord, advocates of multiculturalism are the 'true racists' because they refused the diversity of peoples and cultures. In short, for Lega Nord: 'Patriotism represents the last obstacle to avoid the progress of two imperial powers: the American and the Islam' (Enti Locali, 1998: 14). Those who defend their own *ethnic* community are not *racist*, but *patriots* who are involved in a reactive defense against threats to their identity and their community. For the propaganda of Lega Nord, 'the ideology of the multiracial society is based on two principles, the melting pot that promotes hybrid cultures and the lack of cultural and social roots. In contrast, Lega Nord's stresses the importance of emotional ties, of cultural and *ethnic* continuity' (Enti Locali, 1998: 16). For Lega Nord 'migrants have the right to come and stay', while 'Padanians are invited to forget their history, their culture and their identity' (Enti Locali, 1998: 16).

Lega Nord demanded the establishment of five measures for the *defense* of Padanians against migrants. First, Lega Nord is against the establishment of voting rights for migrants and asks for a restrictive definition of citizenship linked to the principle of *ius sanguinis*. Second, Lega Nord seeks the preservation of 'the specificities of our people, history and traditions in schools', and the need to 'stop multicultural indoctrination in the schools'. Third, Lega Nord asks for 'the priority of Padanians and Europeans in the job market and social services'. Lega Nord has introduced the Italian version of 'Le Francais d'Abord' (FN in France) or Eigen Volk Eerst (VB in Belgium), *Padroni a casa propria*. Fourth, Lega Nord envisages the return of foreigners to their lands of origin, creating a special fund to finance it. In addition, the party program proposes the introduction of a special tax for entrepreneurs that employ new migrants instead of 'Padanians' to cover the social costs of unemployment. Fifth, and last point, the party program asks for the development of a policy of balanced international cooperation with Thirld World countries. For Lega Nord, those countries that refuse the return of migrants must be punished with special sanctions and with their exclusion from international cooperation (Enti Locali, 1998: 30).

Conclusions

In this chapter Lega Nord's construction of *otherness* was discussed. The relationship of politics and prejudice was analysed from the point of view of party mobilisation and party ideology. Under party mobilisation, the main features of Lega Nord's style of mobilisation against migrants—portrait of the criminal *other*, grassroots mobilisation and variation over time in targeted groups—were analysed. The study of party mobilisation has also allowed the consideration of different strategic scenarios in the politicisation of the question of migration during the 1990s and the shifting debates in light of the enlargement of a consensus about the 'question' and 'problem' of migration in Italy. Under party ideology, the chapter discussed the world view of Lega Nord as an increasingly fully-fledged system that emphasises cultural differences as the new markers of migrants groups.

Party politics are important to explain not only the possibility of expressing socially diffused and shared prejudices against Southerners, but also the production and reproduction of *otherness* through political statements and party mobilisation. The chapter showed the specific meaning that *ethnicity* and *race* took in the way in which Lega Nord's politicised the question of migration. Interestingly, it should be noted that the ideological legitimation of anti-migrant rhetoric might be more a matter of internal consumption for party activists, than a relevant political dimension in larger political debates. As Maneri showed in his research on the Italian media, cultural differentialism is only marginally present in the dominant discourse about migrants in Italy. And, although socially the question of migration in Italy involved a variety of migrant 'groups' and was mainly focused on the control of migration flows, the ideology of Lega Nord went one step ahead in the portrait of the cultural incompatibility of groups in Italian society, a question that belongs to a different scenario: that of the integration and incorporation of migrants in host societies.

Notes

[1] For Maneri, the debate that precedes but also foilows the migration legal framework (legge Martelli on February 1990) develops in the context of three new factors: first, the legitimation of the political elaboration of discriminatory and exlusionary practices (which runs parallel to a redefinition in a restrictive sense of the concept of racism), second, the general perception that there is a remarkable change in public opinion and attitudes; and third, the emergence of political entrepreneurs which seek gains in this changing public feelings.

[2] The Italian left had articulated a view in which migration should be regulated around five issues, the regulation of illegal migrants already in Italy, a procedure to expel undocumented migrants, a program to regulate future migrant flows, more strict measures against undocumented immigrants trying to enter the country, and more favorable norms in the context of family reunification (Romano Prodi in Il Corriere della Sera, 19-10-95).

[3] In an interview in 1992, Bossi declared that: 'at the beginning of my political career I remember clearly that in order to gain media coverage your colleagues—the journalists— told me that they would write articles about me but only if I present myself as a racist and, thus, I said that I was a racist although after that it was not easy to go around. But what should I have done?' (Oggi, 21/12/1992).

5 Party Mobilisation and Symbolic Resources

> In theory, Lega Nord is like the rest of us, they have their congresses, they have their rules ... and yet, they are fundamentally different from the rest of us (M. Martinazzoli, last secretary of the DC, Brescia, 1996).

This chapter focuses on Lega Nord's style of mobilisation and organisation. It examines how the party reproduced the new territorial identity of the North, studying mobilisation structures and their effectiveness. Lega is commonly depicted as a populist and charismatic party. Charismatic parties are defined by the presence of a single leader. The party is, in fact, 'the creature and vehicle for the assertion of a charismatic leadership' (Panebianco, 1982: p. 108). Analysts of Lega Nord rightly emphasise Bossi's leadership as a key feature in the party organisation (Biorcio, 1991, 1997; Diamanti, 1993). Bossi is the driving force behind Lega Nord and has fashioned the party as his own political creature. Lega Nord's leader has built his carrier in the creation and reproduction of political controversy and polemic. Described by followers and opponents as a 'political animal', Bossi introduced a popular language in Italian politics and insulted the main societal, institutional and political actors in Italy (Biorcio, 1991; 1997). In fact, one could ask if there is any institution, societal or political actor in Italy who has not been the target of Bossi's attacks, from the Southerners, to his own political allies, to the Pope.[1]

The success of Lega Nord in the Italian party system was explained on many accounts as the result of a cycle of protest in Italian politics and external political opportunities (Diani 1996). Lega Nord's organisation is commonly treated as a secondary development, a minor force in the rise of the Northern question in Italy. Scholars did not explore what the party did—since grievances were conceptualised as the product of public dissatisfaction with political parties and with the impact of the crisis of the welfare state on disadvantaged groups. Lega Nord was conceived as a minimal party in terms of size, membership and mobilisation capacities, although some scholars have even classified Lega Nord as a mass party (Ricolfi, 1995). It is generally assumed that Lega Nord's leader is largely unconstrained by organisational dynamics in a party that he fashioned according to his own political tastes. The presence of Bossi and the emphasis on crisis conditions made the question of following of the party and allegiance to Lega Nord a matter of social pathology (Biorcio, 1991, 1997; Diani, 1994). Journalistic and scholarly writing has incorporated the term *la base*—also used within the party—to describe party activists. Like the characterisations of Communist membership in the cold-war period, Lega Nord's activists are often portrayed as fanatic and irrational creatures.

This chapter examines the mobilisation structures of Lega Nord, collective mobilisation and party resources. Focusing on Bossi tell us nothing about the party organisation and mobilisation dynamics—and whether they constrained and how—the party leadership. Rather than simply categorising Lega Nord as a charismatic party, a neopopulist party, a protest party, a communal party, this chapter focuses on what Lega Nord does. It illuminates the black box of the party organisation and brings evidence to bear in the expansion of the party organisation during the 1990s. This chapter explains the mix of traditional and innovative elements in Lega Nord's mobilisation and organisation. Lega Nord borrows from traditional models of mass party organisations—the Italian Communist party as a source of inspiration—as well as radically departing from them. Lega Nord is closer to a social movement in that direct mobilisation is *essential* for the party.

Second, this chapter combines a classical study of the main features of the party organisation with the description of symbolic structures and their uses. It examines the symbolic elaboration of the party and its ability to generate controversies and public attention with its national symbolism. Lega Nord has captured attention both by making people laugh and worry at their collective representations of nationhood. Lega Nord's gatherings are commonly treated as *folkloristic* events characterised by its limited following. Party demonstrations are considered irrelevant to understand the dynamics of political conflict in Italy. Bossi's fascination with *Braveheart*—the movie that brought Wallace, the Scottish hero, to mass audiences—the four musketeers, and other popular heroes, the rituals of the party with the public enactment of the unity of the North are considered funny, ridiculous, or at best, irrelevant. Yet some scholars have also stressed the role of these events (Diamanti, 1993; Ruzza and Schmidtke, 1994).

Rather than a party ran by a few professional managers, Lega Nord's organisation relied on voluntary participation. Solidarity and normative incentives explain participation in Lega Nord's organisation. Unlike views on the limitless power of new populist leaders, Bossi's leadership is constrained by party organisational dynamics. This chapter aims to show how the need to secure party activism and participation constrained the strategies of the leadership. Bossi has justified the adoption of many decisions on the grounds of the feelings of the party members. This is not a rhetorical device, but a very pressing concern for the party leader. The political trajectory of Lega Nord in the Italian party system reflected radical shifts in elite strategies. The creation of new players and new rules of the game in the Italian party system changed the political environment for Lega Nord. The new political opportunity structure constrained the expansion of Lega Nord and risked its electoral marginalisation. Bossi's choice to enter an electoral alliance with Berlusconi in 1994 was very unpopular within its own party. After the electoral alliance with Berlusconi and the short experience in the Italian government, Lega supported a caretaker government with the Italian left. The political capital of Lega quickly evaporated in this period.[2] Internal conflicts plagued the party.

First, I describe the party organisational format and internal dynamics during the 1990s. Then I explore Lega Nord's symbolic action through two main series of events: the rituals at Pontida and the Parliament of the North. The role of ritual and symbolic politics in projecting the identity and political unity in the party and providing the symbolic linkages between leadership, elite and followers is explained. Rituals provide both an image of the party as a solidarity unit and a means by which the party wins public attention and media coverage.

Lega Nord: Between Tradition and Modernity in Party Politics

Scholarly writing in the post-war period analysed the two major parties in Italian politics: the Christian Democrats and the Communist parties. The Christian Democratic party was characterised by the presence of strong ideological and regional currents within the party organisation and a special relationship with the Catholic world from which it borrowed its organisational and societal resources (Galli, 1978; Menapace, 1974). The Italian Communist party, instead, represented the *ideal* type of mass party organisation. Both parties were mass organisations that consolidated their presence in society and endured stable political and electoral allegiances. Scholars analysed the DC and the Communist parties at the national level, but we have also many studies at the local level (Kertzer, 1980; Evans, 1967; Stern, 1977; Lange, 1977).

Bossi intended to fashion Lega Nord as a powerful mass organisation, to recruit a new political class and to develop party policy and programmatic goals. The imagery of the mass party organisation was behind his attempts to create a powerful Lega Nord and *replace* the presence of traditional parties in the North. Lega Nord's organisational expansion took place combining the entrepreneurship of Lega Nord and the co-optation and negotiations of local politicians with the federal representatives of Lega Nord.[3]

The party organisation was hierarchical. The chart of Lega Nord includes the presence of five organisational layers: federal, national, provincial, district and communal. At the federal level, the Federal Congress is the representative organ of all the members of the national sections of Lega Nord (art. 9 of the current statute). The Federal congress elects both the Secretary and the

President of Lega Nord. The organs of the federation are the Federal Congress, the Federal Council, the Federal Secretary, the Federal President and a Federal board of arbitrators.[4] The Federal Secretariat of the party is in Milan.

Decision-making about the program and strategies of the party is formally in the hands of the Federal Council yet Bossi is, in fact, the single decision-maker. Party statutes have institutionalised the power of the Federal Secretary within the organisation. The secretary represents, political and legally, the unity of the movement. According to the party statute, the secretary coordinates the directives of the Federal Congress, summons and chairs the Federal Council and the Political Secretariat (art. 16). The Federal President cannot be from the same national section as the Federal secretary. The federal secretary of Lega Nord is, since its origins, Umberto Bossi. After a short period in which Bossi combined the roles of *national* secretary of Lega Lombarda and Federal Secretary of Lega Nord—thanks to a transitory clause in the first statute—the federal level and the Lombard national secretary became different organisational layers of the party. In practice, the Federal Presidents of Lega Nord are members of the Venetian *national* section.[5]

The legacies of the Lega Nord's origins as a coalition of parties are incorporated in the party statutes and organisation. The first statute of Lega Nord established the territorial division of the organisation in *national* sections. The current statute of the party includes the national sections that Lega Nord established in Northern Italy in the 1990s. Article 2 of the statute includes 14 national sections: Alto Adige-Sudtirol, Emilia, Friuli, Liguria, Lombardia, Marche, Piemonte, Romagna, Toscana, Trentino, Trieste, Umbria, Valle d'Aosta, Veneto (art. 2 statute Lega Nord). Three Italian regions are split up in two sections Trentino (Trentino and Alto-Adige), Friuli-Venezia Giulia (Friuli and Trieste) and Emilia-Romagna (Emilia and Romagna). The statutes of Lega Nord define a *nation* as 'an ethno-geographical community, identified in the Italian state legal framework, as a region' (art. 6).[6] The primacy of the Lombard national section is institutionalised in party statutes.[7]

The *national* sections of Lega Nord replicate the organisational format of the party at the federal level. First, a national secretary and a national president represent each national section within the party organisation. National sections incorporate a National Congress that represents all the members of the national sections and develops the programs of the party at the 'national' level. The National Council develops the political goals set by the Federal Congress. The provincial and communal sections complete the territorial organisation of the party. At the provincial level, the party includes a provincial congress, an executive council, the provincial secretary and an administrative secretary (articles 44 to 47). The party defines a crucial role for the communal sections as the basic territorial unit dedicated to 'the organisational expansion of the movement and the realisation and diffusion of its programs' (art. 39).

The first statute of the party established three different types of members: ordinary, militant and supporter (art. 26 first statute).[8] Subsequent statutes reduced these categories to only two: ordinary-militant and supporter. Ordinary members have the duty to participate actively in the associative life of the party (art. 34). They are the only ones with the right of speech and vote and have the right to be elected as representatives of Lega Nord.[9] Supporters have neither rights nor duties in the party.

Lega Nord also set up *collateral* organisations to aggregate and represent Catholics, workers, and entrepreneurs. In 1990 Lega Lombarda had already attempted the creation of collateral organisations to the party organisation. Lega Lombard created SAL (*Sindicato Autonomista Lombardo*), a trade union to represent workers outside the channel of traditional Italian trade unions. In addition, the ALIA (*Associazione di Liberi Imprenditori Autonomisti*) sought to organise regional entrepreneurs around the autonomist project. The *Consulta Cattolica*, a special office to represent Catholics within Lega Nord published its own journal and became well known for its position against the hierarchy of the Catholic Church. The formation of technical cadres and a new political class was also attempted during the 1990s. Interviews with party organisers revealed at least three different attempts at the federal level to create a *scuola quadri*.

Lega Nord's objective of becoming a social presence by reproducing the model of the mass party was a failure. The pharaonic proportions of the federal secretary of Lega Nord in Milan and the multiplication of bureaucratic and functional roles within the organisation hide the lack of a functional and hierarchical division of labor. The relationships between the federal secretary and the national secretaries of the party are conflictual. The presence of the collateral organisations of the party is minimal. The efforts to open up the party to society by aggregating and channeling interests and by establishing linkages with organised interests also proved a failure. The linkages and networks between party organisers and representatives are loose. Although the federal level of the organisation has an *Ufficio Legislativo* which, in theory, is in charge of policy proposals, the linkages between the federal secretariat of the party and the parliamentary group are tenuous. Some parliamentarians have informal relationships with local, provincial and local sections. In short, the attempts to institutionalise the party in the *old* style failed.

The *real* party is closer to a social movement than a bureaucratic organisation, becoming a social presence by using other type of resources. Lega Nord specialised in symbolic production since its origins. The party has manufactured from coins—*le leghe*—to ties to perfumes, flags, pins, watches, an entire industry to reproduce Lega's hero Alberto di Giussano and the party's flag. In particular, the graffiti and *attachini* (posters) of Lega Nord were a key means of political communication. As Bossi himself has put it

> In contrast to the opulent tradition of nomenklatura today sunk by Tangentopoli (and in contrast to the conformist and opportunist mass media), I realised that without my journals, my televisions and my messages I still could find the necessary space in the walls of Italy ... A slogan, a manifest of few words (but words can become stones) are a thousand times more worthy than a polished hypocrite political message ... That's the reason I have in great consideration the pioneers of Lega who in the difficult times of our struggle carried, with our *attachini*, the voice of Lega non only in the North, but also in the entire Italy.[10]

For the leader of Lega Nord: 'in order to do politics we need to produce culture' (Lega Nord, n. 41, 1992). Lega Nord is a locus of symbolic production. The party organisation consolidated itself as a machine for symbolic production. Lega Nord symbols are displayed in the cities of Northern Italy, its highways, its secondary roads.[11] Lega Nord specialised in political communication, in the creation of a competing frame with propaganda, slogans and *volantini* and the creation of their own means of political communication (Todesco, 1992).. The organisational identity, as well as the party line—and its changes—are publicised through the party journal, posters, graffiti and pamphlets. Party members are in charge of distributing them. The propaganda resources of the party are concentrated in Via Bellerio. The radio station, the office of the party journal and the production of manifestos are also located there.

Lega Nord's leader uses the rhetoric of the masses but Lega Nord's capabilities to encourage mobilisation are scarce. Lega Nord has claimed a certain following but the party's estimates have been widely questioned (Diani, 1994). In 1992 Lega Nord was adverstising the party as a consolidated organisation. For example: 'To do politics, a big organisation is required. Lega Nord, 400 *sedi*, 700 sections, 200,000 members', Lombardia Autonomista No. 6 (Anno X, March 5, 1992). In June of the same year, the journal of the party included the same advertisement, changing the number of members from 200,000 to 40,000. Later in November of the same year, the party journal claimed again 200,000 members (*Per fare politica occore una grande organizzazione. Lega Nord, 600 sedi, 1000 sezioni, 200,000 members.* Lega Nord No. 42 (Anno X, November 20, 1992).

In absolute numbers, Lega Nord is a small party. Table 5.1 shows the 'real' numbers of party membership and the evolution of membership in Lega Nord during the 1990s.

Table 5.1 Membership in Lega Nord (a.v.)

Year	1991	1992	1993	1994	1995
Total	16912	19951	43308	44186	19501
Ordinary	-	-	6093	9090	9986
Supporter	-	-	37215	35096	9515

Source: Lega Nord (1992 data for Lega Lombarda)

Membership rates in Lega Nord show an expansive trend in the early 1990s.[12]

The presence of the party organisation in most of the regions of the North is very limited.[13] Table 2 shows membership in Lega Nord by region for the same years.

Table 5.2 Membership in Lega Nord by Region (1991-1995) (a.v.)

Region	1991	1992	1993	1994	1995
Lombardy	16912	19951	26334	19852	8474
Piedmont	-	-	8612	7602	3304
Ligury	-	-	929	3346	924
Veneto	-	-	2482	7289	5119
Emilia-Romagna	-	-	2082	2443	596
Tuscany	-	-	1683	1410	5
F.V. Giulia	-	-	418	1450	435
Val d'aosta	-	-	42	39	46
Trentino	-	-	733	643	572
Federal	16912	19951	43308	44186	19501

Source: Lega Nord

In the early 1990s, party membership was growing in all the regions of the North. In absolute numbers, members are concentrated in the Lombard region. During the 1990s, the second position shifted from Piedmont to Veneto. The rise and fall of membership in the red regions of Emilia-Romagna and Tuscany and the special regions reflects the marginal organisational and electoral presence of the party in these regions. Organisational resources are concentrated in the electorally successful regions: Lombardy and Veneto.

Table 5.3 illustrates how the share of the Lombard region has diminished over time. While Lombardy contributed in 1993 with 61% of the total membership rates of participation in Lega Nord, by 1995, its contribution had decreased to 43% of the total. In sharp contrast to the decrease of the Lombard section, the Venetian contributed only a 6% to the membership of the party in 1993 whereas in 1995 contributed with a 26% to the total membership in Lega Nord. The section in Lombardy suffered the struggles that followed from the fall of the Berlusconi government when the national secretary of Lega Lombarda, Luigi Negri, left the party and unraveled a major conflict within the local sections of the party.

Table 5.3 Share of Party Membership by *National* Sections (%)

Region	1993	1994	1995
Lombardy	61	45	43
Piedmont	20	17	17
Ligury	2	8	5
Veneto	6	16	26
Other	12	13	8
Federal Total	100	100	100

Source: Lega Nord

Bossi was supported by local party sections that made Lega Nord's views on the North-South divide a common presence not only in the national media, but also in the Northern regions through the distribution of party propaganda, posters and graffitti at the local level. The tasks performed by Lega Nord's activists in local party sections are both celebratory and proselytising. Party members are engaged in 'face to face' politics, from bars to public markets.[14] Voluntary participation in local party sections evolves around the diffusion of party programs, the distribution of party propaganda and the organisation of public feasts. As one party secretary summarised it:

Until 1990 we did public meetings, distribute propaganda, write slogans and fix posters on the walls. Later there was an organizational effort to do more professional politics, but still today for us public meetings and the distribution of party *volantini* are crucial. They have an educational role; they are a school within the movement, a duty, and a necessary step ... There is a tension between this popular character and the need to form technical cadres within the party (Zanello, Milano, 1996).

Local party sections are in charge of organising party feasts and public meetings on regular basis. For example, the provincial secretary of Lega Nord in the city of Varese described the organisational evolution of the section as follows:

When I started as provincial secretary, we only organised six feasts, today we organize 29 summer feasts. We also bring the tracks to the square and we make public meetings there, because we want to be present over the territory. We all do voluntary work: fix posters, organise public meetings in squares and markets, and of course, we have all the walls of Varese covered with our posters (Reguzzoni, Varese, 1996).

During the 1990s the expansion of the party organisation was extremely vulnerable to two factors. First, the party was vulnerable to changes in voluntary participation. Second, the expansion of the party organisation followed the electoral performance of the party, concentrating resources in the regions of Lombardy and Veneto. The next section looks at party internal dynamics and how they have constrained Bossi's leadership during the 1990s.

Organisational Dynamics: Voice, Exit and Strategic Constraints

Lega Nord's identity was sustained through the creation of controversy and the enemy as a threat that reinforces internal political unity. The creation of tensions with the environment and the activation of a friend-and-foe relationship with outside elements reinforced the organisational and symbolic boundaries of the party. This type of mobilisation dynamics prevented the emergence of procedural mechanisms for the solution of conflicts. Internal conflict over courses of action and strategies fundamentally evolved around issues of loyalty. The external enemy has an internal dimension (traitors) and 'voice' within the movement was constrained by claims of loyalty. 'Exit', instead, was common for both party elites and party activists.

Until 1993 Lega Nord followed a virtous cycle of organisational and electoral expansion. However, collective action problems marked the party during the decade. Internal conflict and polemics around the leader's choices led party elites and members to exit from the organisation. The choice of entering an electoral alliance with Berlusconi in the general elections of 1994, the short participation in the government and the decision to withdraw the support for the government and abandoned the coalition had a devastating impact in the organisation. The organisational dynamics of the party led to *exit* and not *voice*. Bossi had to struggle with the problem of how to maintain voluntary participation. From 1994 to 1995, membership in Lega Nord went down, in absolute numbers, from 44,186 to 19,501 members (see table above). The evolution of membership rates in the organisation reflects the sharp downward cycle that characterised Lega Nord during 1994 and 1995. *Exit* from the organisation was a response to a new political environment where the choices of the party leader became contentious. Bossi's choice had a devastating impact on Lega Nord's membership.

A first step explaining collective mobilisation and party dynamics is to avoid assuming charismatic leadership and unconditional support from its followers as a given. Charisma is a constructed category (Alberoni 1981). Views of Bossi within the party range from the unconditional supporter—who considers Bossi a charismatic leader—to those that merely describe him as the party federal secretary and widely criticised his choices, even if not in public. Bossi needs to assert his *charisma* in order to secure the leadership of the party vis-à-vis both party elites and members. He can only do that by securing participation and votes. Bossi's role as the single interpreter of the North and its interests and its control over the organisation is predicated on his political ability. However, his formula works as long as he can mobilise supporters and votes to gain political credibility.

There were two main mechanisms for the selection of the party elite. First, Bossi's direct appointment recruits the top party elite. The leadership of the party over the last decade shows a group of politicians loyal to the leader, *i fedelissimi*. Second, Lega Nord runs party primaries in which the party 'ordinary' members have the right to vote. While some party organisers claim the primaries are an example of real internal democracy, the *national* secretaries in the regions control the outcomes of these elections. They make sure the right candidates are included and the wrong ones excluded. Two issues should be highlighted. First, the 1996 primaries were precisely used by the hierarchy of the party to give party members more *voice* in the selection of the candidates. In fact, the new parliamentary group of Lega Nord, elected in 1996, had a high rate of party experience at the local level. The party primaries allowed on the one hand, Bossi to retain his power over the party elite—at the mercy of both Bossi's willingness to support their candidacies— and on the other hand, the strenghtening of local party sections where the performance of party representatives was *evaluated* by party members.

Second, the party primaries are, for the leader, a political mechanism to encourage people to participate in the life of the party.

Table 5.4 shows the extent to which the party national elite has been recruited from within the party ranks over the three legislative periods of the 1990s.

Table 5.4 Representatives with Experience in Party Office (%)

	1992	1994	1996
Lega Nord			
No experience	32.7	37.6	31.0
Low appointments	11.5	13.7	36.2
Middle	29.2	28.2	15.5
High	26.5	20.5	17.2
Total Chamber			
No experience	20.4	44.0	36.7
Low appointment	5.6	9.1	24.2
Middle	27.3	20.4	12.1
High	46.7	26.5	17.2

Source: Verzichelli, 1996: p. 754

Lega Nord party elite was entirely new to politics. The year with the highest percentage of representatives with no party experience in office was 1994 (37% of party representatives did not have experience in the party organisation). Over time, the trend is towards recruitment in the lower ranks of the party officials. In 1996, 36% of Lega Nord's representatives had experience in the lower ranks of the party organisation (as opposed to the 24.2% average for the entire Chamber).

Not surprisingly Bossi does not allow this elite to occupy power positions in the party organisation. Those who have attempted to challenge Bossi's leadership or those who Bossi considers as potential challengers were systematically expelled from the party organisation during the 1990s.[15] The trajectory of party elites during the 1990s was shaped by their relationship with the party leader. Bossi's tried to control the relationship between party elites and the party organisation to prevent the creation of alternative power bases within the party. As one ex-representative of Lega Nord in the Italian Parliament clearly put it:

> Lega is Bossi and Bossi is Lega, the last Leninist-Stalinist party. To survive
> within Lega, if Bossi is in the tenth floor, you must stop at the fifth. If you arrive
> at the ninth floor, you will end up down in the cellar. He never allows the growth
> of intermediate cadres and a ruling class.

Bossi's style of command during the 1990s created conflict within party elites and these conflicts resulted in 'exit' from the organisation. While conflicts within the party were common during the 1990s, they had minor consequences for Bossi until 1994.[16] However, the decision to leave the Berlusconi government in 1994—after only eight months in office—divided the parliamentary group and had also a snowball effect at the local level. Out of a parliamentary group of 117 representatives, 59 left the party in the fall of 1994.

La base represents the core of party supporters. Political participation and party activism—given its voluntary nature—are extremely sensitive to changing conditions. Political participation involves an *honorary* system, a learning process designed as a set of steps to become *a leghista*. Becoming a Lega Nord activist involves a process of political socialisation through participation in the life of party sections. The incentives to participate in the party are normative and solidaristic, members use the language moral obligation, commitment, friendship and solidarity. Many representatives of the party recalled their participation in these activities as part of the socialisation process within Lega Nord. The interviews I conducted with party representatives showed that this new political class started working for the organisation by putting posters and *attachini*.

Lega Nord is defined as a revolutionary movement for radical change.[17] The revolutionary nature of Lega Nord and its radical opposition to the current Italian political system is best illustrated by the self-definitions of Lega members. As one member put it: 'We live like an army: the base are those pure and tough who do not go with negotiations and compromises.' The nature of Lega as a movement, and not a political party is a key to explain party dynamics. The self-definition of Lega Nord as a movement marks the politics of radical transformation and revolutionary commitment that, according to the members of Lega Nord, distinguishes their political project from the rest of Italian parties. As one regional councilor of Lega Nord in Veneto put it: '*Sono intrato in Lega per farla morire*' (I entered Lega to make it die).

A good indicator to explore changes in the level of commitment to the party is the type of membership in Lega Nord—ordinary and supporters. The 'core' of party membership is formed by 'ordinary' members. Table 5.5 shows the disparity in the evolution of both categories of membership. Whereas in absolute numbers, ordinary members stagnated or increased slightly during

1994-1995, supporters sharply declined over the same period.

Table 5.5 Lega Nord 'Ordinary' and 'Supporters' (1993-1995)

	1993		1994		1995	
	Ord	Supp	Ord	Supp	Ord	Supp
Lombardy	3026	23308	3189	16663	3724	4750
Piedmont	1067	7545	1916	5686	2342	962
Ligury	164	765	584	2762	428	496
Veneto	946	1536	1757	5533	2732	2387
Federal	6093	37215	9090	35096	9986	9515

Source: Lega Nord

Lega Nord retained and expanded its 'ordinary' members, while the number of 'supporters' was drastically reduced from 35,096 to 9515 members.

By 1995, the journal of Lega Nord was launching campaigns for membership on these grounds: 'Remember, you do not need to participate in order to sustain the party.' Lega Nord retained a core of party members and activists despite the crisis that drastically reduced membership rates in 1995, but Bossi was constrained to radicalise his position to enforce the party organisational and symbolic boundaries. In 1996, the goals of the party leadership shifted from claims of federalism to threats to abandon Italian political institutions and independence of the North. The trajectory of Lega Nord during the period 1994-1996 shows how exit—rather than voice in the form of intra-party democracy—explains elite radicalisation. From the point of view of the party organisation, the launching of secession and independence clarified the goals of Lega Nord and closed the party to external influences.

The first goal of the party leadership in the early 1990s was the expansion of the organisation from Lombardy to the other regions of Northern Italy.[18] Party dynamics were also shaped by the extent to which Bossi could make the idea of a united North a credible reality not only in Lombardy, but also in the other regions of the North, as we saw in Table 2. Party activism in Lega Nord was unevenly distributed across the North. The increasing weight of Venetian membership on the total membership of the organisation paralleled the increasing electoral success of Lega Nord in the Veneto region. The electoral and organisational strength of the Venetian section represented another challenge for Bossi's. His repeated calls for the unity and solidarity of the North were a direct response to the internal challenges of a strong Venetian section. The increasing importance of the Venetian section became a disturbing force within the party, challenging Bossi's control over the organisation.

The first party crisis after the governmental experience showed that the party experienced in this earlier period the growth of membership rates for ordinary members, at the expense of supporters.[19] As table 6 shows 'ordinary' members represented only 14% of Lega Nord members in 1993, yet by 1995 they have grown to represent 51% of the total membership in the organisation. This sharp increase in party membership was most dramatic in Piedmont where Lega Nord suffered a sharp electoral decline (from 12% to 71%). Thus the rate of 'supporters' has drastically decreased at the same time that the core has grown. Over the 1993-1995 period, the only national section of Lega Nord with a positive trend in overall membership was the Venetian section.

Table 5.6 Type of Membership in Lega Nord by Region (1993-1995)

	1993	1994	1995
	Ord/Tot	Ord/Tot	Ord/Tot
Lombardy	11%	16%	44%
Piedmont	12%	25%	71%
Ligury	18%	17%	46%
Veneto	38%	24%	53%
Federal	14%	21%	51%

Source: Lega Nord, Segreteria Organizzativa

Table 5.7 lays out the evolution of both militants and supporters by region in the same period. The weakening of party activism in Lombardy is quite pronounced.

Table 5.7 Lega National Sections by Type of Membership (%)

	Ord '93	Ord '94	Ord '95	Supp '93	Supp '94	Supp '95
Lombardy	50	35	37	63	47	50
Piedmont	18	21	23	20	16	10
Ligury	3	6	4	2	8	5
Veneto	16	19	27	4	16	25
Other	16	18	8	11	12	9
Federal	100	100	100	100	100	100

Source: Lega Nord

In 1993, 50% of all the 'ordinary' members of the organisation were in Lombardy, but by 1995 the share had fallen to only 37%. The percentage of 'ordinary' members in Piedmont slightly increased (18% to 23%). Instead, the situation in Veneto shows how the percentage of 'ordinary' members has been increasing during the 1990s. While the Venetian 'ordinary' members represented only 16% of the total 'ordinary' members, in 1995 they represented 27%. The evolution of 'militant' members shows a similar trend. In 1993, 63% of the members in the organisation were in Lombardy. In 1995 they represented only 50% of the total militant members of the organisation. In contrast, Veneto experienced a sharp increase in its contribution. In 1993, Venetian 'supporters' members represented a mere 4% of the federal total. By 1995, Venetians accounted for a 25% of this type of membership.

Although the data presented in this section only covers the regional distribution of membership until 1995, the importance of the Venetian section in understanding party dynamics accentuated over the 1990s. Conflicts within Lega Nord's elites exploded in the summer of 1998 with the call of Venetians for moderating the party line and attempts to break away from Lega Nord.

Symbolic Action: Party Rituals and Extra-Institutional Means of Action

During the 1990s Lega Nord became a locus of symbolic production in Italy with two main series of events: the rituals and public rallies conducted at Pontida, and the 'Parliament' of the North. The party identity and its political unity were staged in these collective representations. The party rituals at Pontida provided the symbolic linkage between party elites and followers. In turn, the Parliament of the North united party elites around Bossi to assert the rights of political autonomy of the Italian North. I describe first these events and the participation of followers, members and the party elite of Lega Nord. Then, I explain why and how national symbolism were crucial to reproduce the Northern question.

Bossi relied on extra-institutional means of action and symbolic action to reproduce Lega Nord's controversies and to gain mass coverage. Symbolic action serves strategic purposes as well. Party rituals and symbolic politics provide the linkage between what party's elites and members do and how it is represented by other parties and the Italian media. Rituals of political unity of party members and elites also provide for the extensive coverage of Lega Nord in the Italian media (Laurence 1998).

Some authors claim that this—usually negative—publicity is a sign of the *weak* capacities of the party to frame issues (Diani, 1994). Yet negative coverage also reinforces the boundaries between *us* and *them*, it is instrumental for the party leadership. Despite the insults that the leadership of the party reserved for journalists and the common claim that journalists 'serve the regime', during the 1990s Lega Nord lived on the visibility that the Italian media gave to the movement and the leadership of the party knows it. The rule is very simple: *the more controversy, the more media coverage.*

Symbolic Action

The workings of Lega Nord symbolic action can be illustrated through the properties of symbols (Kertzer, 1988). First, during the 1990s, the rituals of Lega Nord used symbolic action to represent the North and its legitimacy with a language of universal rights, freedom and autonomy, but also to launch particularistic demands and fiscal revolt. Second, during the 1990s the symbols of Lega Nord channeled very different meanings of the Northern question. From the North as a macro-region to a Padanian nation, the symbols did not incorporate any specific meaning about what the North is.[20] Third, Lega Nord's symbolic action allow very different interpretations. The parliament was both a party meeting and 'something else'. The Green shirts— *Camicie Verdi*—are both a youth organisation within the party, but also potentially a para-military organisation—for which Lega Nord's leadership was prosecuted in court.

The Rituals at Pontida

Lega Nord initiated its public rallies at Pontida in 1990. The valley of Pontida, a few kilometers outside the Lombard city of Bergamo, was the site of the historical oath of allegiance of the Lombard cities in their fight against the emperor Barbarossa in 1212. In the mythology created by Lega Nord, Pontida is a sacred place that symbolically represents the unity of the Italian North against the 'foreign oppressor'.[21] Today Pontida is a small village without easy access by public transportation. Local trains reach the valley from the city of Bergamo twice a day. Pontida is only a half an hour distance from Milan by car. Lega Nord's supporters arrive at Pontida with their own vehicles or buses rented by local party sections. Lega Nord's supporters from all the regions of Northern Italy gather at Pontida to celebrate and meet with Lega Nord's leadership, party members and friends. The weather is humid, cold and very unpleasant in the winter, sunny and warm in late spring.

The first public ritual celebrated in 1990 started a tradition in the life of the party. Lega Nord's rituals play out the themes of political unity between the leadership and the followers of the party. Lega Nord's representatives pledge allegiance to the movement at Pontida on every election since 1990.[22] The ritual at Pontida mixed sacred and secular elements. On the one hand, the *sacred* part includes the oath of allegiance of party representatives and members to the freedom of the North and the party ideals and goals. Political rituals enact the unity of the Northern nation and the loyalty to the cause of autonomism. Pontida is a feast of flags, symbols, customs, food, and singing. One has the opportunity to listen to autonomist hip-hop and rap in the local dialects, participate in raffles and eat *panini*. Posters covered with the phrase 'Bossi, you are the Mike Tyson of the North' and the flags of Lega Nord surrounded the stage. It is a public rally and a public feast in the traditional sense and it recalls the traditional feasts organised by the Communist party.

Bossi's addressed the Leghista people describing the wrongdoings of the Italian political class, the state, the exploitation of the economic resources of the North by Southerners with an incendiary yet convoluted language that mixed the principles of liberalism with Marxian dialectics and Gramscian terms. The normative language was that of universal rights combined with *symbolic* violence. In the rituals at Pontida, the party leader sent his threats— *Il Nord se ne va* (the North is leaving) if the demands of the movement on the Italian state and the government were not met. However, these threats were always combined with remarks about the need to use democratic means for achieving a peaceful solution to the Northern question—such as the 'Ghandian revolution' launched by Bossi in May 1996. Other members of the party elites also addressed the Leghista people in the rituals. The small group of *fedelissimi*—the loyals—includes Francesco Speroni, Gianfranco Pagliarini, Roberto Maroni and the ex-mayor of Milan, Marco Formentini.

As table 5.8 shows, participation at these public rituals has fluctuated over last decade. Only 500 people attended the first rally at Pontida. After the elections of 1996—in which obtained the highest percentage of votes in its short history—the party gathered between 60,00 and 100,000 members and supporters at the valley.

Table 5.8 Participation at Pontida

Dates	Participation
25 Marzo, 1990	500 (LN)
May 20, 1990	8000 (LN)
June 16, 1991	25,000 (LN) 10,000 (Corriere della Sera)
May 10, 1992	25,000 (Corriere della Sera)
March 28, 1993	8,000 (LN)
July 11, 1993	10,000 (Corriere della Sera)
September 26, 1993	10,000(Corriere della Sera)
April 10, 1994	30,000 (Corriere della Sera)
June 19, 1994	5000 (Corriere della Sera) 20,000 (LN)
April 9, 1995	10,000 (Corriere della Sera)
July 9, 1995	10,000 (LN)
November 26, 1995	7,000, 8,000 (LN) 8.000 (Corriere della Sera)
March 24, 1996	40,000 (LN) 25,000-30,000 (Corriere)
June 2, 1996	100,000 (LN) 60,000-80,000 (Corriere)

Sources: Lega Nord; Il Corriere della Sera

Lega Nord's rituals provided the linkage between micromobilisation and mass coverage through the reproduction of party events in the Italian and international media.

Party rituals serve two main purposes. On the one hand, rituals serve to enact in the public sphere the identity of the party, its political unity and the commitment of the leader, the party elite and its members to Lega Nord's goals. The use of rituals of political unity between the party leadership, the party representatives in local and national institutions and party activists gave an image of unity to a party that was characterised by collective action problems and 'exit' as the common solution of these conflicts. On the other hand, rituals serve to generate public controversy about the organisation and are used as a provocation to established Italian institutions. In the language of the party leadership, 'strong signals' are sent to the Roman parties.

The substantial shifts in Lega Nord's position in the Italian party system were processed through ritual action. Lega Nord's rituals gave an image of continuity to a project that was radically changed. Party rituals suggested the revolution advanced by Lega Nord is coming, no matter how different the framing of the revolution involved in the revolt of the North is. The novelties of advancing the demands and rights of the North were a breakthrough in Italian politics. However, during the 1990s the party leadership made sure that the challenge advanced by the party remains such. Table 5.9 also summarises the shifts in the party position since 1993 and the various threats launched by the leadership in the form of 'strong signals'.

There were fundamental shifts in the way the Northern question was defined during the 1990s—as a macroregion, a nation, a state. They were also substantial changes in the party elites' policy positions and agenda during the 1990s. However there were also major continuities. First, one of the common elements used by the party leader to generate controversy and activate organisational and symbolic boundaries within the organization was the threat to abandon Italian political institutions. Second, during the early 1990s the official platform of the party was *no* to secession, *yes* to federalism (Lega Nord, January 29, 1993). This situation was reversed in 1996: the party seeking independence of Padania from the Italian state. Rituals and symbols became a collective mechanism to process these political shifts and changes in the party position by enacting the party identity and unity. The party leadership used the ritual to explain and reinterpret political reality. Bossi's language of radical change, revolutionary goals and insults did not change. There was always an enemy and always the identity of the North to be preserved. However, as Table 9 shows the content of what the leadership said profoundly changed during the 1990s. Third, Lega Nord's symbolic action provided the linkage between micromobilisation and mass coverage. During the 1990s, the party leadership not only made rituals a standardised form of interaction between leadership, elite and followers, but also learned by doing it that symbolic action was a very effective way of attracting media coverage.

Table 5.9 Rituals 'Strong Signals' at Pontida

Dates	Strong Signals
March 25, 1990	First Rally to Pontida
May 20, 1990	First oath allegiance of party representatives after local elections to the cause of a free North
June 16, 1991	The Republic of the North is born, election of Sun Ministers
May 10, 1992	War against partitocrazia,
	the peoples of the North will claim independence, now Padania libera
March 28, 1993	Federalism reborn,
	strong signal to Scalfaro,
July 11, 1993	Fiscal strike,
	majors oath allegiance to the party
September 26, 1993	Fiscal protest,
	threats of removal of representatives from the parliament,
	formation of the constituent for the Republic of the North elections or secession
April 10, 1994	Celebrate victory, federalism now, the Lega of government is born
	Institutional reforms or the North will leave, federalism within six months
June 19, 1994	Two souls a federalist one within the government and an independentist one
	Bossi la lega is only one division between governmental and independentists
April 9, 1995	Operation freedom, conduced by Pagliarini
July 9, 1995	War to the party system,
	the birth of the third Pole, il Guerriero
	Da soli
November 26, 1995	Impossible to make federalist reforms with this parliament, the federalist way is an ilussion, lega is one,
	independentism is the second soul of Lega
March 24 1996,	Bossi proposes the draft for the Constitution of Padania, vote for declaration of rights, oath constitution of the North
June 2 1996	Oath allegiance provisory government of Padania
	Freedom, secession.
	Self-determination of the Padanian nation
	Fiscal resistance
	One for all and all for one

Sources: Lega Nord; Il Corriere della Sera

The Parliament of the North

In addition to the rituals at Pontida, Lega Nord organised a 'parliament' of the North—the parliament of Mantova. The party leadership launched the Parliament in June 1995. Lega Nord's claims of political autonomy and self-government for the North were given renewed attention with the writing of the Constitution of the North in the fall 1995 and the official birth of Padania in 1996. The parliament launched in 1995 was the most systematic attempt to create a symbolic institutional framework to legitimise the claims of the party, yet these were *old* ideas within the party. The first time Lega Nord launched the independent Republic of the North with an alternative government—*il governo sole*—was in 1991.

In his inauguration speech Bossi explained the creation of the Parliament of Mantova as follows:

> Dear colleagues, Lega Nord is not a party, that is, it does not represent a political faction, but a broader political movement for the freedom of the North and Italian federalism, today creates the Parliament of Mantova, that is, the Parliament of the peoples of the North ... Today here at Mantova we are not only a people, but also we have been elected by the people ... Therefore our meeting at Mantova is absolutely legitimate, because nobody can debate the right of this parliament: its purposive, critical and indicative function for the achievement of essential objectives among, which federalism is the first one ... (Lega Nord, Ufficio stampa, Parlamento del Nord, intervento del on, Umberto Bossi).

The sessions of the Parliament of the North took place in a villa—often used for wedding banquets—that Lega Nord's organisers rented on Saturdays or Sundays. The villa is located in a small village, Bagnolo San Vito, near the city of Mantova—chosen for its *geopolitical* position in the middle of the North. The building, an old construction with high ceilings and very poor heating also had a nice garden. In the ground floor, there was a bar—with coffee and panini to fight the cold in the winter—and a pressroom with phones and TV cameras to follow the sessions. In the upper floor they used a big chamber for the sessions of the Parliament decorated with the flag of Lega Nord.

The Parliament became an alternative symbolic *institution* that represented the North, to Italian and foreign observers, as an *oppressed nation*. For Bossi: 'Since the creation of the Parliament of Mantova, the conflict between centralism and federalism has become institutional. It is no longer an abstraction but a very concrete thing' (L'Indipendente February 11-12, 1996: p. 2). Members of the Parliament of the North were all party representatives in political institutions: deputies, senators, European Members of Parliament, majors, regional councilors and presidents of the provinces. Table 11 shows the absolute number of Lega Nord representatives who were also members of the symbolic Parliament of the North and their regional distribution.

Table 5.10 Representatives in the 'Parliament of the North'

	a.v.	%
Lombardy	207	52,3
Piedmont	89	22,5
Veneto	39	9,8
Friuli	31	7,8
Other	30	7,6
Total	396	100

Source: Lega Nord [23]

The Parliament became the center of attention with the passage from federalism and independence to secession as the official line of Lega Nord. There, the writing of a constitution for the North also took place, as Lega Nord recognised the *inevitability* of secession and separation from the Italian state (Lega Nord, n 38, 1995; Lega Nord n 10, 1996).

Members of the Italian parliament arrived on the weekends to attend the parliamentary sessions at Mantova. The sessions started with the meetings of 12 Commissions specialised by function—such as Transportation, Health or Social Services—to discuss Lega Nord's proposals and their coordination at the local and national level. The Parliament also provided the opportunity to chat with colleagues and to visit the *osterie* of the area—famous for their hunting dishes—and meet old friends. The sessions were, in theory, opened to the public, yet visitors were rare. After the meetings of the commissions, the parliament had a plenary session with the attendance and speech of Umberto Bossi. He arrived at the sessions of the parliament in the early afternoon. At the sound of Wagner's Walkirie or sometimes without music, and with the entire parliament standing up, Bossi made a dramatic appearance. Plenary sessions included the presentations of proposals, discussion of international and domestic issues, and ended with the leader's speech. Not surprisingly, voting in the plenary sessions was always by unanimity.

The Parliament of the North was moderately attended by Lega Nord representatives. Table 11 shows the participation rates in the parliament of the North during the sessions organised by Lega Nord in 1995 and 1996.[24]

Table 5.11 Participation in the 'Parliament' of the North

	%Tot.	National	Local
07\06\95	55,7	80.0	46.3
30\06\95	40,5	67.3	30.0
24\07\95	32,1	57.3	22.3
08\09\95	23,6	45.4	15.2
27\10\95	22,1	37.2	16.4
18\11\95	37,9	76.3	23.5
16\12\95	23,8	41.8	17.1
20\01\96	26,1	48.9	17.7
10\02\96	29,3	50.9	21.2
09\03\96	29,5	54.5	20.1
04\05\96	42,3	62.3	8.50
12\05\96	44,6	83.6	21.5
Average	31,3	59.7	21.6

Source: Lega Nord

During this period, the rate of participation was, on average, only 31.3% of the members of the parliament. However, participation rates widely fluctuated, from 55% in the first session—the peak of participation—to the lowest point in October 1995, when only 22.1% of Lega Nord's representatives attended the session. Bossi was more successful in bringing the national representatives to Mantova than in securing the participation of local politicians. As Table 13 shows, the participation rates of national politicians was much higher than that of Lega Nord's local representatives. The participation of national politicians varied from 83.6% and 80% in the last and first sessions, to 41.8% in December 1995. The participation of local politicians fluctuated from 46% in the first session to a 8.5% in May 1996.

Participation rates in the Parliament do not show regional differences. As Table 5.12 shows, representatives from the other regions of the North participated as much—or as less—as the representatives from Lombardy.

Table 5.12 Participation in the 'Parliament' by Region (%)

	%Tot.	%Lo.	%Other.
07\06\95	55,7	54,8	54,4
30\06\95	40,5	43,2	34,8
24\07\95	32,1	28,1	32,2
08\09\95	23,6	25,2	24,0
27\10\95	22,1	21,8	19,3
18\11\95	37,9	35,1	35,4
16\12\95	23,8	22,3	23,0
20\01\96	26,1	23,6	27,3
10\02\96	29,3	24,6	29,2
09\03\96	29,5	29,3	26,7
04\05\96	42,3	37,9	38,6
12\05\96	44,6	31,7	30,4
Average	31,3	31,4	31,2

Source: Lega Nord, Organizational Secretariat [25]

Discussions of the parliament of the North reviewed international developments on the right of self-determination.[26] With the help of the Parliament of the North, the imagery of the principle of self-determination moved to the front to advance the claims of Lega Nord.

The sessions of the Parliament became the platform for the escalation of conflict as the 1996 general elections in Italy approached. In December 1995, the party leadership decided to *dissolve* the Parliament of the North and recall it as a Constituent Assembly, 'the Constituent of the North' with the task of writing a new Constitution for Northern Italy. For Bossi: 'Mantova was no longer the headquarters of federalism, but the one for the freedom of the Northern nation'(L'Indipendente, December 17-18, 1995). There, the party leadership initiated its threats to withdraw Lega Nord's representatives from the Italian parliament. Bossi declared:

> That's enough! I won't go to Rome anymore ... and this is the last week our representatives will put their feet there, in that *Palazzo*. This is the last week because then we will only have Mantova, the parliament of the free North (L'Indipendente).

Francesco Speroni, one of the *fedelissimi* and ex-Minister for Institutional Reform in the Berlusconi government, was put in charge of writing the Constitution of the North. The Oath of Allegiance to the new Constitution took place at Pontida.[27] In the session of the Parliament of Mantova on May 4, 1996, Bossi accelerated the strategy of conflict. He proposed to 'put our Parliament as an instrument of mediation inserted in the Parliament of Rome and to launch an alternative triangle formed by Lega, the Parliament of the North and the Committee for the Liberation of Padania'.

The leader of Lega Nord used the 'parliament' to radicalise Lega Nord's position. Bossi brought about again that the lack of national integration in Italy was due to 'the problem of affections, culture and morals'. Lega Nord's role was then defined as the preservation of territorial diversity. According to Bossi, within Italy there was a 'systematic effort of the *colonial* and *racist* Italian state to control the economy, the schools, the judicial system with the intention of controlling the culture of the North'. Lega Nord, thus, transformed the North in Padania: 'We live in difficult times because of the unsustainability of the Roman burden on the Padanian productive model'. One of the members of the parliament asked the leader what kind of mobilization he had in mind ... Do you also consider violence—*lotta armata*? Bossi simply did not answer, leaving in the air an open question (my trascripts Parliament of the North, May 4, 1996).

On May 1996, the parliament of Mantova was renamed the Parliament of Padania: 'to discuss the political mechanisms to achieve the independence of Padania from Rome'.[28] After the 1996 general elections, the Parliament itself became the locus for launching a new set of political institutions for the representation of Padania. The party leadership decided to form the Padanian government and also organised a Committee for National Liberation on the grounds of the principle of self-determination and the right to resistance (Lega nord, no. 19, May 6, 1996). The organisation of the 'Green shirts' in the spring of 1996 transformed the open nature of these events. In the last session of the Parliament I attended, access to Bossi and the main party representatives was blocked by this new group and the sessions were closed to the public, although microphones outside the building permitted one to follow the discussions taking place inside.

At the parliament of the North, Bossi addressed his followers while at the same time he sent his message to the Italian parties and the Roman state.[29] The parliament of the North was the most systematic attempt by the party to use symbolic action to manipulate the media and public opinion. Mantova became an obliged stop for Italian journalists. Threats of secession and independence, a language of insult and provocation attracted the attention of the media. The use of medieval myths, the dramatic enactment of loyalty, the flags and the self-representations of the party as a solidarity unit have attracted the Italian media and the international press. Thus, these were the resources the party can activate in mobilising and sustaining political controversy.

Bossi made the Parliament a platform to address his colleagues in the Italian parliament. The creation of a symbolic and alternative Parliament served to relaunch the *non-negotiable* nature of Northern claims and distance the position of Lega from the other parties. Political distance was staged by placing the party leadership in a different geographical setting, the Northern city of Mantova. The Parliament had a fundamental ambiguity. On the one hand, the symbolic parliament passed as a party gathering whose declared objective was the development and coordination of the party program. On the other hand, the Parliament became the symbolic nucleus to assert new legitimacy and blackmail Italian parties. Bossi turned the official party line from federalism and institutional reform to independence. The policy of compromise was transformed into a non-negotiable territorial conflict.

The Parliament of Mantova was very effective in building up conflict in two related ways. First, the uses of an alternative legitimacy and the creation of a paralleled institutional framework generated a new wave of controversies in Italian politics. The other Italian leaders were *forced* to take sides on the issue of independence. The territorial dimension of conflict in Italy evolved not only from Lega's claims of secession for Padania but also from the common position taken by the parties with regard to independence: asserting the fundamental unity of the Italian state. Lega's claims to verticality in the Italian political space and representation of a territorial dimension of political conflict became self-fulfilling prophecies. The negative responses of the leaders of the main Italian parties—from Berlusconi, Dini, Prodi, Buttiglione, to the president of the Republic, the hiearachy of the Catholic Church and Italian journalists—helped to define the boundaries between *us* and *them*. The common response to Bossi's provocations with his parliament reinforced Bossi's claims that the conflict was *all* against Lega Nord.

The second success of the party leadership was that the media rewarded the extra-institutional means of action and Lega Nord's succeeded again in manipulating attention cycles. At Mantova, Italian journalists mixed with foreign correspondents to follow the evolution of the Northern question. The staging of the Parliament attracted the attention of the Italian and international media that reported Bossi's declarations from Mantova and kept the Parliament alive. Both political controversy and political visibility gave momentum to Lega Nord during the spring of 1996. While some laughed at the prospects of independence for the Padanian nation, others worried that the escalation of conflict would lead into a serious conflict. The party leadership played with this ambiguity, using a language of violence while claiming that Lega Nord supported a peaceful solution to a political conflict Lega Nord had ultimately created itself. In the midst of all this speculation, Bossi kept public opinion talking politics and discussing the *Northern question*.

The result of this type of mobilisation and the need to create political controversy was the accentuation of the fringe character of Lega Nord between 1996 and 1998. The party stretched the boundaries of the Italian legal framework by playing with the idea of a para-military organisation (*le camicie verdi*), using a language of insults, violence and threats. Lega Nord continued to secure access to the media by bringing renewed political controversies into Italian politics. The ways in which Lega Nord attracted media attention has forced the party leadership to push further the political and democratic boundaries of the Italian state. The prosecution of Bossi and other party leaders in recent times—illustrates the extent to which Bossi is 'playing with fire'. Lega Nord acts at the boundaries of what is legitimate, legal and democratic.

The leader is *forced* to innovate in his symbolic production and to create new controversies to gain attention. The 'birth' of Padania appeared to mark a turning point in the history of Lega Nord. The symbolic production of Lega Nord continued after the summer of 1996. The party launched in September 1996 a demonstration along the Po river to signal the birth of the Padanian nation and elections for the parliament of the Padania in the spring of 1997. Today, the symbol of Padania is *la stella delle Alpi*, the star of the Alps. However, Lega Nord has continued to organise new events, new celebrations (referendum for the self-determination of Padania, celebration of elections for the Parliament of Padania) in the party efforts to recreate the novelties of Lega Nord's symbolic action … a very time and energy-consuming exercise.

Conclusions

This chapter explained the party organisational dynamics and mobilisation structures. This chapter showed the role of the party organisation, party activism and party rituals in the reproduction of the territorial identity of the North. This chapter showed the real dimensions of the party organisation. Rituals of unity of nationhood provided the symbolic linkages between the party leadership, elites and party activists during the 1990s. Symbols of nationhood were coupled with calls for fiscal revolt and threats to the Italian political class. The rituals provided an image of fundamental continuity in the politics of Lega Nord. They covered up the substantial shifts in the politics of the leadership and collective action problems within the party.

The main and unintended consequence of reinforcing the collective identity of Lega Nord with this type of political action is that it undermined the strategic aims of the party leadership. The organisational dynamics of Lega Nord encouraged direct mobilisation, but Lega Nord's capabilities for aggregation of interests and representation were clearly constrained. Internally the party organisation was weakened in its efforts at societal penetration by the reinforcement of organisational and symbolic boundaries. In short, Lega Nord's style of mobilisation subverted the goals of the party leadership. Using symbolic action to maintain the identity boundaries of the North, creating controversy and winning media attention weakened the attempts to consolidate the party organisation and represent interests. While the leadership coupled the 'heart and the pocket'—the identity and the economic interests of the North—this style of politics uncoupled identity and interests, mobilisation and representation. In this political logic, the party ended up supporting the movement. Ironically, a party specialised in identity and symbolic production could poorly represent the economic interests of the Italian North, allegedly one of the main priorities of Lega Nord.

Notes

[1] As Bossi put it: 'We are a long way from the times of Pope John XXIII, the great Lombard, who said the church's interest in politics was finished and it was time for people to busy themselves only with their consciences ... since then the Polish pope has arrived and taken over the church, and invested in secular powers.' L'Osservatore Romano, the Vatican newspaper answered back by portraiting Bossi as 'a dwarf who thinks himself a giant'. *The New York Times* (August 20, 1997): 7.

[2] Accusations of *consociativismo* and corruption, could be easily made against the party leadership. Bossi was sentenced for the *tangenti* Enimont for accepting monies to finance the 1992 electoral campaign.

[3] In the case of Friuli Venezia Giulia—the fourth region of the North in terms of Lega's electoral strength—internal infighting in the regionalist Movimento Friuli led to contacts between one of the splinter groups and the federal secretariat of Lega Nord. The result was the creation of the Friulian national section of Lega Nord in 1991-1992.

[4] The federal Assembly is the permanent organ of the federation and is composed of 100 members of the party elected at the Federal Congress and the Secretary, the President, the secretaries of the national sections and the parliamentary representatives and regional councilors (article 12 statute).

[5] After the *transition* period, the presidency of the party has been in the hands of Venetian members: Marilena Marin, Franco Rochetta and currenlty Stefano Stefani.

[6] The expansion of Lega Nord's territorial organisation beyond the regions where the party is currently present will respond, according to the party statutes, to a decree of the Federal Council establishing the 'birth of other nations' (article 6 statute).

[7] The Federal Council—whose goal is the definition of the programs and priorities of Lega Nord—is elected on territorial basis with a quota system. The members of the Federal Council—in addition to the Secretary, the President, and the Secretaries of all the national sections of the party—are representatives of the national sections of Lega Nord. In the first statute, the council included 14 members elected with a quota system (three representatives from Lombardy and one for each other national section (article 11 statute Lega Nord). In the current statute, the quota system includes four representatives from Lombardy, two from

Veneto and Piedmont and one for each other national section whose territory includes more than one million inhabitants (article 11 statute Lega Nord).

[8] In 1984 Lega Lombarda had introduced two types of tessere, that of *amico del popolo lombardo* and that of *aderente* (Lombarda Autonomista, 15 Settembre 1984). In 1986, the categories have changed to include *socio* (member of the Federal council), *Lumbard* (supporter with voting rights), *Amis* (members without voting rights) and *Riaa* (torrenti in dialect) for the young.

[9] Thus, all candidates of the party in local national or European elections have to be 'ordinary' members. Rights of participation also include voting in the party primaries. Ordinary members vote to elect their candidates in national elections.

[10] 'Nomenklatura' refers in Bossi's political language to the old Italian political class. I translated *politichese* for political message. Umberto Bossi, preface to Roberto Iacopini and Stefania Bianchi, *La Lega ce l'Ha Crudo. Il Linguagio del Carroccio nei suoi Slogan, Comizi e Manifesti* (Milano: Mursia, 1994): VI.

[11] Any traveller in Northern Italy—either by car or train—can have the opportunity to see all the manifests and slogans of Lega Nord displayed over the walls and highways of the North.

[12] Although in absolute numbers Lega Nord has more members than political parties such as Democrazia Proletaria (DP)—which in the decade from 1979 to 1989 increased from 2,500 to 10, 310 members—still the figures cannot even compared with the small political parties of the first Italian Republic, such as PRI (99,386 members in 1988), PLI (40, 491 in 1988) or PSDI (110,000 in 1988). Data from Leonardo Molino, 'Italy', in Richard S. Katz and Peter Mair, eds. *Party Organizations. A Data Handbook on Party Organizations in Western Democracies 1960-1990* (London: Sage Publications, 1990).

[13] I don't have data on party sections on the other national sections of Lega Nord. To assess their strength, I substituted basic units for data on party membership in these regions.

[14] The importance of 'face to face' politics in Lega Nord's style of political mobilisation is highlighted by Ruzza and Schmitdke. See Carlo Ruzza and O. Schdmitke, 'Roots of Success of the Lega Lombarda: Mobilisation Dynamics and the Media', *West European Politics* vol. 16 (no.2 April 1993): 1-23.

[15] I asked for data on the number of people expelled from the organisation but the party does not keep records.

[16] Bossi's conflicts with his sister and brother-in-law led to a splinter party, Lega Alpina Lombarda, in 1990. In 1991 the president of Lega Lombarda, Roberto Castellazi was expelled from the party as a traitor. In 1991, the first congress of Lega Nord included a power struggle to define the rules of the organisation and the leadership. The potential alliance of the Bergamasco provincial section and the Venetians against Bossi was undermined by Bossi himself.

[17] According to the first statute of the party, Lega Nord was: 'a federalist movement for the transformation of the Italian state through democratic means'. The statute approved in the Third Federal Congress of the party, 14-16 February 1997, changed the content of article 1. Now article 1 reads: 'the political Movement named Lega Nord for the Independence of Padania has as its goal the independence of Padania through democratic means and the recognition of the latter as an independent and sovereign republic' (Lega Nord party statutes 1997).

[18] The original idea was to launch the 'Republic of the North' dividing Italy, not in two, but three regions or cantons: North, Center and South. In 1993 Lega Nord sought to organise in the Center and in the South of Italy with no success (interview the Organisational Secretariat of the party, Alessandro Patelli, Lombardy, 1995).

[19] This is not the case, however, for the *red* regions of Tuscany and Emilia-Romagna, where Lega Nord lost over time most of the party members.

170 Ethnicity and Nationalism in Italian Politics

[20] As Kertzer stresses: 'It is the very ambiguity of the symbols employed in ritual action that makes ritual useful in fostering solidarity without consensus. Symbols can have a strong emotional impact on people, rallying them around the organisational flag, in spite of the fact that each participant interprets the symbols differently', D. Kertzer, *Ritual, Power and Politics* (New Haven: Yale University Press, 1988), 69.

[21] In fact, the move to Pontida was a political response to the Socialist leader Betino Craxi's attempts to pre-empt Lega Nord's agenda for autonomism. Craxi launched a Declaration of Pontida in 1990 requesting the autonomy of local governments in Italy.

[22] In the second gathering at Pontida all the local councilors elected in the local and provincial elections of 1990 swared allegiance to the cause of autonomy and freedom of the regions of Lombardy, Veneto, Piedmont, Ligury, Tuscany and Emilia-Romagna people.

[23] The number of representatives in the Parliament slightly varied in the last sessions to accommodate the changes in representation produced by the outcome of the local and general elections of 1996.

[24] Two of the sessions of the Parliament were held at the demonstrations at Pontida. I don't have participation rates for those sessions.

[25] Others include the representatives from the Veneto, Piedmont and the Friuli regions.

[26] I was approached to call United Nations to ask for information about the office in charge of denouncing state violations against national minorities.

[27] The oath was the following: 'Sons of the Great People of the North, sons of the Padanian Nation, aproving this constitution we assert our undisclaimable right of Padania for independence'. Declaration of Self-Determination, Sovereignty and Asosociation of the Peoples of the North, aproved by the Constituent Assembly of the Parliament of the North at Pontida. Lega Nord, No. 12 (Anno XIV, March 25, 1996).

[28] As Speroni put it: 'the self-determination of the people does not mean to introduce a border, a free Padania will not have borders because it will be an integral part of Europe'. *Il Corriere della Sera* (May 19, 1996).

[29] In these attempts to open the party to society, the Parliament of the North also launched a campaign of meetings with citizens to explain the new policy of the party (*incontri del Parlamento del Nord con I cittadini*). Lega Nord No. 39 (Anno XIII, November 7, 1995).

6 An Ethno-Territorial Cleavage in the Italian Party System?

The erosion of traditional cleavages in European party systems—in their different dimensions: party organisations, party identification and electoral alignments—has provided a new political space for the mobilisation of new conflicts. Over the past two decades scholars have studied the rise of new cleavages in European party systems. Systemic change is explained as a function of changing public opinion and new attitudes and values. The rise of new politics in the form of Green parties and left-libertarian politics marked the 1980s (Kitschelt, 1989). The emergence of the new radical or populist right marked the rise of a new family of parties in the 1990s (Kitschelt, 1995; Betz, 1994).

The rise of territorial political mobilisation in Northern Italy provides a puzzling case to explore both the rise and/or failure of old and new political cleavages in European party systems. The Italian party system fell apart in the early 1990s, traditional parties disappeared in the midst of corruption scandals, institutional change provided new electoral rules and a new party system emerged in this process. The rise and success of Lega Nord—the last *new* political party to emerge in the traditional Italian party system but one of the oldest in the new Italian party system—is usually analysed within the framework of a new political cleavage manifested by the rise of new radical right wing parties (Kitschelt, 1995; Biorcio, 1991; 1997).

This chapter discusses the rise of a territorial cleavage in the Italian party system and its persistence. In analysing the trajectory of Lega Nord, one should keep in mind that focusing on the territorial dimension of new political space does not prevent the analysis of Lega Nord for its right-wing agenda. Muller-Rommel considers the contemporary wave of *ethno-territorial* mobilisation as part of a 'collective identity mood' (Muller-Rommel, 1997, p. 24). In addition, scholars mention the potential of these parties to receive protest votes. For Muller-Rommel, 'it is well known that many adherents of ethnoregionalist parties in Europe are more critical of governmental and party politics than the average voter' (Muller-Rommel, 1997, p. 24).

The nature of systemic change in the Italian party system during the 1990s is closer to the creation of new party systems in Eastern Europe than to the changes at the margins that characterise the transformation of West European party systems over the past two decades. While the rise of new parties of the left and right in West Europe has not substantially modified main electoral alignments, this transition has radically changed the Italian party system. The transition from the so-called First Republic to the Second Republic, as several scholars have noticed, has almost no parallels in comparative terms in the electoral history of European party systems (Cartocci, 1996; Bartolini and D'Alimonte, 1994). The 1994 Italian general elections marked the demise of the old party system and the creation of a new one.

The political trajectory of Lega Nord during the 1990s shows substantial changes in its short history. First, the strategies of the party leadership radically changed as it attempted to adapt to new rules and new patterns of electoral competition. In 1994 Lega Nord became part of a awkward electoral coalition with a new party, Forza Italia and the ex fascist Alleanza Nazionale. The electoral coalition won the general elections and formed a government under the leadership of Berlusconi. Lega Nord's decision to withdraw from the government unraveled the Italian political scenario once more. After 1994 Lega Nord became a political failure and marginalised player with the normalisation of the Italian party system, only to obtain, in the 1996 general elections, the best electoral results in its short history. Then the results of the 1999 European elections and the 2000 regional elections—in coalition with Berlusconi—fixed the position of Lega Nords as a secondary player in Italian politics.

The first *electoral winning formula*—to use Kitschelt's formulation—used by the party leadership was undermined by the disappearance of the political opportunities that favored the early electoral expansion of Lega Nord. Kitschelt's hypothesis predicts major setbacks if protest parties pursue office-maximising strategies. After the 1994 governmental experience, Lega Nord's setback was a major one: it lost voters, activists and representatives. To many analysts of Lega Nord, this period marked the decline of Lega Nord and its marginalisation in the Italian party system. Instead, the party leadership found a new *electoral winning formula*. The party leadership managed to reshape a political space by emphasising the non-negotiable nature of their claims for autonomy of the North. The strategy of radicalisation of party demands that followed the experience in the Berlusconi government was a surprise. Nobody predicted the radicalisation of a party that was struggling to moderate its demands to 'normalise' and consolidate its position in the Italian party system (Diamanti, 1995). Quite the contrary, expectations were against the radicalisation of Lega Nord (Trigilia, 1994).

This chapter seeks to explain the ability of the party leadership to introduce the territory as a discriminating issue in electoral alignments in Northern Italy. The chapter focuses on the strategies of the party leadership and how they adapted to changing opportunities in the Italian party system. After the cycle of protest that marked the first success of Lega Nord. Lega Nord leadership pursued two very different strategies during the 1990s. First,

Lega Nord engaged in a strategy of moderation, downplaying the more radical elements within the party, and sought to enter office and gain respectability as the party of the 'center' in the North. Second, the party leadership pursued a strategy of mobilisation and radicalisation claiming independence for the Padania.

Next section presents the explanations of the electoral success/failure of Lega Nord during the 1990s. Then I examine the nature of institutional and political changes in the Italian party system and the increasing difficulties of the party leadership to exploit the North-South divide. The party leadership adopted a strategy of moderation and a strategy of radicalisation. The opportunities and costs of each strategy are evaluated in light of the views of the party elites. The last section of the chapter considers the implications of the changing trajectory of Lega Nord for our understanding of cleavages as structures for the institutionalisation of political conflict.

Explaining the Electoral Success of Lega Nord

Two different explanations emphasise the long-term nature of Lega Nord's electoral success. The first explanation considers the electoral success of Lega Nord is driven by the support from the 'typical constituencies' of new right-wing politics (Biorcio, 1991; 1997). As we saw in the first chapter, the electoral support for Lega comes from 'disadvantaged' constituencies and social groups that are more prone to right-wing authoritarian politics. The populist explanation stresses Lega Nord was considered in the early 1990s the party of the *ceti medi produttivi* (the productive middle class); artisans, shopkeepers, and local entrepreneurs who were particularly hurt by state fiscal pressures (Trigilia, 1994). By 1994 instead, Lega Nord was becoming the party of workers of the North (Calvi and Vanucci, 1994; Riccamboni, 1997). The second explanation, in contrast, stresses the geographical location of Lega Nord's voters. The electoral success of Lega Nord is explained by the erosion of the functional role played by the Christian Democratic party. The Christian Democratic party lost its centrality in national politics. The clientelistic power of the DC was eroded during the 1980s. Diamanti stresses a fundamental continuity between the electorates of the DC and Lega Nord in the Catholic subculture (Diamanti, 1993; 1996).

The chapter does not investigate the relationship between the political construction of *otherness*, electoral success and the underlying motivations of Lega Nord's voters. However, research during the past decade provides sufficient evidence of the anti-migrant attitudes of Lega Nord's voters (Biorcio, 1991, 1997; Van Der Brug, Fenemma and Tillie, 2000). A survey conducted in 1996 confirmed earlier analyses on the anti-migrant attitudes of

Lega Nord's voters. Fifty-eight percent of Lega Nord voters agreed with the assertion: 'too many migrants disturbe', compared to a population average of 40% in the Northern Italian regions. Fifty two per cent of Lega Nord's voters agreed with the assertion 'it would be better to return migrants to their countries of origin', compared with a population average of 38.7% in these regions. 14.6% of Lega Nord's voters agreed with the assertion: 'migration was one of the three more important problems in Italy', compared to a population average of 10.3% in the Italian North (Biorcio, 1997: 258) (Biorcio, 1997).[1]

Diamanti characterises the electoral support for Lega Nord in geographical terms. He defines a new area—the *Pedemontana*—encompassing the Friuli region (Pordenone and Udine), Veneto (Belluno, Treviso, Vicenza and some districts in Padova, Verona and Venice), Lombardia (Bergamo, Sondrio and Brescia, Varese and Como) and one province in Piedmont (Cuneo). Diamanti argues that this area represents a competing socio-political model to the industrialised North. As Table 6.1 indicates, the Deep North (*profondo Nord*) exhibits distinctive socio-economic and political characteristics: the lowest rates of unemployment in the North of Italy, the highest percentage of employment in industry, the highest number of firms per inhabitant, the lowest number of urban electoral districts, and the highest percentage of votes for the Christian Democratic party in the post-war period.

Table 6.1 Diamanti's *Pedemontania*

	Comp. North	Left North	Deep North	Right North	Total North
Electoral Districts					
A.V.	97	21	31	22	179
%	54.2	11.7	17.3	12.3	100.0
Urban	30.9	61.9	3.2	63.6	33.5
1996 Elections					
%Pds	15.0	25.9	8.3	17.7	15.2
%Forza Italia	21.3	18.8	17.5	28.8	20.9
%Lega Nord	23.4	10.5	40.4	12.4	23.0
1992 Elections					
% DC	25.5	18.1	34.3	18.1	25.1
% Pds	11.9	19.8	6.8	13.9	11.9
% Lega Nord	19.8	12.9	23.8	17.5	18.9
Firms (1000 pop)	75.4	65.2	80.7	68.9	75.0
% employ					
Industry	44.7	36.2	55.9	30.0	43.3
Commerce	21.8	22.6	18.6	24.8	22.1
Services	33.5	41.2	25.5	45.2	34.6
Unemployment	9.9	13.3	7.5	10.1	9.7

Source: Diamanti, 1996, pp. 87-88

Diamanti considers that voters in the areas of the *Pedemontania* use Lega Nord to protest against the central government. In Diamanti's interpretation, voting for Lega is a manifestation of local interests. Localism accounts for the electoral homogeneity of Lega Nord in the 'deep north'. The Pedemontania represents areas that shifted from 'white' vote (Christian Democratic) to 'green' vote (Lega Nord). Diamanti argues that Lega Nord represents 'an answer and an alternative' to the erosion of the role the DC played in these areas (Diamanti, 1996, p. 27) According to Diamanti,

> Voting for Lega does not reflect an *ethnic* identity but rather, a local identity that finds the source of integration and economic regulation in the local environment, in its social milieu, in its system of relationships and traditions. Therefore, it is in

the *Pedemontana* and in localism, where one should dig to find the sources of the electoral success of the Leghista phenomenon: to find the reasons of its persistence and strengths but also the limits to which it is constrained (1996, p. 27).

The replacement of the Christian Democratic party by Lega Nord in the Pedemontana seems to be an inevitable and predictable process driven by the local economies. Diamanti's interpretation suggests the importance of exploring the political legacies of traditional parties, yet other evidence points to a fluid and flexible political environment characterized by electoral uncertainty. The electoral market in Northern Italy is much more in flux than this interpretation seems to suggest. As Table 6.1 shows, displaying Diamanti's findings, 54.2% of the electoral districts in the North—beyond the Pedemontania—belong to what Diamanti defines as the 'competitive' North. Diamanti's explanation only focuses on the *Pedemontania*, yet in the 'competitive' North Lega Nord is also the first party in terms of votes. The 1996 general elections in Italy were marked by increasing electoral competitiveness and electoral change in these areas (Riccamboni, 1997; Natale, 1997).

It is in a political environment of uncertainty, complexity and political change that we have to situate the electoral success of Lega Nord during the 1990s. The rapid changes taking place in Italian politics shaped the struggle of party elites to adapt to the transformation of the system. The ability of Lega Nord's to cater to uncertain voters was mainly concentrated in the areas of the North where the erosion of the Christian Democrats was widespread. These areas determined a scenario under which the party leadership gained a peculiar *market niche* in the Italian party system. In local contexts dominated by the DC in the past—where traditionally the distinction between identities and interests was of little relevance to explain politics—the party found its electoral stronghold. Political uncertainty was widespread in the 1990s. Zucchini's analysis shows that Lega Nord's voters were much more uncertain about their choices than voters for the left and right-wing coalitions were. 61 per cent of Lega Nord's voters made their choice during the electoral campaign of 1996, while 64.7% of voters for the right-wing coalition decided much earlier. Only 20% of voters for the left coalition and 16% for the right coalition declared that they made their decision between a few weeks and a week before the elections, compared to 30% of Lega voters (Zucchini, 1997, p. 7).

The Italian Party System During the 1990s

The transformation of the Italian party system redefined the players and the rules of the game. The investigations of the Italian judiciary had three main consequences. First, the corruption scandals were so effective in displaying the system of bribes to the parties and the extent of corruption in the system that many of the party leaders and parliamentary representatives of the parties were prosecuted (Waters, 1994). Second, the investigations of the judiciary gave momentum to the agenda for institutional reform in Italy. Although some attempts at institutional reform took place during the 1980s under the Socialist governments of Bettino Craxi, it is after *Tangentopoli* that institutional reforms became a political priority. Third, public dissatisfaction with political parties peaked and voters *eliminated* traditional parties from the electoral arena between the 1992 and 1994 Italian general elections.

Institutional Change

Institutional reform became the top item on the agenda for political change. A consensus among Italian elites emerged about the need for electoral reform. The system of proportional representation—the pillar of Sartori's model of polarised pluralism, consociational practices and multiparty governments— was blamed for the scale of corruption and clientelism in Italian politics. In 1991 a referendum already eliminated the possibility of expressing individual preferences for candidates on party lists. Another referendum allowed the use of single-member districts and plurality voting for the Senate in 1993. The Italian Parliament passed the new electoral laws (*leggi* 276 and 277) in August 1993.

The result was that the introduction of new electoral laws in Italy that are unique in comparative terms (D'Alimonte and Chiaramonte, 1995). The introduction of the new electoral laws eliminated the system of proportional representation with a 'hybrid' system that combines plurality and proportional features. The mixed system was the product of the compromises and negotiations between the parties in Parliament and accmmodated the demands of small parties threatened by the possiblity of eliminating proportional representation in the new Italian party system (Sani, 1994).

Under the new *hybrid* electoral system, 75% of the seats are assigned in single member districts. The remaining 25% is distributed to party lists under proportional representation. The Italian state is divided in 26 electoral districts (*circoscrizione*). The number of single member seats is distributed according to the size of the population in each district. Single-member districts are distributed first-past-the-post. The distribution of seats for candidate's lists under proportional representation takes place at the national level. The electoral threshold is established at 4% of the vote at the national level. Both systems—plurality and proportional—are interdependent. The elections take place in *turno unico*. As Chariamonte and D'Alimonte point out, plurality and proportional representation are not different formulae to be applied in different contexts. In each single member district there are district candidates and list candidates and the former must be linked to at least one district list. There are two votes cast—one for the plurality and one for the proportional part—yet there is not differentiation of competitive arenas.

In addition to the new electoral rules for the election of the Parliament and the Senate, the Italian Parliament also passed new legislation to change the electoral rules for local, provincial and regional governments. In March 1993, new laws introduced a plurality system in local and provincial elections. The local system of governance was fundamentally transformed. Mayors are now directly elected under majority voting (Di Virgilio, 1994). Changes in the regional electoral systems introduced a proportional system with a majoritarian premium to achieve political stability in regional governments (D'Alimonte, 1995). Thus, all systems, national, regional and local are 'mixed' systems, although they are different among them.

The new electoral systems had a mixed effect. On one hand, and despite the contrasting views on the impact of the electoral laws in the Italian party system (Bartolini and D'Alimonte, 1995), the most clear-cut result of the electoral reform has been the introduction of very strong incentives for aggregation and coalition-building. On the other hand, political parties also have strong incentives to run by themselves. Parties can rely on gaining representation through the proportional system—25% of the Italian parliament is elected on this basis—yet they run the risk of remaining marginal players. Thus, if the new electoral system has removed the old patterns of coalition-government in Italy by introducing incentives to form coalitions before elections, the new electoral laws have also allowed the consolidation of a new fragmented multi-party system in Italy.

Electoral and Party Change

Between 1992 and 1994 the Italian party system fell apart. The transformation of the Italian Communist party had taken place in 1991 with the consolidation of its two heirs, the moderate PDS (*Partito Democratico della Sinistra*) and *Rifondazione Comunista*. While the refounding of the Italian left was relatively smooth, the collapse of the governmental parties in 1993 opened a political vacuum. The DC elected on October 12, 1992 Martinazzoli as general secretary, who declared 'I am a secretary elected by despair. The party is a cemetery'. Martinazzoli was elected, de facto, the last general secretary of the DC. In the 1993 local elections, the Christian Democratic party disappeared as an electoral force everywhere. The most active Christian Democrat politician in introducing institutional reforms, Mario Segni, also left the party after Giulio Andreotti was prosecuted for his alleged relationship with the Mafia. Segni founded *Popolari per la Riforma* in March 1993. In 1993, the party reemerged as the Popular Party. The Centro Cristiano Democratico (CCD) became another splinter of the DC.

The PSI dissolved in the middle of corruption scandals and its leader Bettino Craxi fled to Tunisia. In January 1994, the fascist MSI changed its name to become Alleanza Nazionale. Excluded from consociational practices and multi-party governments in the post-war period, Alleanza Nazionale underwent the transition from fascism to the new right (Ignazi, 1994). Finally, the media entrepreneur Silvio Berlusconi launched the party-firm, Forza Italia. The first convention of Forza Italia presented officially the party on February 6, 1994. To some, Berlusconi's Forza Italia became the new *populist* in Italian politics (Paolo Flores d'Arcais, 1996; Revelli, 1996).

The coupling of the disappearance of the old Italian political class in 1993 with the passage of the new electoral laws created an environment of profound political uncertainty in the Italian party system. Three clear indicators of the political uncertainty facing Italian voters in the 1990s are: 'voter turnout', 'wasted votes' and 'electoral volatility'. The first clear indicator of political uncertainty is the decreasing trend in voter turnout during the 1990s. Table 2 shows the percentage of voter turnout in Italian general elections since the late 1970s.

Table 6.2 Voter Turnout (1976-1996)

Election Years	Participation (%)
1976	93.4
1979	91.4
1983	89.0
1987	90.5
1992	87.4
1994	86.2
1996	82.9

Source: Caramani, 1996, p. 587

Participation rates in the 1994 and 1996 general elections were the lowest in the entire history of Italian elections in the post-war period. This is not surprising, given public dissatisfaction and the fact that Italian voters had three general elections every two years (1992, 1994, 1996), local elections in 1992, 1993, 1995; 1998, regional elections in 1995 and 2000, European elections in 1994 and 1999, and a variety of referenda. The complexity of the new electoral system can be measured by the significant rate of 'wasted votes'. The complexity of the new electoral rules led voters to make mistakes in casting their votes. Third, electoral volatility in Italian elections during the 1990s achieved unique proportions in comparative perspective. In the 1994 general elections, aggregate volatility was the highest in the entire Italian electoral history (Cartocci, 1996). Bartolini and D'Alimonte only found four similar cases in the entire electoral history of European party systems.

The introduction of new electoral rules did not bring political stability in party alternatives and Italian political elites. First, the mixed effects of the new electoral laws shaped the fragility of the new electoral coalitions—that were completely rearranged from 1994 to 1996 (di Virgilio, 1996). Second, the loopholes for small parties provided by the electoral law increased their political leverage and maintained political fragmentation (de Virgilio, 1996). Third, Italians continued to have fragile multi-party governments. Italians had care-taker governments with the end of the first Republic but they also had care-taker governments with the new Italian party system. The technical government of Lamberto Dini replaced the disastrous experience of the Berlusconi government supported by Alleanza Nazionale and Lega Nord. The uncertainty of the political scenario and the multiple coalition games in which parties were involved opened up *again* a new agenda for institutional reform.

Lega Nord Between the Old and the New Italian Party System

Interviews with Lega's representatives on the question of the new electoral laws, revealed that the party elites were divided over the best electoral system to adopt at the time of the reform. For those who participated in the drafting of the new electoral laws, the outcome of these institutional changes and its impact on Lega Nord was not clear. Some favored a pure plurality system with single-member districts. Others prefer to maintain proportional representation. Although some worried about the potential risks of introducing a plurality system, their expectation was that the new rules would not change their prospects for replacing the Christian Democrats in the North. The choice to vote for the new electoral laws was made on the basis of Lega's anti-system platform—to put it simply, they could *not* vote for the maintenance of an electoral system which was blamed for *consociativismo*.

Changes in the Italian party system shaped a new strategic scenario for

Lega Nord along three lines. First, the reconfiguration of the Italian party system structured a new political space for reshaping the left-right dimension. Second, institutional change provided strong incentives for electoral coalition-building. The introduction of the mixed electoral system with a strong bias towards plurality voting, hindered the electoral prospects for a party that was poorly equipped for coalition building. Although some scholars have argued that single-member districts and plurality voting always favour parties with concentrated territorial support (Riccamboni, 1997), the *viability* of this strategy was not self-evident to party elites. Third, a broader proyect of reform of the Italian political system became a priority. While its position as the challenger to the political system was Lega Nord's main resource in the late 1980s and early 1990s, the new task was *how* to introduce the necessary reforms to meet these challenges. On this question, Lega was poorly equipped to propose concrete institutional reforms.

The *Northern Question* in the Italian Party System

Lega Nord's leadership introduced a new dimension defining the political space in the Italian party system: the territory needed to mobilise the North as a 'discriminating' issue to force voters to take sides. As one party representative defined it: 'We are neither left nor right. *We are for verticality. We represent a new axis centralism-federalism.*' The party leadership has always claimed an electoral space of its own. As Bossi put it:

> For a federalist, the true alternative is not left or right. One who is convinced that only a true federalist reform of the state can transform Italy into a modern and European country knows that the true alternative is another one: federalism or centralism (1995, p. 57).

However, the very definition of the Northern question was rather malleable. During the 1990s, the Italian North evolved from a *macroregion*, to the *Nord-Nazione* to *Padania*. During the early 1990s, the official platform of the party was *no* to secession, *yes* to federalism (Lega Nord, 20 January 1993). The situation was reversed in 1996: the party seeking the secession of Padania from the Italian state. In 1998, the party leader announced yet another shift by proclaiming the willingness of Lega Nord to support *devolution*, no longer claiming independence from the Italian state. As one senior member of Lega Nord explained these shifts: 'In 1991-1992 we talked about macroregions while the other parties talked about regional autonomy. Otherwise there was *confusion*. Now, they all talk about federalism ... we talk about independence.' One of the leaders of the party put it shortly: '*We did politics as we moved along.'*

From 1996 to 1998 Lega Nord was involved in a major exercise in symbolic politics with the declaration of the birth of the Padanian nation, the declaration of the Padanian Republic, the referendum for the self-determination of the Padania, the Padanian elections to elect a Northern parliament, the referendum to aprove the Constitution fo the Padania. In 1998 Bossi publicly renounced independence and secession from the Italian state to adopt a moderate line: this time the *Northern question* was about territorial *devolution*.

Until 1994. Lega Nord's leadership followed a short-term electoralist strategy to downplay its radical opposition to the Italian political system. A strategy of moderation attempted to transform the image of Lega Nord, from a challenger to *partitocrazia* to a respectable reformist party. The party leadership aimed to cater to multiple constituencies in the North. However, there were significant trade-offs involved in this strategy. The space created by Lega Nord had a crowd-in effect. The new Berlusconi's Forza Italia benefited from it. As we saw in the previous chapter, the strategy of moderation and coalition seeking tested the loyalties of party activists. The weakening of Lega Nord's image along these lines led to the withdrawal from the Berlusconi government in the fall of 1994. Lega Nord's entered a profound crisis that risked the very sustainability of the party in the long run. Elite, members and voters deserted the party. The party leadership pursued subsequently a strategy of radicalisation. Lega Nord started to claim the independence from the Italian state. The strategy of radicalisation presented a revolutionary image of Lega Nord. Lega Nord launched its 1996 electoral campaign with the party *against all*, rejecting electoral coalitions and specialising its appeals with demands for the independence of the North. With this strategy, the party obtained the highest percentage of votes in its short history. This strategy, however, also involved trade-offs. Radicalisation tested once more the loyalties of party elites and representatives, and risked the political marginalisation of Lega Nord at the national level.

Federalism for Italy

The unraveling of Italian politics since 1992 modified the political scenario for Lega Nord. The Northern question was framed as a demand for a federalist structure. The North could be 'accommodated' within an Italian federation. The party leadership embarked on a strategy of moderation, encouraged by the extent of electoral de-alignment in 1992. Lega Nord's leadership was convinced that the erosion of traditional parties and the extent of electoral dealignment in the North after 1992 would have turned Lega into the first party in the North and the *natural* heir of the Christian Democrats. As one party representative explained:

> At that time, there was left and right, but we talked about the North and federalism versus centralism as an alternative model. We always thought that in Italy there would be a party of the center. We thought we would become the party of the center in the North. With the disappearance of the DC we thought all those votes would have come to Lega Nord (interview no. 15).

In this period Lega Nord's short-term electoral strategists made it a clear-cut example of catch-all politics. The party leadership catered to a broad electoral constituency, trying to attract votes from left and right, appealing to workers and Catholics:

> The period I remembered most happily was in 1993 when we were playing politics like a coordinated team (*gioco di squadra*). It was almost natural; I played the left of the party, Formentini dealt with the economic questions, Miglio provoked strong reactions with the territorial question, Pivetti appealed to Catholics and Gnutti catered to the moderates (Maroni, Milano 1996).

Bossi presented himself as a moderate and tried to control radical factions within the party. In addition, both calls for independence and the rhetoric against migrants were downplayed. The adoption of three macro-regions (North-Center-South) became the party goal to transform the state structure in Italy. Umberto Bossi even downplayed the project of Gianfranco Miglio of dividing the Italian state in three cantons—considered at the time *too* radical. The party elites publicly declared the end of their period of opposition to become a party of government. In Bossi's words, Lega was 'both a force of struggle and a force of government'—*La Lega è forza di lotta e di governo*—(Bossi 1993: 216). The objective of becoming a party of government moved center stage. In the local elections of June and November 1993. Lega Nord's program in the 1993 local elections in Milan stated:

> Lega Nord does not intend to retain its role as a force of political opposition. Lega Nord—a main interpreter of the need for new forms of democracy, of new institutional models among which federalism constitutes the essential component of a more advanced system of government—considers that a mature and organized political force cannot restrain itself to represent only a fraction of the electorate, it has to present itself as a force for government (*Un Programma per Governare Milano*, 1993).

In the local elections of 1993, Lega Nord's electoral success that allowed the party to enter local governments in Northern cities. Lega Nord significantly improved, both in June and November, the percentage of votes the party had gained in the general elections of 1992 (Di Virgilio, 1994). Moreover, Lega Nord gained even more political visibility with the election of Lega Nord's candidate, Marco Formentini, as major of Milan in December 1993.

However, Lega Nord's leadership also realised that the strategic scenario for seeking office was more complicated than they had initially thought. While most parties engaged in coalition building, Lega Nord competed in these elections alone. The effects of coalition building against Lega Nord were most clearly seen in the 1993 November elections (Di Virgilio, 1994, p. 155). Although Lega Nord became the first party in terms of votes in many Northern cities, the candidates of the new left-wing coalition—the *Progressisti*—won the local elections in the cities of Torino and Venice. In the cities of the North, competition in the second round between Lega Nord candidates and left-wing candidates supported by coalitions showed the vulnerability of Lega Nord's electoral strategy to achieve office.

The victory of the left coalition in the 1993 local elections encouraged the media entrepreneur Silvio Berlusconi to launch his own political party, Forza Italia, *il partito-azienda* (the firm-party). Berlusconi's Forza Italia was the new successful alternative to reform Italian politics. Surveys revealed the increasing popularity of Forza Italia in the months previous to the 1994 general elections (Sani, 1994; Diamanti, 1994). The novelties of Berlusconi's political project were too close to the moderate strategy pursued by Lega Nord. Forza Italia could also claim the status of the *new* political party as an outsider to politics, sharing the same position with Lega Nord against *partitocrazia*. Both parties advocated the need for reducing state intervention in the economy, the cult of entrepreneurship and economic success, and the the introduction of a neoliberal right-wing agenda. These similarities did not pass unnoticed to Lega Nord's elites. The party leadership feared that Forza Italia would replace Lega Nord among Northern voters.

> Lega had a modernising and innovative proposal for the reform of the country. Forza Italia had the same image ... yet it was a form of cheating, they wanted to preserve the system ... For Berlusconi, federalism was simply a word (Speroni, Busto Arsizio 1996).

Finally, Lega Nord's leadership was also involved in a scandal of political corruption: the monies received from the Ferruzzi group. This scandal became known as the *Tangente Enimont*.

Thus, the party leadership decided to embark on coalition-building to run in the 1994 general elections. As Bossi put it,

By the end of 1993, Lega Nord came to terms with the question of the passage from the old to the new regime. Our revolution had the strength to uproot the centralistic system, but to gather the consensus required for the new Republic, with a plurality system, we needed an alliance with other political forces (Bossi, 1995: p. 35).

Bossi considered three alternatives. The first option was abstaining from coalition building, competing in the elections alone. Yet this possibility was soon ruled out. As Bossi explained: 'It was a fascinating perspective, maybe desired by the hard-liners within the movement who insisted on this choice, but destined to end in a major political failure. Under the plurality system, we wouldn't have obtained more than twenty seats' (Bossi, 1995, p. 38). The second option was to make a coalition of center parties with the reformist lists and the newly found *Partito Popolare*, one of the heirs of the DC. Roberto Maroni, reached an agreement with Mario Segni. However, Bossi backed away almost immediately from it.

In January 1994 I talked to Segni and I reached an agreement with him, but within three days the electoral agreement was over because Segni had introduced the condition that Martinazzoli and the Popolari with Formigoni would be with us. But Bossi said no (Maroni, Milano 1996).

According to Maroni, Bossi did not want the party to be perceived as allying with the Ppi and the remnants of the *old regime* (Galli, 1994; Diamanti, 1995). The third option was an electoral coalition with Berlusconi's Forza Italia (Bossi, 1995: 38). In 1994 Bossi and Berlusconi reached an agreement and formed their first electoral coalition, *il Polo della Libertà*. The coalition was presented as a political platform to introduce a new neoliberal right in the Italian party system. The alliance favored Lega Nord in the composition of the lists. This electoral coalition was officially approved in the second federal congress of Lega Nord in Bologna in February 1994.

The alliance with Berlusconi was, to say the least, very contentious within Lega Nord and the source of new and pressing dilemmas for the party leadership. First, as Bossi himself recognised, the electoral coalition was not popular within the party. Interviews with party organisers revealed the difficulties of explaining the alliance to party activists. As one member put it: 'I did not agree with the 94 alliance. I had a hard time accepting the agreement with Berlusconi ... but Bossi kept on saying that there were no alternatives.' Second, the lack of popularity of the electoral coalition was further compounded by the fact that Berlusconi's party made a parallel electoral coalition in the South with Alleanza Nazionale, *Il Polo del Buon Governo*. The electoral alliance was paradoxical in that it linked a new pro-unity party

Forza Italia, the fascist AN, and the autonomist Lega Nord. The tactic for the party leadership was the following: by embracing the enemy and making its main competitor in the North a partner, Lega could counterbalance the *novelty* effect of Forza Italia.

At the same time, however, Lega Nord attempted to discredit Berlusconi during the electoral campaign:

> If Lega Nord wanted to survive, it had to make an electoral alliance with Berlusconi. We knew it was a very risky operation, but the only one possible with that electoral law (Maroni, Milano 1996).

Despite the 1994 electoral alliance, Lega tried to maintain a distinctive and *floating* position vis-à-vis the Italian left and right. In fact, Lega ran the campaign for the elections of 1994 against Berlusconi (Bossi, 1995; Diamanti, 1995): 'We ran all the electoral campaign in 1994 against our ally, against Berlusconi. We couldn't do otherwise. We simply couldn't go with Berluconi and Fini.' The attacks during the campaign also targeted on Alleanza Nazionale and the Italian South.

The electoral alliances were a success, both in the.North and the South. The agreement with Berlusconi in the formation of the coalition lists allowed Lega Nord to win 180 seats between the Parliament and the Senate, becoming the largest parliamentary group. Despite the strenght of Lega Nord's representation in parliament, in fact, the electoral expansion of Lega Nord was arrested and the party lost 0.4% of the votes at the national level (Diamanti, 1995). Lega Nord obtained five ministries in the new government. Bossi requested the introduction of federalist reforms within six months. Fancesco Speroni, instead of Miglio, became the minister for Institutional Reform. Lega Nord had become a party of government and also controlled a key ministry for introducing institutional changes and reforming the Italian state structure. Scholars marked here the period of adaptation and evolution towards the moderation of Lega Nord in the Italian party system (Diamanti, 1995; Trigilia, 1994).

However, the governmental experience proved unsustainable even in the short run. The experience in the Berlusconi government was short-lived. Accountability in office proved a major factor in deteriorating the image of Lega Nord. The lack of popularity of the government further compromised Lega Nord's image of a party for radical reform and institutional change. Lega Nord's parliamentary group opposed government policies and Lega Nord's ministers faced widespread criticism from their own parliamentary group.

Within a few months, the costs of participating in the Italian government became clear. The electoral results of the European elections of June 1994 were a shock for the party leadership. Lega Nord obtained its worst electoral results in the 1990s while Forza Italia increased its electoral gains in the North. In these elections, Lega lost votes in its electoral strongholds in the North (Diamanti, 1996, p. 150). The party leadership decided to bring down the government in an attempt to stop crisis.

> We talked about our withdrawal from the government from May to September although Bossi announced in the federal assembly in Genova in the fall of 1994. Yet we started to talk to d'Alema and Buttiglioni about our decision and the possible alternatives already during the summer.

Lega Nord's withdrawal from government—known as *il ribaltone*—involved the formation of a care-taker government led by Lamberto Dini. The new government was supported by the votes of the Left coalition and Lega Nord. Although Lega Nord's political support for the government was only *external*, it was another contentious choice for the party.

As one party leader described the perception of an ideological shift: 'we found another majority, but the media started to say that we were shifting towards the left' (interview no. 7).

To summerise, the experience in the Berluconi government ended for Lega Nord with the lost of votes, party activists and party representatives.

> It was difficult to make people understand our withdrawal from the government. It was difficult ... some have not realized what Lega is. We are a revolutionary movement. We cannot accept small reforms. Many have become party members and voted for us only for small change, but we are for the independence of Padania. We have always worked along the same lines but unfortunately we couldn't make the revolution (Speroni, Varese, 1996).

Thus, by the end of 1994, Lega Nord exhibited divided party elites, a shrinking party membership and a reduced electoral base. The lowest point in the political history of the party-movement also found the issue of territorial conflict submerged in widespread debates about modernisation and Italy's position in the European Union.

The governmental experience is recalled differently by party representatives. As one party leader told me: 'We only made an electoral agreement. The plan was to find a majority after the elections to make reforms. Bossi wanted to open discussions to all parties, but the *Progressisti* refused the offer. They *forced* us to make a government with the right' (interview no. 28). A perception of the lack of alternatives for Lega Nord was common within the party leadership:

That electoral coalition should not have taken us to the government with Berlusconi and Fini. In 1994 we were hoping nobody would win and form a government. Instead, the alliance won. We were *constrained* to go into the government (interview no. 37).

For the party leadership, the worst outcome of this political crisis was the lost of Lega Nord's distinctiveness in the Italian political scenario. By the end of 1994, federalism had become a transversal issue in Italian politics. First, some politicians from the PDS strongly favored the introduction of a federal state structure in Italy. Franco Bassanini and Mario Cacciari, both considered *filo-leghisti*, became the advocates within the left of a federal Italy. Second, the PDS's leader, D'Alemma, in a polemic interview released in the newspaper *Il Manifesto* had also expressed the similarities between the political projects of Pds and Lega Nord. For D'Alema:

Lega is absolutely related to the left, this is not blasphemy, between Lega and the left there is a strong social continuity. The biggest workers' party in the North is Lega ... Lega Nord is like our appendix (Il Manifesto, 1995)

In the fall of 1995, the ideological distance of Lega Nord vis-à-vis the Italian left was called into question. Not only Lega Nord was supporting a technocratic government with the left, but also the PDS had showed its opening to Lega's political project.

Moreover, federalism had become a transversal question to which both left and right politicians in Italy could adhere. The party leadership desperately fought to claim that the real federalism was that of Lega Nord. As an article by one of Lega Nord's representatives in Parliament put it:

The term federalism belongs to Lega. The federalist idea belongs to Lega. Lega is the only one that really wants federalism ... Today emerge presumed federalists and autonomists everywhere. Nice game ... maybe they think they can dilute a revolutionary concept, by simply chatting about it? The federalist concept is revolutionary (Simoneta Faverio, L'Indipendente 17-18, December 1995: p. 3).

Independence for Padania

The care-taker government supported by the left and Lega Nord was short-lived. A conflict involving one of the ministers in Lamberto Dini government in the fall of 1995 led to Dini's resignation after the approval of the budget. The winter of 1996 started with a fundamental political uncertainty about the prospects for a new Italian government. Italian parties engaged in negotiations for the formation of a new government and for the setting up of the agenda for institutional reform. The failure of the parties to secure an agreement led to new general elections in the spring of 1996.

In the 1996 elections the party leadership adopted what at the time was considered a *suicidal* strategy. Lega engaged in a strategy of conflict and radicalisation without precedents. The party leadership moved from demands to reform the Italian state along federalist lines to demands for independence and secession of the North from the Italian state. As last chapter explained, the escalation of the Northern conflict was staged by using symbolic politics. Lega Nord's party elite engaged in extra-institutional means of action, inaugurating the symbolic 'Parliament of the North'. The existence of the Parliament asserted the non-negotiable nature of Lega Nord's demands. Lega Nord projected a fundamental ambiguity, displaying 'radical flank effects' with the presence of an independentist faction within the party.

In October 1995, Bossi declared in the Italian Parliament:

> I considered that the timing is ready for the political struggle of the independence of the North. I am telling you very clearly: it is not possible to stay within a Parliament that calls himself democratic and does not make the rules of democracy ... You'll see that the game is not over! You deceived yourselves thinking it is over: (the game) begins know and starts with the awareness that there are not democratic rules. Therefore, each of us will make our own calculations ... Let's see if the North is ready to go on like this, to live in a system like this, a Third World system, and an anti-democratic system! The North does not deserve this! (Camera dei Deputati, Atti Parlamentari XII Legislatura. Seduta Pomeridiana, October 24th, 1995).

In the fall of 1995, Lega Nord's displayed a radical faction led by two members of Lega Nord in the Italian parliament: Mario Borghezio and Erminio Bosso. Both politicians scandalised the country with initiatives to launch the Northern police, the Northern Church, the Northern soccer league, the Northern judiciary and a Northern military guard. In November 1995 both became the most aggressive speakers against migration flows into Italy. Initially, Bossi maintained an ambiguous position with the independentists. He presented himself as the controller, rather than the instigator, of a bunch of radicals within Lega Nord. On the occasion of one of the demonstrations at Pontida, he warned both politicians to 'behave seriously or to leave the party'. Later Bossi openly embraced the radicalisation of the party line.

In the 1996 general elections Lega Nord chose to compete alone. From November 1995 to February 1996 the party leadership explored the prospects for entering electoral coalitions. The possibilities offered by a pact with the left-wing coalition were first considered, either as an active agreement or as a *patto de desistenza* that involved party cooperation by abstaining to compete in certain electoral districts. By February 1996, the leader of l'Ulivo, Romano Prodi, publicly declared that there would not be any agreement with Lega Nord until the closing of the Parliament of the North. The federalists within the PDS agreed with their leader. Two other alternatives in coalition building were available. Berlusconi also attempted to approach Lega Nord to seek the formation of a new right-wing coalition. In January 1996, Berlusconi met with Roberto Maroni in an exploratory meeting, in which, according to Maroni, Berlusconi made an offer to 'prevent the victory of the Communists in Italy'. Berlusconi had publicly supported Lega Nord's proposal of a Constituent Assembly to introduce institutional reforms and change the Italian constitution. There was another attempt to reconstitute the center' of the Italian political space. Irene Pivetti, from her position as President of the Chamber of Deputies, tried to create a moderate coalition of centrist parties with Lega Nord as the main party. Her exploratory attempts failed.

Lega Nord's leadership became more explicit about the need for running aloane: 'our idea is to bet for our identity and our project, rather than being homogenised to the logic of left and right' (interview no 29). Lega run the 1995 regional elections and 1996 general elections with a different electoral strategy: *Lega da sola*. On March 2, 1996, after a meeting of the federal Council, Lega Nord announced officially that the party would also run the general elections alone. Bossi wiped out the history of negotiations with other parties declaring that 'Lega has *never* dealt neither with the right nor with the left'. Lega Nord would pursue the independence of Padania. In the words of the party leader, the quest for the independence of the North had been always part of Lega's objectives.

> For the past fifteen years, the independentist goal has been always inherent in the thinking developed within Lega. It has been, so to speak, a bit shadowed during the period 1993-1995, when Lega became a parliamentary and governmental force, following the diffusion in our electorate of more moderate positions than the original formulation of our project (Bossi, Parliament of Mantova 1996)

This strategy of radicalisation implied that for Lega Nord there was no solution to the *Northern question* within the Italian state. The alternative became reform or revolution:

> The process of reform is no longer possible, the one solution is the independence of Padania. The situation is changed. When Lega was in the government there was a magic moment in Italian politics, but the conditions for reform are no longer there (Speroni, Busto 1996).

The party leadership decided to suffer the consequences of running 'against all' in the 1996 general elections. Lega Nord's elites emphasised the transformation of the Italian party system from 1994 to 1996, and the new conditions that allowed them to avoid coalition building:

> In the 1996 elections electoral competition for us was already different. We run the electoral campaign with a heavy emphasis on independence. We thought we had been able to stop the trend. Berlusconi was no longer the new man in Italian politics.

Bossi's decision to run the 1996 general elections without electoral coalitions allowed the party leadership to replicate again the position of Lega Nord as challenger to the system and *partocracy* in the early 1990s. Lega Nord was *again* struggling against party politics and institutional actors in Italy. For Bossi:

> Lega does not fear to stand alone in the battlefield to defend the essential values upon which the faith of its base and its program is founded. A new fraud (*truffa*) is in the making to challenge democracy, true popular sovereignty, and the federalist impulse ... This is why Lega will compete alone (*La Lettera di Bossi: Perché da Soli*. Camera dei Deputati, Gruppo Lega Nord, March 4, 1996).

The strategy of radicalisation gave Lega Nord its best electoral results in 1996. Lega Nord gained also more votes under the plurality part than under the proportional system. This result has puzzled Italian scholars (Chiaramonte and Bartolini, 1997). However, Lega Nord's presence in the Italian parliament was sharply reduced. Table 6.3 shows the allocation of Lega Nord's seats during the elections held in the 1990s.

Table 6.3 Distribution of Seats in the Italian Parliament (1992-1996)

Lega Nord	Proportional	Single-Member	total seats	% Votes Italy	% votes Northern regions	total seats (%)
1992	55					
1994	10	107	117			18.6
1996	20	39	59			9.4

Source: Bartolini and D'Alimonte, 1997: 112

The results of the 1996 general elections were surprising in two main ways. First, there was a widespread assumption about the marginalisation of

Lega Nord in Italian politics. Radicalisation was considered a poor strategy to gain votes. Some argued that the party would be able to gain support in its electoral strongholds in the peripheries of the Northern cities, but the overall asessment was one of electoral marginalisation. Second, the presence of a new electoral system providing strong incentives for coalition building was considered a major impediment to the success of Lega Nord. In light of the results of the regional elections in 1995, when the party chose to run alone, some scholars argued that Lega Nord would lose visibility in Italian politics.

The expectations of the party leadership were rather modest. In February 1996, Roberto Maroni, declared that Lega could perhaps 'take 15 electoral districts running and aggressive campaing over the territory'. Although Bossi's expectations were much higher, the *fidelissimi* did not expect the electoral results of April 1996.

Lega Nord risked its marginalisation in Italian politics and its ability to continue playing a key role in government formation. If the party leadership did not count on having a big parliamentary group, Bossi *did* count on playing a pivotal role to become *l'ago della bilancia* in Italian politics. In the political uncertainty that characterised Italian politics in the spring 1996, Bossi hoped that the outcome of the elections would give none of the coalitions the possibility of forming a government. However, the 1996 elections gave the victory to the multi-party left wing coalition *l'Ulivo*. The prospects of a stable Italian government for the next four years were extremely disappointing for Bossi. As one of the ex-party representatives explained:

> Before he played a pivotal role (*l'ago della bilancia*). Now he needs elections within two years or the breaking up of Prodi government. If we vote in five years, Lega will be arrested. One should distinguish between static and dynamic politics. Bossi needs elections, needs political confrontation (Marano, Varese 1996).

The creation of the new governments led to new negotations for completing the agenda for institutional reform. Federalism was one of the items of the agenda ... without Bossi. As one of the party politicians put it assessing the implications of this new political scenario,

> Now there is a danger. They talk about federalism, another attempt of *gattopardismo*. The state will decentralize some of its powers to the regions ... This is something we are trying to avoid, but we don't have the parliamentary force to do it, that is why we make the demonstration on the Po River and the referendum for the independence of Padania (Pagliarini, Milano 1996).

Cleavage Replacement? **The Paradox of the Northern Question**

Rather than an evolution from extra-institutional means of action to institutional means of action, from mobilisation to representation, Lega Nord followed during the 1990s the opposite trajectory to the one predicted by evolutionary models of party adaptation. The reconfiguration of the Italian party system and the persistence of Lega Nord in the new Italian party system *accentuated*, rather than eliminated, the importance of party mobilisation.

The results of the elections of 1996 led to a public debate on the causes of the electoral success of Lega Nord and the motivations of Lega Nord's voters. The journalist Giorgio Bocca published an article on the newspaper *La Reppublica* entitled '*Bossi il Tribuno del Popolo*'. Giorgio Bocca explained voting for Lega Nord as a mystery, an *irrational* outcome of Italian politics. The national secretary of Lega Nord in Lombardy, Roberto Calderoli, published an open letter to respond to Bocca. He outlined the understanding of the party leadership about Lega Nord's electoral success. According to Calderoli:

> We are the spokesmen of a people, yes, a people who is rottenly tired of the conditions under which it lives. A people who started to think and search for solutions, and found them … If you think that the independence of Padania is an example of a deteriorated localism you are making a conceptual mistake: Padania is not a geographical area drawn with the rule of a geometrist of politics, Padania defines instead the identity of a nation because it is a nation … Padania is a part of Europe and in a united Europe imagines its future … Lega is the force of liberation of the North and *Lega expresses, the number of votes speaks for itself, the will of an entire society* (my emphasis) (*Roberto Calderoli , "Lettera aperta a Giorgio Bocca, Lega Nord-Lega Lombarda, ufficio stampa", 24-5-26*).

Lega Nord's is a clear-cut example of the non-congruence of attitudes between party elites and party voters: elites are more radical than its electorate. In the 1996 general elections, the party gained its best electoral result with a ticket advocating the independence of Padania. However, despite party elites' claim that voters support the independence of the North, the official party line is not a popular idea in Northern Italy, not even among Lega Nord's voters. Most Lega voters agree with the transformation of the state structure along federal lines. While the Italian average is only 19.8%, the percentage for Lega is much higher (33.8%). Public opinion polls revealed that there is neither consensus nor support for the idea of independence. Only 3.1% of Italians favor independence. Support for the idea in the North-West and the North-East is 5.9% and 5.7% respectively. Lega voters distinguish themselves from the other parties on the question of independence. However, *only* 13.0% of Lega voters agree with the self-government and independence for the North. The majority of Italian respondents prefer strengthening the current regions or a federal system (24.8% and 27.0% in the North-West; 26.2% and 24.0% in the North-East) (Renato Mannheimer, Ipso Survey 15-9-96).

The party elite understands its role as a party vanguard in the transformation of people's attitudes about the autonomy of the North. Lega Nord's elites agree their role is purely political: to change the system and to mobilize and make people aware of the situation in the North. The party leadership claimed that: 'People in the North want secession'. As one party leader put it:

> This is a diffused idea in people's consciousness ... The situation in the North is clear for the citizens, all have understood that our project and it is the best, clearest and most comprehensible of all. They (the other parties) have been unable to eliminate us and to destroy the Lega anomaly. Our territorial representation is central to Italian politics. They are scared. They have failed to isolate us, to buy us; the only choice is to solve the problem of the North (interview no. 42).

The 1996 general elections in Italy brought to closure the window of opportunity opened with the transformation of the Italian party system. Federalism, independence and secession do not appear as real choices for the party leadership, but as the outcome of a political process and an environment of fundamental uncertainty. In the views of the party elites, federalism, independence and secession are basically the same thing. As an ex-minister of the Berlusconi's government put it:

> Our political project has not changed a bit. We are culturally and economically different and we want a separate administration. Call that regions, cantons or pippo, I don't care, that's all we want (Pagliarini, Milano, 1966).

However, the restructuring of the Italian party system in the last two general elections in Italy undermined the previous malleability of Lega Nord's politics.

Institutionalisation of Conflict?

The results of a decade of territorial mobilisation in Northern Italy are here summarised in three main points. First, the need to mobilise in the short-term to keep the unity of Lega Nord undermined the goals of the party in the long-term. Second, the increasing tensions between mobilisation and representation resulted in the instablity and increasing weakness of the party elites. If a decade of electoral studies have shown the limits of defining Lega Nord's voters as *protest* votes, the *protest* character of Lega Nord's leadership and elites defined the rise of this new political class. Third, if the political linkages between *center* and *peripheries* remain today central for the articulation of a territorial politics, Lega Nord's local and national party linkages were subject to broader considerations of party strategy and therefore, suffered the consequences of a decade of radical shifts in party strategy.

In 1995, regional elections under the new system were held. The regional elections were a major success for the center-left coalition in Italy. However, in the regions of the North, the right-wing coalition won the control of Veneto, Lombardy and Piedmont.

Table 6.4   Lega Nord's Results in Regional Elections (1995-2000)

Regions	1995(%)	2000(%)
Piedmont	11.1	7.6
Lombardy	17.66	15.47
Veneto	17.5	11.96
Liguria	6.5	4.3
Emilia-Romagna	3.8	3.3

Source: D'Alimonte, 1995: 533

According to D'Alimonte, Lega Nord was the most punished party with the introduction of the new regional electoral rules with the majoritarian premium. The so-called Lega Nord *Third Pole* did not break the bipolar competition between left and right in the Northern regions (D'Alimonte, 1995: 535). The 2000 regional elections had a similar result. Table 6.4 shows the results of Lega Nord in the regional elections of 1995 and 2000. Paradoxically, during the 1990s Lega Nord played a marginal role in the Northern Italian regions, while the party managed to retain, for whatever means, a prominent role in national politics.

Mobilisation against Representation: The Weakening of Party Elites

The strategy of radicalisation initiated in 1995 tested the loyalty of the party elites. Moderates within the party parliamentary group were both interested in securing an electoral coalition to compete in the elections and in moderating the image of the party. The *exit* of this group from Lega Nord took two forms. Some of the most well known moderates within Lega Nord left the party before the general elections of 1996. Others who were perceived as too moderates, such as Bonomi and Marano—known as the *Serpentone Varesino*—were excluded from Lega Nord's party lists since they were not elected in the party primaries. Later they were expelled from the party.

The result of this process of creation of political controversies during the 1990s was a fundamental instability of party elites. Lega Nord's politicians considered that electoral alliances were no longer possible.

> We live like an army: the base of tough and pure does not agree with negotiations and alliances. We are diffident of *poltrone* ... to mediate and to soil I, personally, if there is a coalition I don't run as a candidate, I am one of those pure and tough.

Already in 1994 Bossi's decision to abandon the Italian government fractured the parliamentary group. Table 6.5 shows the number of representatives who left the party then.

Table 6.5   The 1994 Breaking-up of Lega Nord's Parliamentary Group: Loyalists and Defectors

	Loyalists		Defectors	
Total		**117**		**59**
Role in party Organisation	Yes	82	Yes	34
	No	35	No	26
Parliamentary experience	Yes	49	Yes	14
	No	68	No	46

Source: Diamanti, 1995: 159-160

The withdrawal from government generated a profound crisis in party elites. Although the party leader claimed that these *traitors* were not *real leghisti*, some of the parliamentarians who left the party were founding members and key players in the organisation. Table 6.6 shows the distribution of loyalists and defectors by region of origin. Belonging to the Lombard national section was a strong factor in predicting the likelihood of the candidates to support Bossi's choice. Venetian and Piedmonts representatives were more likely to leave Lega Nord and joined Forza Italia.

**Table 6.6   The 1994 Breaking-up of Lega Nord's Parliamentary
Group by Region**

	Loyals	Defectors
Lombardy	62	16
Veneto	22	13
Piedmont	15	18
Other regions	18	12
Total	117	59

Source: Diamanti, 1995: 161

The turnover in the parliamentary group shows that, Lega Nord's image of political continuity during the 1990s, hides significant changes in the composition of the party elites. Conflicts about policy choices led to 'exit' from the organisation. Table 6.7 shows the extent to which the parliamentary group has changed during the 1990s.

Table 6.7 Turnover of Lega Nord's Parliamentary Group (1992-1996)

	1992	1994	1996	92-94	94-96	92-96
Chamber	55	120	60	34	19	13
Senate	25	60	27	18	12	5
Total	80	180	87	52	31	18

Source: Lega Nord

Discontinuity in Lega Nord's political elites has not passed unnoticed to party organisers. As one of them put it:

> We had a very high politicians' mortality rate. I believe this is a positive sign of the integrity of the Movement. This is positive because it allows us to remove these foreign bodies (*corpi stranei*) and continue to be a revolutionary movement and create a new political class (Ronchi, Milano, 1996).

The mistrust of *le poltrone* and power and the constant rhetoric of revolution introduced an element of uncertainty undercutting the position of party representatives. Party representatives are faced with a political dilemma: their *dual* loyalty to the organisation and their electorate. Lega politicians faced these double loyalties when the party elite shifted again in 1996 to make Lega Nord a revolutionary movement against the state.

Not surprisingly, Lega Nord's party elite—both at the national and at the local level—refused to define their role as representing interests. Representation of interests was equated, in their views, with clientelistic politics. Mediating interests is at odds with Lega Nord's self-definition as a *revolutionary* movement for political change.

> I don't want to be a traditional parliamentarian, to go to Rome to split up monies ... some *leghisti* mediates interests at the local level ... Sometimes even we must participate in this structure, but we don't want to do it, sometimes we are constrained to do it (Irene Pivetti, Milano 1996).

Party representatives vigorously refute parallels between the Christian Democrats and the Lega.

> The parallel people make between Lega and the DC is a stupidity. We don't have a project of mediation of interests. Votes have become free, unlike with the Dorotei ... Lega is more political. We don't go around saying we will bring you this or we will bring you that. At the end, there are always interests, but there are material and moral interests (Covre, Oderzo 1996).

In short, party mobilisation during the 1990 resulted in a profound instability both in the party organisation and party representatives. The list of *disegni di leggi* introduced by party representatives in the Italian Parliament in the 1992-1994 and 1994-1996 legislatures indicates the interests of party representatives on a wide variety of issues, many of them completely unrelated to territorial issues and the political autonomy of the North.

Strategic Scenarios at the Local, Regional and National Level

Local politicians have been particularly vulnerable to the tensions between mobilising and *revolutionary* rhetoric and the daily needs of local administration. Party local sections can pressure local administrations to pursue the revolutionary struggle. Lega Nord's party coordinator of local governments at Lega Nord's federal level illustrated the demands the party puts on its local representatives:

> Our political struggle is a risky and slow process. We have decided that local governments, communes, provinces and regions contribute to accelerate this

political process, contribute to unhinge this system of power. In this phase, the strategy for unhinging the system is that Lega has to govern at the local level. It has to be present in order to make visible the contradictions in local institutions. Lega has as its mail role to make explode the internal contradictions of the system and not to give legitimacy to the system. If our politicians would limit themselves to honest and efficient, then we would legitimate the system every time a commune is well governed and becomes an example of efficiency ... We live an absurd situation, Lega majors swear loyalty, they are borrowed from this state but they have their hearts with Lega, though they have to serve the Constitution. Yet Lega is born to fight against the system, Lega is a revolutionary movement (Moltifiori, Milano 1996).

Many representatives at the local level struggled to balance the tensions and contradictions of representing while revolutionising the state. For one of the them:

It is a mistake to mix national politics with administering, when one wants to politicise everything ... political battles are sterile, they don't solve problems, when one does national politics in local governments one does not solve the problems over the territory. I cannot do a political battle because problems remain unsolved (interview no. 52).

Local representatives are also more accountable to voters. In 1993 the new electoral law improved the visibility of majors with their direct election under a plurality system. As we saw, in those elections some northern cities elected for the first time Lega Nord's majors. In the views of one of them: 'I represent citizens, but I do not mediate interests.' Lega Nord's local representatives emphasised their distinctiveness from the *old* political class.

The Dorotei current of the Venetian DC busied themselves with the political mediation of interests. To assimilate us to them is not fair ... they use Veneto as a reservoir of votes but thought more about Rome than about bringing welfare to Veneto.[...] We want the transformation of the state. Under the name of federalism are the interests of the area where citizens live and produce ... Our philosophy is the opposite of the Dorotean system (Covre, Oderzo 1996).

During the 1990s, conflicts at the elite level had a snowball effect in the local party sections. Events at the national level were followed by the breaking-up of conflicts at the local level during the fall of 1994 and the spring of 1995. In the provinces of Mantova, Milano and Pavia, conflicts about the loyalties of majors vis-à-vis Lega Nord and the erosion of the coalition with Forza Italia led to the demise of Lega's local governments in many towns. For example, in the province of Pavia, in 1993 Lega Nord had elected new majors to the three main cities of the province. Divided by internal power struggles and conflicts between the local party sections and the new elected mayors, from 1993 to 1996 Lega went from being the most voted party to a marginal position in the province.

The Lega Nord's ex-president of a Lombard province explained to me the failures of the experience of Lega in local governments:

> Why things went wrong? … for stupidity, for lack of knowledge of the problems and experience. People who previously did not have any political experience (coming from a revolutionary movement and not acknowledging that they were moving from a revolutionary to a management moment), continued to act as revolutionaries, to maintain the purity of the organisation. They prevented us from conquering the hill. Then, people also came to Lega at the last minute because they thought they could benefit from it, and ended up seeding conflict, clicks and accusations. As a revolutionary movement we were fractured by these events and the other parties found the space to gain votes (Enzo Casali, Pavia, 1996).

The changing position of Lega Nord at the national level had very different consequences for the type of politics Lega Nord could pursue in different institutional and political contexts. In the past the DC's presence both in the region and the center provided political linkages between center and periphery. Instead, Lega Nord's changing position in national, regional and local governments made the formation of center-periphery linkages through the party an impossible task.

Lega Nord's current position in the Italian party system suggests the emergence of three different scenarios for the party. First, Lega Nord faces in the old industrial and metropolitan areas of the North a situation in which the party is in a minority position and bi-polar competition takes place between left and right coalitions. Where the party is in a clear marginal position and needs to mobilise to gain votes vis-à-vis the left and the right coalitions, the sections of the party tend to operate as sects with a closure of the organisation to any external collaboration. In this scenario, ironically, the party needs to open-up if Lega Nord's wants to win votes. Second, Lega Nord faces a very different scenario in the local peripheries of the North-East. The party is in a dominant position and has engaged in a virtuous cycle of electoral growth, stability and local government.[2] Where the party represents a majority of the electorate and does not require political compromises, alliances or external support, Lega Nord tends to offer more moderate political lines at the local level and therefore it is in a much better position to secure political consensus and votes.[3] The third scenario is characterised by political uncertainty. The trade-offs between mobilisation and representation are more visible in competitive scenarios, as the ones identified by Diamanti in his classification of the Northern electoral districts. This scenario is highly unstable and requires all the political ability of local politicians and local party sections in order to improve Lega Nord's position.

Conclusions

Academic emphasis on the peculiarities of Lega Nord's electoral success is explained by scholars as follows: although Lega Nord's claims to represent a territorial identity, the electoral success of Lega Nord *is not* about a territorial identity. Evidence about other nationalist parties in European party systems shows that we should keep analytically distinctive three issues: the claims of party elites; the patterns of self-identification with the territory, and voting behavior. Thus, the lack of congruence between elite's claims and public self-identification is not unique to the Italian case. The extent to which this is the case, however, is characteristic of the Italian case.

This chapter reviewed two alternative explanations of the electoral success of Lega Nord. The populist explanation emphasised the power of populist persuasion to attract disadvantaged constituencies in the crisis and transition towards postindustrial society. Instead, the territorial explanation stresses the salience of local interests in the peripheral areas of the North-East and the continuity between the Christian Democrats and Lega Nord's electorates to explain the electoral success of Lega Nord.

The chapter explained the trayectory of Lega Nord in Italian politics during the 1990s. The alternative strategies of the party leadership and their different effects were presented, as well as the party elite's assessment of their political opportunities and constraints in the Italian party system. First, Lega Nord followed a short-term electoralist strategy that moderated the party line with a platform on federalism. The pay-offs for this strategy were more seats and more visibility for Lega Nord in national politics. However, the trade-offs of pursuing this strategy were very high. New parties—Forza Italia—inherited the moderate electorate of Lega Nord. Moderation and office seeking tested the loyalties of party activists. A strategy of radicalisation followed. Lega Nord's leadership substituted moderation and federalism for claims of independence for the North. Institutional politics were replaced with symbolic politics and the creation of the Parliament of the North. Lega Nord distanced itself from other competitors and regained a core but uncertain electorate. The trade-offs, however, were also significant. The strategy of radicalisation tested the loyalties of party elites and representatives. Radicalisation risked the marginalisation of the party in Italian politics with the victory of the left-wing coalition and the formation of the Prodi government. In the late 1990s the party suffered again from electoral failures in the 1999 European elections and 'exit' problems with the breaking-up of Lega Nord in the Veneto region. The coalition with Berlusconi in the 2000 regional elections, however, shows the persistence of Lega Nord in the Italian party system.

Notes

[1] The same survey shows the overlap between the attitudes of both Lega Nord's and Alleanza Nazionale's voters. The percentages of voters agreeing with the assertions that 'too many migrants disturbe' (58% Lega Nord, 58.1% AN), 'it would be better to return migrants to their countries of origin' (52.6% LN, 54.7%) and 'migration is one of the three most important problems in Italy' (14.6% LN, 15.7% AN) are almost identical (Biorcio, 1997: 158).

[2] This is consistent with the findings of several scholars. The differential ability of local party sections and their relationship with the local environment determines the extent to which they can advance the long-term goals of party elites. Panebianco on Hellman and the comparison between the sections of the Communist party in Veneto and Emilia.

[3] The provinces of Belluno and Treviso are clear-cut examples of the second type of strategic scenario and institutional equilibrium. Lega Nord engaged in a 'virtuous' cycle of expansion and consolidation to become the first party in these areas and to rule at the local level.

7 Conclusions

The rise of Lega Nord in Italian politics in the 1990s raises some fundamental questions about change in contemporary European politics. Is this *real* nationalism? What kind of identity politics is at stake? How persistent are these demands? Is this type of politics sustainable in the long run? This chapter addresses these questions and opens up the findings of the study to three main debates in the literature of political science. First, it considers the lessons of the rise and success of Lega Nord for students of *peripheral* nationalism and the ethno-territorial cleavage in European party systems. Second, it examines the implications of Lega Nord's style of political mobilisation and organisation for our theories on party formation and consolidation. Third, it draws the implications of Lega Nord's electoral success for analysis of the relationship between party elites and voters in European party systems.

The rise and success of Lega Nord higlights some fundamental novelties in European politics. The rise of this party is an excellent case to explore a new political space, and its limits, to redefine territorial identities and new interests. The rise of Lega Nord challenges our received wisdom about territorial cleavages in European party systems. A decade ago, neither Padania existed in the collective imagination—a common claim by scholars and politicians—nor the Italian North as a homogenous economic or social unit within the Italian state. Today, the persistence of Lega Nord has made the *Northern question* part of political reality in Italy. Moreover, the claims advanced by the party constructed a new category of belonging—Padania— and put forward new demands for the right of self-determination within an integrated Europe.

This book focused on explaining why and how this happened. The argument advanced here challenged the classic causality in the rise of new ethno-territorial parties. Rather than defining ex-ante the dimensions of conflict generated by the transition to post-industrial societies, this book focused on how a new territorial cleavage was constructed in political processes. In short, what this book aimed to show was a new cleavage *in the making*. Conflict, in this work, is seen as the outcome, and not the pre-existing condition, for political mobilisation. There were alternative scenarios and directions for political change in Italian politics during the 1990s. Lipset and Rokkan paid crucial attention to the *translation* mechanisms that locked social conflict with political alternatives (Lipset and Rokkan, 1967). The book moved center stage political and institutional variables. By focusing on the political process that led to the construction of the Northern question, I sought to build a theoretical bridge between agency and structure.

Some objections can be raised on the grounds of the methodology used in this study. Case studies are questioned on the grounds of their generability. Moreover, case studies of Italian political economy, party government and public policy commonly face objections on the grounds of the comparability of their findings. As Richard Locke explains, Italian *exceptionalism* is usually brought to the fore (Locke, 1995). However, this was a deliberatedly chosen 'case study' approach. The case study was justified on two grounds. First, the uneasy location of Lega Nord in the typologies of political parties and in our explanations about political change offered the opportunity to explore an *anomaly* for the purpose of theory building and hypothesis generating. In this regard, the case study was an effort to make a very simple and obvious outcome in light of some scholary research, into an open-ended, constructed and problematic one that targets contemporary academic debates. Second, the collapse of the Italian party system also offered a unique opportunity to explore the rise and success of new parties in European party systems. Unlike the changes at the margins that have taken place in the party systems of Western Europe, the transformation of Italian politics has no parallels in contemporary European politics. The Italian party system and the rise of Lega Nord can be fruitfully used as a magnifying glass to study political change in European party systems.

The first part of this book is, in fact, built upon a traditional comparative design that aimed to re-introduce within-country comparisons as a useful methodological device for exploring political change.[1] Within-country comparisons—first introduced by Linz and de Miguel as a strategy for comparative research—were ideal to explore the mobilisation potential of the different Northern regions of Italy. These later comparisons provided the background to understand the difficulties Lega Nord had in sustaining the unity of the North as a homogenous social and cultural category in Italian politics.

An unlikely reform of the Italian state structure—in light of contemporary developments in Italian politics—won't provide a *solution* to the Northern question. Ultimately, as I showed in this book, during the 1990s Lega Nord's political elites were in search of *conflict*, not of solutions. In the past, the formation of cleavages was about the structuring of conflict and its institutionalisation in party systems (Lipset and Rokkan, 1967). Today, the rise and success of new political parties is also about the structuring of conflict.

In this concluding chapter, I will review first the main findings and then explore their implications for contemporary debates in the literature.

A Review of the Findings

For modernisation theories in the post-war period Europe was the home of the nation-state. Instead, the wave of new political mobilisation in the 1970s made Europe the home of multi-ethnic states (Esman, 1977). If Italy defied the idea of a nation-state—as a case of weak *national* integration—neither was *ethncity* part of the political landscape. Local, but not *ethnic*, identities were part of the Italian political system. Chapter 2 explained the sources of new political mobilisation in Northern Italy. If modernisation, industrialisation and migration processes help to erode the enclosure of culturally distinctive groups in European states, institutional designs provide a contemporary structure of incentives for reinventing cultural differences to claim new rights. *Ethnicity* and *nationhood*, as discursive and institutionalised practices, provide in pluralist democracies the structure of incentives for new political mobilisation. The evidence presented in chapter 2 showed how ethnicity as a normative principle became available in Italy. The institutionalisation and success of the German-Speaking minority in the special region of Trentino Alto-Adige as an *ethnic* group provided the stimulus for new demands for recognition and for new mobilisation efforts in the Nothern regions of Italy.

Nationalism is a principle of legitimacy that holds that the political and cultural unit should be congruent (Gellner, 1983; Hobsbawm, 1990). Chapter 2 showed how this principle can be used for claims-making in contemporary politics regardless of the presence of objective or subjective differences to identify collectivities. In the Northern Italian regions, the *ethnic* wave of the 1970s gave rise to the mobilisation of minorities in the 'special' regions of the North *but also* to new political mobilisation in the 'ordinary' regions of Piedmont, Lombardy and Veneto. These new parties claimed the ethnic and cultural distinctiveness of nations that matched the administrative boundaries of the 'ordinary' regions introduced by the Italian state in 1970.

Chapter 2 also assessed the mobilisation potential of the various regions of Northern Italy. The chapter explored the determinants of political mobilisation in Piedmont, Lombardy and Veneto in light of traditional theories of ethno-territorial conflict developed in the 1970s. The Lombard and Piedmont regions were the 'core' of Italy in political and economic terms, eliminating, on theoretical grounds, the possibility of the rise of political mobilisation. The Veneto region, however, experienced a rapid process of industrialisation that was coupled with the erosion of the political linkages between the Venetian Christian Democrats and the Italian central governments. In contrast to Piedmont and Lombardy, the mobilisation potential of Veneto made the region an *ideal* case for the rise and success of territorial political mobilisation.

The second wave of ethno-territorial mobilisation in the 1970s—with the first signs of electoral de-alignment—did not fundamentally change European party systems. In Italy new political parties appeared and developed at the margins of the Italian party system. Their trajectory in the Northern ordinary regions during the 1980s responded to the traditional scenario of minority nationalism and marginal electoral gains. The outcome of political mobilisation, however, yielded unexpected results. Liga Veneta was a political failure while Lega Lombarda became an electoral success by the end of the 1980s. This was a political breakthrough between minority nationalism and mass 'populist' success.

The trajectories of these parties during the 1980s offered some lessons to understand the conditions under which parties can make identity a successful principle of political mobilisation. For new political parties, collective action is the *problem* as well as the *solution,* to overcome 'entry costs' in the political system. I demonstrated how the *recipe* and party platform for these parties was the same, but the outcome of political mobilisation was very different. Political factionalism was a key factor in undermining the prospects of the parties in Piedmont and Veneto during the 1980s.

Chapter 3 explained both the contingent nature of the Northern question and the political reinvention of Italian geography. Economic, cultural and political differences are brought to the fore to explain why North and South in Italy *are* different. In some views, the growing economic gap between North and South, the cultural differences between North and South and the clientelistic patterns of political involvement in the South explained the rise of Lega Nord in the Italian party system. The revolt of the North against a clientelistic and underdeveloped South would have expressed the failure of national integration in Italy and the erosion of national boundaries in the context of a global economy. Territorial disparities and the dualism between North and South are long-standing features in political and economic analyses of Italy as well as are widespread prejudices against Southerners. However, I argued in this chapter that there was nothing inevitable about the rise of the *Northern question.*

Chapter 3 explained the political process that led to the rise of the Northern question. I showed how the North as a unified category was not the response of an old North to the crisis of the state, but a new category of belonging. The category of the North (later Padania) was the product of the political choices of the party leaders of the 'ordinary' regions of Northern Italy. Cooperative strategies and coalition building led to the centralisation of all the parties under a single leader, Umberto Bossi, and single party label, Lega Nord. The assessment of the political scenario led to a strategy of centralisation and concentration of resources to compete in the electoral arena. Under the leadership of Bossi, Lega Nord went beyond the boundaries of the Lombard region to expand in the other ordinary regions of the North. Chapter

3 showed that the timing and sequence of mobilisation was the critical intervening variable to explain why the North, and not other territorial identities, gained political visibility. An exogenous shock—the fall of the Berlin wall—had a snowball effect in undermining traditional electoral alignments in Northern Italy. Thus, the chapter showed how small events can have large consequences for explaining the trajectory of political change.

In scholarly writing the absence of an *ethnically* distinctive North made the question of Lega Nord's nationalism as epiphenomenal since Lega Nord's categories of nationhood were invented. In these views Lega Nord is an anti-tax revolt (Melucci and Diani, 1992). Chapter 3 went beyond the distinction between identities as *authentic* or *invented* to explore the categorical remaking of Italians introduced by Lega Nord. The chapter showed—through the party production of pamphlets, journals, manifests and elite interviews—how Lega Nord constructed the category of Padania as an internally homogenous political, economic and cultural unit. Lega Nord constructed a new category of belonging while at the same time 'hiding' the contingent history by which Padania came about. In the construction of this category, social stereotypes, social-scientific discourse and European integration provided the material to construct and represent cultural differences. On the one hand, the party elites built on old prejudices and stereotypes against Southerners to shape the image of North and South as internally homogenous units. On the other hand, the party leadership used the process of European integration to fashion a view of a future Italian North bounded by European borders. Europe marked the boundaries between the 'Mediterranean and African Worlds' on the one hand, and the core European regions on the other.

Populist political leadership has been emphasised in all studies about the rise and success of Lega Nord. The party, relative to the leader, has received secondary attention. Chapter 5 went beyond Bossi's charismatic leadership to show the role of Lega Nord's organisation and mobilisation structures in the rise of the *Northern question*. Rather than defining what Lega Nord is—a populist party, a protest party, a communal party—the chapter explained what Lega Nord *does* to create controversies. This chapter challenged common views on the irrelevance of new party organisations on two grounds: the importance of the style of mobilisation and organisation to explain Lega Nord's success, and the relevance of organisational constraints. The chapter examined the internal dynamics of the organisation, showing how the party leader was constrained by the territorial expansion of the organisation and decreasing party membership to radicalise the party's platform and assert its political unity.

This chapter also showed the limits of Kitschelt's mirror image of the New Left and the New Right as polar opposites of political involvement. Lega Nord is a party characterised by the importance of voluntary participation and activism. Solidarity incentives explain participation in Lega Nord. Chapter 5 showed how Lega Nord combined traditional and innovative elements in party politics. Local party sections do what local party sections did in the past: organise feasts and proselytise. The use of traditional means of communication, such as the party journal, party posters and slogans reproduced the image of Lega Nord across Northern Italy. However, in absolute numbers, participation resembled more small social movement organisations than traditional mass party membership.

In addition, Chapter 5 showed how Lega Nord's organisation introduced a competing frame to interpret political reality in Italy by using symbolic politics. Here Lega Nord was analysed as a locus of symbolic production. Lega Nord's rituals and symbolic action used public space to enact the collective identity and unity of the Italian North. I described these events and presented evidence on participation of Lega Nord's followers. I explained how rituals combined sacred and secular elements, and provided a space for interaction between the party leadership, the party elites and its followers. This chapter also argued that these symbolic resources could be analysed as a *functional equivalent* to mass mobilisation. The chapter suggested that the strength of this type of political action is in their ability to gain media coverage. First, symbolic and ritualistic action attract media attention. Symbolic action and extra-institutional means of action with collective representation and drama provided the linkage between micro-mobilisation and mass audiences. The Italian and international media extensively covered these theatrical and ritualistic events. Second, rituals made people appeared as a solidarity unity. During the 1990s and despite fundamental collective action problems—*exit* of party elites and members—continuity in the rituals at Pontida made the party appear as a solidaristic unit around the leader. Third, symbols projected an image of profound ambiguity that allow Umberto Bossi to manipulate the attention of his political competitors and the general public. Are they joking or are they serious? Do they really want secession from the Italian state or are they just provoking us? In the midst of speculation, Lega Nord kept people talking about the Northern question.

Lega Nord has not established institutional networks or linkages with economic and social actors and associations in these territorial economies to represent these interests in the center of the political system. The political radicalisation of the party with claims of independence and secession has produced an environment of political instability and uncertainty that does not match the moderation predicted and required by analysis that emphasises the regionalisation of economic interests and their need of representation (Trigilia, 1994).

Chapter 6 examined the construction of new political space with the shifting electoral trajectory of Lega Nord during the 1990s. Rather than defining ideological space *ex-ante*, the chapter showed how party elites struggled to construct a territorial dimension of political space, a *vertical* position of Lega Nord, a new axis centralism-federalism in the Italian party system. Party elites redefined the distinctiveness of Lega Nord in different ways. Lega Nord's is a clear-cut example of non-congruence in elite and voters' attitudes and despite the claims of party elites, Lega Nord's voters do not support independence or secession from the Italian state. The chapter explored the political processes that shape the interaction between elites and voters in Italian politics during the 1990s. The institutional and political environment shaped the goals of the party leadership over time. The transformation of the Italian party system with the disappearance of the traditional governing parties, the refounding of the Communist party and the creation of new players and new rules of the game substantially modified the conditions for electoral competition. Chapter 6 examined the strategic dilemmas of the party leadership as they pursued two very different courses of action during the 1990s. On the one hand, they followed a short-term electoralist strategy that led the party into moderation, compromises and instititutional politics. On the other hand, the party leadership pursued a strategy of long-term mobilisation, radicalising the party platform claiming independence from the Italian state.

In contrast to common views on a linear trajectory of new parties that leads from radicalisation to moderation and catch-all strategies, Lega Nord's followed the opposite direction. The party elites learned the payoffs of radicalising the party platform. By examining the *mis-match* between Lega Nord's elites and voters, chapter 6 explored the paradoxes of political representation. Support for independence among Lega Nord's voters is minimal. The party leadership however, has used its electoral support as an indicator of the support for independence of the North.

In the remaining of this chapter I focus on the lessons that this case offers for those interested in nationalism and identity politics, more specifically, to those interested in *peripheral* nationalism in European party systems. Then I explore the relevance of this study of Lega Nord for scholars interested in party and electoral change in European party systems.

Revising Nationalism: New Party Mobilisation

In the universe of *peripheral* nationalist parties, Lega Nord is an uneasy latecomer. In classical approaches to the study of *peripheral* nationalism, the Italian case is an anomaly on two main grounds. First, some scholars argue that this is *not*, in fact, *peripheral* nationalism. Both scholars and politicians have guarded the *real* distinctiveness of old nationalisms vis-á-vis these newcomers.[2]   Second, the electoral success of Lega Nord has undermined a central assumption of the literature: ethno-territorial parties specialise their electoral appeals to culturally distinctive collectivities and this limits their ability to gain votes. The rise of Lega Nord illustrates in an extreme form, how claims of cultural distinctiveness are successfully tied with distributive demands.

The rise and success of Lega Nord in Italy offers important insights to understand not only future, but also past developments on *peripheral* nationalism in Europe. This relevance might seem paradoxical since the claims of nationhood are commonly considered in academic and journalistic writing ridiculous and/or funny. What follows, however, is an effort to take this public amusement seriously and provide some insights about identity politics and contemporary forms of nationalism in Europe.

Nationalism: Theoretical and Methodological Implications

This section considers the theoretical, normative and methodological implications of Lega Nord's rise in Italian politics. The first question that I address here is the possibility of deriving any conclusions about nationalism. Is this *real* nationalism? From the point of view of any external observer, the invented nature of Padania is self-evident. From the point of view of Lega Nord's party leadership and elites, the answer is also self-evident. The party elites appeal to the universal right of self-determination on the basis of the distinctiveness of the Northern people. However, we need to explore the question of reality and invention a step further. Constructivist approaches criticise an interpretation of nationalism which only consider invention and manipulation at the elite level and neglects the role of everyday practice in the construction of categories. Sociologists and anthropologists such as Herzfeld, Brubaker and Calhoun highlight the importance of the study of the *reification* of the nation as a practical category in social processes (Herzfeld, 1992; Brubaker, 1996; Calhoun, 1996). Herzfeld focuses on *practical* nationalism that is, how identities, classifications and stereotypes defined ordinary social interaction. For Herzfeld: 'if nationalist ideology represents cultural units as social units, practical nationalism is the result of the conversion of this logic in everyday practice' (Herzfeld, 1992, p. 174). From the point of view of the citizens of Northern Italy, we simply do not know. This is a question this study did not investigate but leaves open to future research. However, when scholars, journalists and the public spend their time and energy in asserting that Padania *does not exist*, the power of new categories to define political debate is clearly displayed.

The trajectory of the new peculiar peripheral nationalism in Northern Italy during the 1990s provides evidence against views on the strengthening of the European Union and the undermining of nation-state politics. If the fragile Italian *nation-state* did not break up during the 1990s, who will? Evidence from Belgium case points to a contemporary scenario where multiple identities are at stake and where national identity can be reconstructed and reinvented in new ways with the addition of a new layer: attitudes against migrants (Maddens, Billiet and Beerten, 2000). One also wonders whether one of the effects of the rise of the leghe in the Italian party system has been an increase in *national* identity.

The rise of Lega Nord can also help us to revise our theories about the old *peripheries*. Brubaker has made an important contribution to eliminate *nations* as analytical categories (Brubaker, 1996). In this study *national* and *ethnic* minorities were no longer the unit of analysis, nor the history of nation-formation was introduced to assert or refuse the legitimacy of alternative claims. My analytical framework claims that all identities are historically constructed and articulated, and politics plays a crucial role in these cateogorical constructions. The *essentialism* of Lega Nord in the construction of categories of belonging is, in its simplicity and visibility, a guideline to understand all *essentialism* as well. Agency in the construction of differences is hidden by the denial of agency itself in political mobilisation.

However, it is also obvious that there are crucial differences in the extent of construction and invention, in the extent to which these categorical constructions have public support, and in the power of the different actors participating in the construction of categories. However, instead of locating differences and fixing traits in substantial entities and the 'nature' of identity, here the emphasis is on the political processes that shape the boundaries of new categories and reify them in social and political processes.

The identity politics of Lega Nord is also relevant to current debates on multiculturalism. *Culture* has re-entered contemporary debates in European politics in two main forms: 'multicultural' citizenship and 'cultural differentialism'.[3] The first debates focus on the possibility of a citizenship decoupled from a national identity but coupled with the recognition of multiculturalism in pluralist democracies (Kymlicka, 1992; Taylor, 1992). The way the concepts of 'culture' and 'groups' are introduced in these debates is often times unproblematised. They take cultural differences as given and understand the political process as recognising them, not about producing and reifying culture by human agency. Debates focus on inclusion of groups and leave largely unexplored the other side of the coin: cultural differences as the tool to assert political exclusion. It is on the name of respecting cultural differences that the new right in Europe uses *cultural differentialism* to argue against the compatibility of groups and the need to terminate with migration towards European countries.

Hardly anybody would take Lega Nord as a manifestation of pluralism in

European party systems. However, the principles upon which the new party based its claims are those of an *oppressed minority* by the Italian nation-state, a minority in search of its official recognition as a culturally distinctive collectivity. Lega Nord shows how culture is used today as a force of political exclusion in contemporary European politics and how it is also incorporated in right wing politics against migrants (Balibar, 1991). A sharp distinction between culture and politics, society and political institutions, is misleading one and calls for a systematic examination of the role of institutions in reifying existing categories. The key question we need to address relates not only to the right to have one own's culture, but on how cultural differences entered politics in European societies.

Claims of nationhood and identity politics are, in the analytical framework presented here, and running the risk of stating the obvious, neither pre-modern nor post-modern but very contemporary developments. Identity politics has moved center stage in current debates in political science and sociology. This book suggests some caution in assessing the implications of this new type of political mobilisation. I think in some contemporary literature there is a very problematic assumption about the fact that modern liberal democracies are held capable of *negotiating* identities in the political system. Benhabib introduces a radical distinction. In her words:

> ... But the politics of identity/difference, emerging out of the experience of new social movements in liberal capitalist democracies, and the politics of racial, ethnic, linguistic and religious difference developing in former communist countries, North Africa and the Middle East are radically different. Whereas the former kind of identity/difference politics focuses on the negotiation, contestation, and representation of difference within the public sphere of liberal democracies, the politics of ethnonationalisms seek to redefine the constituents of the body politic, and aim at creating new politically sovereign bodies. [...] The essays in this volume shared the assumption that the institutions and culture of liberal democracies are sufficiently complex, supple and decentered so as to allow the expression of difference without fracturing the identity of the body politic or subverting existing forms of political soverignty (Benhabib, 1996: 4-5).

The rise of political mobilisation in Northern Italy raises some fundamental questions about the possiblity of *negotiating* identities in liberal democracies. The question of the negotiation of identity/difference as a yardstick for democratisation has to be considered in specific contexts. *Ethnic* violence is not the terrain of weak states and unstable democracies, but as we all know, a very contemporary feature in some countries of Europe, Spain and Ireland providing the most outstanding examples of the non-negotiable nature of collective identities. Democratic theory does not offer a key to the problem of territorial boundaries and the public space of liberal democracies can be broken by the rise of new claims of distinctiveness. I believe it is in *specific* political processes that we can assess on normative grounds the positive or negative effects of the politics of difference in contemporary democracies. This is an unhappy solution, but as Etienne Balibar and Edward Said write, we have to face the uncomfortable vicinity of progressive nationalism as a form of resistance and liberation, and nationalism in its extreme forms as a form of exclusion.

As we saw, the normative basis of nationalism—the congruence between the cultural and political unit—is institutionalised in world politics and in pluralist democracies (Brubaker, 1996). The principle of congruence can be continously used in politics to draw new boundaries of social and political exclusion/inclusion. The rise of claims of nationhood in Northern Italy is a case to explain the modernity of nationalism and its contemporary relevance in defining new political and social boundaries. In the most 'modernised' part of Italy, claims of national distinctiveness are being advanced to demand political autonomy and self-government as a tool of political exclusion. Finally, the malleability of the idea of national distinctiveness in contemporary politics also suggests that, as the nation as a principle of legitimacy has gained recognition as an institutionalised form, the multiplication of new claims of nationhood are, paradoxically, de-legitimising the very idea of national self-determination. As Lega Nord has shown, today *everybody* can assert cultural differences and national distinctiveness in the public sphere.

Comparative Research on Peripheral Nationalism

This section offers some thoughts on future research on comparative *peripheral* nationalism. The study of *peripheral* nationalism has been a challenge for comparative research (for an exception see De Winter and Tursan, 1998). First, in the past scholars have taken the periphery as the unit of analysis; the ethnic minority or the peripheral nation as the pre-existing condition that explain the rise of political mobilisation (Lipset and Rokkan, 1967; Rokkan and Urwin, 1983; Gourevitch, 1979; Hueglin, 1986). Second, classical analyses emphasise the differences, rather than the similarities, in *peripheral* nationalism in Western Europe. Since all these nations were *different* among themselves—because of different trajectories of state and nation formation—comparative work stressed the impact of these differences in explaining variation in the outcome—the presence and relative success and failure of party mobilisation. For example, the strength or weakness of *peripheral* nationalism in European countries was explained by the processes of nation-formation that produced different types of national minorities in European countries (Linz, 1967).

214 Ethnicity and Nationalism in Italian Politics

My work suggests that comparative work on past and present peripheral nationalism in Europe can be conducted on two premises. First, this book suggests dropping the study of *nations* and *ethnic minorities* as social units and substantial entities, exploring instead the historical processes that construct collective differences as *ethnic* and *national*. In these processes we have to pay attention to the construction of differences as *essential* traits of collectivities, as well as to the institutional processes that recognise, reproduce and reify collective differences in pluralist democracies. In addition, we can explore the ways in which institutions reproduce differences and how categorical identities—whether old or new—are represented in discursive practices. My current research explores these questions: how do *peripheral* nationalists define their cultural distinctiveness and nationhood in light of European integration? How do these categories define new boundaries between insiders/outsiders? How are new migrants defined vis-à-vis the *other* minorities?

Second, this book suggests conducting comparative work on *peripheral* nationalism taking political parties as the unit of analysis. What is distinctive about these types of parties is the nature of their claims. As Urwin remarks: 'What separates these parties out from the mass of European parties is the nature of their claim upon the state. They identify with, and make claims upon the central government on behalf of, territories and groups that are not coincident with state boundaries and national populations' (Urwin, 1983, p. 232). These parties want to gain institutional recognition and the granting of rights for collectivities and they subordinate all other issues, agendas and demands to this claim.[4]

While we can count today with excellent scholarly work on *peripheral* nationalism, most of the research conducted focus on case studies. The question of overselection on the dependent variable is a traditional problem for comparative research. Future work on *peripheral* nationalism in Europe needs to illuminate three key questions. First, we lack a systematic comparative analysis of the trajectories of these parties since the 1970s with the first erosion of traditional electoral alignments. We lack studies on *failures*, and not successes, on the mobilization of claims of nationhood on the peripheries of Europe.

Second, the *floating* position of these parties with regard to major ideological divisions in European states is a well-known phenomenon in the study of the rise of *ethnic* claims (Berger, 1977; Urwin, 1983). What shapes the trajectory of these parties towards to left-wing or right-wing politics, and towards 'old' and 'new' politics? My current research maps peripheral nationalist along the left-right dimension, in *old* and *new* politics. Third, the rise of Lega Nord problematises long-standing assumptions in the study of ethno-territorial parties. The literature on these parties has traditionally assumed that what explains the electoral base of these parties is the presence of *encapsulated* constituencies and the specialisation of voters' appeals along cultural demands (Lipset and Rokkan, 1967; Bartolini and Mair, 1990). Comparative research in the future also needs to uncover the strategies and political opportunity structures that allow these parties to expand their electoral basis.

Explaining Political Change and New Party Formation

The Rise of New Conflict

The rise of Lega Nord offers the opportunity to recast debates about political change and party politics in contemporary European party systems. The findings of this study can be applied to all new processes of political mobilisation. These findings are rather disturbing for our current theories on party formation and political change. The traditional model on the formation of party systems holds that the translation of structural cleavages formed by national and industrial revolutions shaped the main dimensions of political conflict in European party systems (Lipset and Rokkan, 1967). New models replicate old ones. Kitschelt explains the rise of the new left and the new right on the basis of the structural dislocation in the transition from industrial to postindustrial society (Kitschelt, 1995). Cleavages are rooted in the social structure and are translated in new political mobilisation. Social location in the economic structure explains the rise of new mass attitudes: new political entrepreneurs then translate a new ideological cleavage in post-industrial societies. Political parties mediate between voters and the institutions of political representation of liberal democracies.

Rather than thinking about parties as translators of conflict, this dissertation showed that political elites are actively engaged in politicising issues and mobilising the public. The problem for new political elites in the Italian case was not how to solve unsolved problems of territorial dualism or represent underrepresented regional interests, but how to construct and sustain the conflict itself over time. While all explanations about political change allowed some form of political entrepreneurship, this book suggests that political elites play a crucial role in mobilising and politicising issues, and that political parties are key actors in political change.

Political processes and institutional factors play a crucial role in two main ways. First, the rise of Lega Nord and the transformation of the Italian party system during the 1990s strongly indicate that political change is a slow process and that political *inertia* prevails in many instances. Moreover, the trajectory of Lega Nord points to the importance of exogenous shocks and critical junctures in providing avenues to redefine conflict and structure new political space. In light of the Italian example, neither apocalyptic images of the changing face of European politics nor images of profound stability are adequate. In Italy we have seen a critical juncture that opened up the redefinition of the main dimensions of conflict in Italian politics, but we have also seen the narrowing of political options in a new party system. Second, rather than defining ideas, strategies and goals as independent from the institutional and political context, this study showed that it is in interaction and endogenous processes that party competition structures political space.

Party Organisations and Resources

Conventional politics heavily influence the literature on political parties in Western Europe. Scholars have analysed the impact of modernisation in undermining the functions of parties in the management of political conflict, political integration and socialisation. Evolutionary approaches to the study of parties highlight the shift from mass to catch-all and finally, today the cartel party (Kircheimer, 1967; Bartolini and Mair, 1991; Mair and Katz, 1995). These views link the organisational and political transformation of traditional parties to the effective 'oligopoly' they exercise over the electoral market. Parties follow a trajectory that erode their societal links and reinforce their ties to the state apparatus. Protest parties can be undertood, in these views, the logical byproduct of trends towards partocracies in European polities.

Instead, this book showed the importance of party politics by focusing on what parties do and how they do it: systematically investigating the kind of resources that are crucial in contemporary politics. This book incorporated the tools of social movement research to explore the kind of political resources that matter to explain political mobilisation. However, these tools can also be used to explain what old parties do to mold public opinion and attract voters. In the traditional divisions of labor in the literature, social movements mobilise and parties represent. However, Lega Nord is a clear example to show this distinction to be of little relevance. What parties do to frame reality and define identities and interests is a key to explain the formation of political preferences.

Political organisation is as important today as it was in the past. First, the setting up of political parties, how political entrepreneurs solve 'entry costs' and collective action problems has crucial implications for explaining the rise of new political conflict. This study showed how Lega Nord combined old and innovative features in its party organisation. It is not in the size of membership but in the type of political participation and organisation that we find today the *old* features of political parties. The uses of symbolic resources and the role of the media today in providing the context in which conflicts are represented and reproduced needs to be systematically explored (Ruzza and Schmidtke, 1993). Focusing our attention on the old field of political communication and rethinking party resources can help illuminate the mechanisms and the different tool-kits political parties use to reach potential voters in the absence of strong organisational capacities. Strategic action can achieve media coverage in the absence of other resources to gain mass audiences.

Between Continuity and Change

The transformation of the Italian party system during the 1990s and the differential erosion of traditional electoral alignments within Northern Italy suggests a peculiar combination of *old* and *new* features in electoral change. The Italian political earthquake of the last decade offered a mixed result for those interested in political change. The rise and electoral success of Lega Nord involves a political paradox. On the one hand, everything seems possible in a political scenario in flux. After all, we have seen the birth of the Padanian nation in front of the TV cameras and we have seen the mass electoral success that Lega Nord obtained with claims of secession from the Italian state. On the other hand, the rise of political mobilisation in Northern Italy shows that not everything is possible. If a major process of political transformation and electoral re-alignment took place in Northern Italy, there was a fundamental continuity in the electoral alignments in the *red* regions of Central Italy.

The Communist territorial subculture showed its resilience to the mobilisation efforts of Lega Nord. The different legacies of traditional parties in these areas, and not socio-economic or structural differences between them, explain the ability of new political entrepreneurs to shape electoral alignments in different contexts. Despite the political earthquake that characterised Italian politics during the 1990s, electoral alignments in the *red* regions exhibited a remarkable continuity with electoral alignments in the post-war period. Votes for the two heirs of the Italian Communist party—the PDS and Rinfondazione Comunista—is concentrated in these regions. This striking outcome needs to be highlighted in analysis of political change in European party systems. Why and how do old electoral alignments retain their resilience today? Research conducted at the local level appears as the ideal strategy to illuminate continuity and change in party politics and electoral alignments in these areas.

Are new parties likely to create and stabilise new electoral alignments, and if so, how? Explaining the rise of new parties and their electoral success also begs the question of their persistence and consolidation in European party systems. In the past, the literature on electoral stability in European party systems predicated the stability of traditional cleavages on the organisational encapsulation of electoral constituencies (Bartolini and Maier, 1990). However, organisational encapsulation is no longer an option for parties in contemporary European politics.

The rise of Lega Nord suggests that our traditional conceptions of parties as constituency representatives and as political actors mediating the relationship between organised interests, associations and the state has to be revised. In his study of Green parties in West Germany and Belgium, Herbert Kitschelt explored a new pattern of politics. Kitschelt identified a new development: the ability of new political parties to achieve political realignment without introducing organisation linkages with constituency groups (Kitschelt, 1989). As Kitschelt showed in his study, organisationally the ties between new parties and their electorates are weak. The findings of my study suggests a similar dynamic for new radical right-wing parties. Lega Nord has developed an organisation for mobilising rather than representing specific constituencies and interests. Lega Nord's efforts to enlist key societal actors and to build stable networks with organised interests failed.

What are the implications of these findings for our analysis of the relationship between party elites and voters? Public opinion, as Iversen points out, 'is itself an object of, and not merely a constraint, on political contestation' (Iversen, 1994: p. 160). The emphasis on symbolic resources, framing and rituals, is not a purely decorative aspect of party politics, but a central mechanism that can explain how party elites can influence public opinion and change political attitudes. Political parties—as key institutions in liberal democracies—are actively engaged in influencing the public and do not merely respond to mass attitudes. In the conclusions to his study on Green parties in Germany and Belgium, Kitschelt writes, 'postindustrial political entrepreneurs rely on persuasion' (Kitschelt, 1989). This work leaves open the question of the individual motives of voters, but strongly suggests that neither traditional theories of party identification, organisational encapsulation nor rational choice emphasis on utility functions, adequately answer the question of the formation of political preferences and voting behavior. In light of empirical evidence on the Italian *Northern question*, we can question not only the tight connection between the voters' expression of party preference and party elites' actual behavior, but also the very notion of political representation in light of what new political entrerpreneurs do.

Finally new party organisations are less equipped to face the traditional functions of political parties and their organisations are weakly present in society. They resembled more new social movement organisations. However, unlike social movements, political parties recruit political elites to represent their constituencies in political institutions. Unlike social movements, moreover, parties need to consolidate their position as stable players in the political system.

In light of Lega Nord's experience with the institutionalisation of the Northern question, persistence is a major issue for new parties of the radical right. The presence of these new parties brings about three types of problems in European politics. First, the specialisation and narrowing of party agendas risk their ability to consolidate their position in party systems when issue attention cycles or external conditions changed. Their persistence relies on their ability to reproduce controversies and conflict over time, manipulating attention cycles. Second, in the trade-offs between mobilisation and the specialisation in political representation and institutional politics, the specialisation in the production of symbols can undermine the actual advancement of their own agendas. This peculiarity creates collective action problems as soon as party representatives entered political institutions and they are confronted with choices that go beyond the party agenda. Third, these parties are extremely vulnerable to internal organisational dynamics—regardless of the style of leadership—that risk their sustainability in the long run.

Rather than following a trajectory from mobilisation to representation, the persistence of Lega Nord in the Italian party system relied on its ability to continue creating controversies by engaging in extra-institutional means of action. The key strategic dilemma for Lega Nord's leadership was how to adapt to the new institutional environment: either moderating or radicalising the party demands. New challenges in European politics, in light of Lega Nord's trajectory, can be thought of as potential 'free riders' in party systems, since they have less incentives to moderate their claims. Pushing the boundaries of the establsihed political sphere, they also bring fundamental problems of governability in liberal democracies.

A Note on Rationality and Passion

Identity and strategy support two competing paradigms in the study of political action. The identity-paradigm argues that people mobilise because they share a common identity. Collective action, needs, at the very least, a common definition of 'who we are' (Pizzorno, 1966). From collective identities we can then derive political preferences. In contrast, the interest-paradigm argues that preferences are given and instrumental rationality accounts for collective action. Individuals participate and vote because they maximise their utility functions (Olson, 1965). Cultural explanations emphasise the impact of collective identity on individual behavior. They tend to assume a collective actor and consider identity a dimension of politics which is not concerned with choices. Instead, rational choice explanations take individuals maximising their utility function as the unit of analysis:

collective actors are treated as the sum of aggregated individuals. For the first paradigm political action is mainly expressive, whereas for the second paradigm political action is instrumental. In short, these paradigms profoundly diverged in their methodological and epistemological assumptions. In choosing one or the other, we are also forced into categorical distinctions between interpretation and explanation, meaning and choice.

Here I attempted to depart from this alternative. The identity paradigm forces the study of identity politics as expressive action. However, as Cohen argues: 'the category of expressive action cannot give adequate account of the problem of identity for two reasons: first, because it misses the normative components of a shared social identity, and second, because it excludes the strategic dimension of conflicts concerning the latter's interpreation' (Cohen, 1985: p. 694). This paradigm derives individual identities and preferences from collective ones, yet it cannot explain how collective identities are constructed. The second paradigm explains a collective identity by aggregating individual preferences and cannot explain how a collective identity can define and constrain individual behavior. In my study politicians are assumed to behave in opportunistic ways, by political entrepreneurship is explored within the context of the ideas and values that support political action. In short, I sought to explain the strategic uses of identity, but also the constraints on strategic behavior that claims to a collective identity create.

Rather than taking individuals or groups as the unit of analysis, I focused on how political processes shape both collective identities and individual preferences. As Cohen put it, 'there is no reason why the analysis of the various logics of collective action should be seen as incompatible, so long as they are not construed as the sole rationality of collection action to the exclusion of others' (Cohen, 1985, pp. 707-708). My study was an inquiry on why and how nationhood as a collective representation links territory, identity and interests in political action. I was interested in the producing of meaning and shared values on the one hand, and on strategic behavior and manipulation on the other.

Still today David Laitin's study of the Yoruba provides the most interesting attempt to bridge a gap between these competing paradigms. In his study of politics and religious change among the Yoruba, David Laitin reconciled what he called 'the two faces of culture'. He put together the empistemological basis of social systems and rational choice approaches. On the one hand, Laitin studied how culture orders preferences, the impact of sharing a culture on political values. On the other hand, he claimed that shared cultural identities facilitate collective action and explored culture as a political resource. For Laitin, 'the political power inherent in shared cultural symbols is what lies behind the Machiavellian smile of culture's second face' (Laitin, 1986: p. 11).

In its more simple formulation, rational choice approaches explain identities as coalition of groups glued by material interests, assuming the *ethnic* element (Bates, 1983). They are not only reductionist, but also unable to provide an explanation of why and how material coalitions are formed, and why identity as opposed to any other principle of political organisation becomes the basis for political action, from votes to violence and war. I strongly believe that identity politics and nationalism defy and challenge a reductionist view of the complexity of the human soul. Even in such a clear-cut case as the rise of Lega Nord in Italian politics.

Notes

[1] See Juan J. Linz and Amando de Miguel, 'Within-Nation Differences and Comparisons: The Eight Spains', in Richard L. Merritt and Stein Rokkan, *Comparing Nations. The Use of Quantitative Data in Cross-National Research* (New Haven: Yale University Press, 1966).

[2] Interview with Pujol. *Il Corriere della Sera* (February 2, 1998).

[3] See Will Kymlicka, *Multicultural Citizenship* (Oxford: Clarendon 1995); Amy Gutman ed., *Multiculturalism and the Politics of Recognition* (Princeton, Princeton University Press 1992); Yasemin Soysal, *Boundaries and Identity: Immigrants in Europe* (Harvard University, 1996, unpublished manuscript).

[4] As Urwin writes: 'Regionalist parties are more disparate in the specificity of their demands. There is little in the way of a common economic policy or common view of the structure of society. Few if any, could be said to have a 'Weltanschauung'. Not all are linguistic. All are rather small.' Derek Urwin, 'Harbinger, Fossil or Fleabite? Regionalism and the West European Party Mosaic', in Peter Mair, *Western European Party Systems: Between Continuity and Change* (Beverly Hills, CA: Sage Publications, 1983).

References

Acquaviva, Sabino and Eisermann, Gottfired (1981). *Alto Adige. Spartizione Subito*. Bologna: Patron Editore.

Agnelli, Arduino (1987). 'Il Friuli-Venezia Giulia dalla Resistenza allo Statuto Speciale' in Agnelli and Bartole, eds. *La Regione Friuli Venezia-Giulia*. Bologna, Il Mulino.

Agnelli, Arduino and Bartole, Sergio (1987). *La Regione Friui-Venezia Giulia. Profilo Storico-Giuridico Tracciato in Occasione del 20 Anniversario dell'Istituzione della Regione*. Bologna: Il Mulino.

Agostini, Piero (1986). *Alto Adige. La Convivenza Rinviata*. Bolzan: Praxis, 2nd edition.

Alberoni (1981). *Movimento e Istituzioni*. Bologna, Il Mulino.

Alleanza Nazionale (1995). Tesi di Fiuggi. Capitlo Secondo: La Comunitá Nazionale.

Alleanza Nazionale (1998). Tessi di Verona. Parte Seconda: Popoli, Conoscenza, Identitá, tra Innovazione e Tradizione.

Allevi, Stefano (1992). *Le Parole Della Lega*. Milano: Garzanti.

Almond, Gabriel A. and Verba, Sidney eds. (1965). *The Civic Culture: Political Attitudes and Democracy in Five Nations*. Boston: The Little Brown Series in Comparative Politics.

Amantia, Agostino e Vendramini, Ferrucio (1994). *Lega e Localismo in Montagna. Il Caso Belluno*. Belluno: Istituto Storico Bellunese della Resistenza e dell'Età Contemporanea.

Anderson, Benedict (1991). *Imagined Communities: Reflections on the Origin and Spread of Nationalism*. London: Verso.

Apalategui, Jokin (1979). *Los Vascos de la Nación al Estado*. Zarauz: Elkar.

Bagnasco, Arnaldo (1977). *Tre Italie. La Problematica Territoriale dello sviluppo Italiano*. Bologna: Il Mulino.

Bagnasco, Arnaldo (1996). *L'Italia in Tempi di Cambiamento Politico*. Bologna: Il Mulino.

Balbo, Laura e Manconi, Luigi (1992). *I razzismi Reali*. Milano: Feltrinelli.

Balibar, Etienne with Wallerstein, Immanuel (1991). *Race, Nation and Class. Ambiguous Identities*. London: Verso.

Banfield, Edward C. (1958). *The Moral Basis of a Backward Society*. New York: The Free Press.

Barnes, Samuel (1974). 'Italy' in Richard Rose ed. *Electoral Behavior. A Comparative Handbook*. New York: The Free Press.

Barth, Frederick (1968). *Ethnic Groups and Boundaries. The Social Organization of Culture Difference*. Boston: Little, Brown and Company.

Bartolini, Stefano and D'Alimonte, Roberto (1997). 'Electoral Transition and Party System Change in Italy' in Bull and Rhodes, *Crisis and Transition in Italian Politics*.

Bartolini, Stefano and D'Alimonte, Roberto eds. (1997). *Maggioritario Per Caso. Le elezioni politiche del 1994 e del 1996 a confronto: il ruolo del sistema elettorale, le coalizioni, le scelte degli elettori*. Bologna: Il Mulino.

Bartolini, Stefano and Mair, Peter (1990). *Identity, Competition and Electoral Availability. The Stabilisation of European Electorates 1885-1985*. Cambridge: Cambridge University Press.

Bates, Robert (1983). 'Modernization, Ethnic Competition and the Rationality of Politics in Contemporary Africa' in Rotchild, Donald and Olorunsola, Victor eds. *State Versus Ethnic Claims: African Policy Dilemmas*. Boulder CO: Westview Press.

Benhabib, Seyla (1996). *Democracy and Difference. Contesting the Boundaries of the Political*. Princeton, Princeton University Press.

Bereciartu, Gurutz Jauregui (1981). *Ideología y Estrategia política de ETA. Análisis de su*

Evolución entre 1959 y 1968. Madrid. Siglo XXI de Espana. Editores: S.A.

Berger, Suzanne (1972). *Peasants Against Politics. Rural Organization in Brittany 1911-1967.* Cambridge: Harvard University Press.

Berger, Suzanne (1977). 'Bretons and Jacobins: Reflections on French Regional Ethnicity' in Esman Milton, ed. *Ethnic Conflict in the Western World.*

Berger, Suzanne (1979). 'Politics and Antipolitics in Western Europe in the Seventies'. *Daedalus,* Winter issue: 27-50.

Berger, Suzanne (1987). 'Religious transformation and the future of politics' in Maier, Charles S. ed. *Changing Boundaries of the Political.* Cambridge: Cambridge University Press.

Bertolessi, Mario (1987). 'La Regione Friuli-Venezia Giulia dalla Costitutente allo Statuto' in Agnelli e Bartole eds. *La Regione Friuli-Venezia Giulia.*

Betz, Hans-George (1994). *Radical Right-Wing Populism in Western Europe.* New York: St. Martin Press.

Biorcio, Roberto (1992). 'Neopopulism in Italy and France', *Telos,* no. 90, Winter 1991-1992.

Biorcio, Roberto (1997). *La Padania Promessa. La storia, le idee e la logica d'azione della Lega Nord.* Milano: Il Saggiatore.

Blackmer, Donald and Tarrow, Sydney, eds (1977). *Communism in Italy and France.* Princeton: Princeton University Press.

Bocca, Giorgio (1990). *La Disunità d'Italia. Per venti milioni di italiani la democrazia è in come e l'Europa si allontana.* Milano: Garzanti Editore.

Bossi, Umberto (1992). *Vento del Nord.* Milano Sperling and Kupfer Editori.

Bossi, Umberto (1994). *Tutta la Verità. Perché ho partecipato al governo Berlusconi. Perché l'ho fatto cadere. Dove Voglio Arrivare.* Milano: Sperling and Kupfer Editori.

Bossi, Umberto (1996). *Il mio Progetto. Discorsi su federalismo e Padania.* Milano: Sperling and Kupfer Editori.

Bossi, Umberto e Daniele Vimercati (1993). *La Rivoluzione. La Lega: storia e idee.* Milano: Sperling and Kupfer Editori.

Bourdieu, Pierre (1991). *Language and Symbolic Power.* John B. Thompson, ed. Cambridge: Harvard Universtiy Press.

Briggs, Charles L. (1996). 'The Politics of Discursive Authority in Research on the 'Invention of Tradition''. *Cultural Anthropology* 11 (4): 435-469.

Brodero, Antonio e Gremmo, Roberto (1978). *L'Oppressione Culturale Italiana in Piemonte.* Ivrea: Editrice BS.

Brubaker, Rogers (1996). *Nationalism Reframed. Nationhood and the National Question in the New Europe.* Cambridge: Cambridge University Press.

Budge, Ian, Newton, Kenneth et al. (1997). The Politics of the New Europe. London: Longman.

Bull, Martin and Rhodes, Martin (1997). 'Party Organisations and Alliances in Italy in the 1990s: A Revolution of Sorts' in Bull and Rhodes eds. *Crisis and Transition in Italian Politics.*

Bull, Martin and Rhodes, Martin eds. (1997). *Crisis and Transition in Italian Politics.* London: Frank Cass.

Calhoun, Craig ed. (1994). *Social Theory and the Politics of Identity.* Cambridge: Blackwell Publishers.

Calise, Mauro and Renato Mannheimer (1981). 'I Governi Misurati'. *Il Mulino* 4\81, anno XXX no. 276.

Calvi, Gabriele and Vannucci, Andrea (1995). *L'elettore Sconosciuto. Analisi socioculturale e segmentazione degli orientamienti politici nel 1994.* Bologna: Il Mulino.

Caramani, Daniele (1996). 'La Partecipazione Electtorale: Gli Effetti della Competizione

Maggioritaria'. *Rivista Italiana di Scienza Politica* a. XXVI, no. 3, Dicembre 1996.

Cartoci, Roberto (1994). *Fra Lega e Chiesa*. Bologna: Il Mulino.

Cartocci, Roberto (1997). 'Indizi di un inverno precoce: il voto proporzionale tra equilibrio e continuità' in Bartolini and D'Alimonte eds. *Maggioritario per Caso*.

Cecovini, Manlio (1985). *Trieste Ribelle. La Lista del Melone. Un Insegnamento da Meditare.* Milano: Libero Scambio, SugarCo eds.

Chiaramonte, Alessandro (1997). 'L'effeto mancato della riforma maggioritaria: il Voto strategico' in Bartolini and D'Alimonte eds. *Maggioritario per Caso*.

Clark, Robert P. (1984). *The Basques Insurgents. ETA 1952-1980*. Madison: The University of Wisconsin Press.

Cohen, Jean L. (1985). 'Strategy or Identity: New Theoretical Paradigms and Contemporary Social Movements'. *Social Research* vol. 52, no. 4, Winter 1985.

Corbetta, Piergiorgio, Parisi Arturo, and Schadee Hans M.A. (1988). *Elezioni in Italia. Struttura e tipologia delle consultazioni politiche*. Bologna: Il Mulino.

Corti, Michele Padania (1995). 'Italia, Quale 'Questione Nazionale?'. *Quaderni Padani*, Anno 1, no. 2, Autunno 1995.

Costabile, Antonio (1991). 'Il fronte dell'uomo qualunque e la Lega Lombarda'. Working paper n. 48. Messina, Armando Siciliano Editore, Università di Messina.

Costituzione della Repubblica Italiana (1995). Maglioli Editore, Rimini.

Cotta, Maurizio and Pierangelo Isernia (1996). *Il Gigante dai Piedi di Argilla*. Bologna: Societa Editrice il Mulino.

Cuaz-Chatelair, René (1971). *Le Naufrage du Val D'Aoste francophone*. Paris: La pensée universelle.

D'Alimonte, Roberto (1995). 'La Transizione Italiana: Il Voto Regionale del 23 Aprile' in *Rivista Italiana di Scienza Politica* a. XXV, no. 3, December 1995: 515-559.

D'Alimonte, Roberto and Chiaramonte, Alessandro (1995). *Maggiortario Ma Non Troppo*. Bologna: Il Mulino.

Della Sala, Vincent (1997). 'Hollowing Out and Hardening the State: European Integration and the Italian Economy' in Bull and Rhodes eds. *Crisis and Transition in Italian Politics*.

Dente, Bruno (1997). 'Subnational Governments in the long Italian Transition' in Bull and Rhodes eds. *Crisis and Transition in Italian Politics*.

De Winter, Lieven and Tursan, Huri (1998). *Regionalist Parties in Western Europe*. Routledge, London.

Di Virgilio, Aldo (1994). 'Elezioni Locali e Destrutturazione Partitica. La Nuova Legga all Prova'. *Rivista Italiana di Scienza Politica* a. XXIV, no. 1, April 1994: 107-165.

Di Virgilio, Aldo (1997). 'Le Alleanze elettorali: identità Partitiche e logiche coalizionali' in Bartolini and D'Alimonte eds. *Maggioritario per Caso*.

Diamanti, Ilvo (1993). *La Lega*. Roma: Donzelli.

Diamanti, Ilvo (1994). 'Lega Nord' in *Milano a Roma. Guida all'Italia elettorale del 1994*. a cura di Ilvo Diamanti and Renato Mannheimer. Roma: Donzelli Editore.

Diamanti, Ilvo (1994). 'The Northern League. From Regional Party to Party of Government' in Gundle, S. and Parker, S. eds. *The New Italian Republic. From the Fall of the Berlin Wall to Berlusconi*. London and New York: Routledge.

Diamanti, Ilvo (1995). *La Lega*. 2nd Edition. Roma: Donzelli.

Diamanti, Ilvo (1995). "La Lega' Ilvo Diamanti and Renato Mannheimer'. *Da Milano a Roma. Guida all'Italia Elettorale del 1994*. Roma: Donzelli.

Diamanti, Ilvo (1996). *Il Male del Nord. Lega, Localismo, Secessione*. Roma: Donzelli Editore.

Diamanti, Ilvo and Allum, Percy (1995). 'The Autonomous Leagues in the Veneto' in Levy, C.

ed. *Italian Regionalism. History, Identity and Politics*. Oxford, Washington DC: Berg.

Diamanti, Ilvo and Mannheimer, Renato (1994). *Milano A Roma. Guida all'Italia elettorale del 1994*. Roma: Donzelli Editore.

Diamanti, Ilvo, Ricciamboni, Gianni (1992). *La Parabola del Voto Bianco. Elezioni e Società in Veneto* (1946-1992). Vicenza: Neri Pozza Editore.

Diani, Mario (1993). 'Lo Sviluppo dei Movimenti Etnico-Nazionali in Occidente 1960-1990' in Gian Enrico Rusconi ed. *Nazione Ethnia Cittadinanza*. Brescia: La Scuola.

Diani, Mario (1996), 'Linking Mobilization Frames and Political Opportunities in Italy'. *American Sociological Review*, vol. 61, no. 6: 1053-1069.

Diani, Mario and Melucci, Alberto (1992). *Nazioni Senza Stato. I movimenti etnico-nazionali in Occidente*. Milano: Universale Economica Feltrinelli.

Edelman, Murray (1985). *The Symbolic Uses of Politics*. Urbana: University of Illinois Press.

Einaudi, Mario and Goguel, Francois (1969). *Christian Democracy in Italy and France*.

Esman, Milton (1977). *Ethnic Conflict in the Western World*. Ithaca: Cornell University Press.

Europa Ethnica (1961). Virteljahresschrift fur Nationalitatenfragen. Mit offiziellen Mitteilungen der 'foderalistischen Union Europaischer Volksgruppen'. Revue Trimestrielle des Questions Ethniques. Contenant aussi des Communiques officiels de l'Union Federaliste des Communautes Ethniques Europeennes. A Quarterly Review for Problems of Nationality. Containing Official News of the 'Federal Union of European Nationalities'. Guy Heraud, Johann Wilhelm Mannhardt, Povl Skadegard and Theodor Veiter Wilhelm Braumuller eds. Universitats. Verlagsbuchhandlung. Wien IX Stuttgart.

Evans, Peter (1976). *Coexistence. Communism and its Practice in Bologna*. Notre Dame: University of Notre Dame Press.

Evans, Robert (1967). *Life and Politics in a Venetian Community*. Notre Dame: University of Notre Dame Press.

Fassini, Morena (1997). *La Vera Storia della Lega Nord 'Federalismo e Liberta' dalle Origini ad Oggi*. Lega Nord Ufficio Elettorale Federale.

Fearon, James D. and Laitin, David D. (1996). 'Explaining Interethnic Cooperation'. *American Political Science Review* 90, December 1996: 715-735.

Fenemma, Meindert (1997). 'Some Conceptual Issues and the Problems in the Comparison of Anti-immigrant parties in Western Europe'. *Party Politics*. London: Sage Publications, 473-492.

Fifteen Years of Problems in Alto-Adige. Fifty Clear Replies to Fifty Define Questions. Roma: Istituto Poligrafico dello Stato.

Flores d'Arcais, Paolo (1996). *Il Populismo italiano. Da Craxi a Berlusconi. Micromega*. Roma: Donzelli.

Flores d'Arcais, Paolo (1996). *Il Populismo Italiano. Da Craxi a Berlusconi*. Roma: Donzelli.

Follini, Marco (1992). *La DC al Bivio*. Roma: Laterza.

Follini, Marco (1994). *La DC al Bivio*. Roma: Saggi Tascabili Laterza.

Fontan's, Francois (1961). *Ethnisme. Vers Un Nationalisme Humaniste*. Bagnols: Librerie Occitaine.

Friedman, Debra and Dough McAdam (1992). 'Collective Identity and Activism. Networks, Choices and the Life of a Social Movement' in Aldon D. Morris and Carol McClurg Mueller eds. *Frontiers in Social Movement Theory*. New Haven: Yale University Press.

Fusella, Ambrogio ed. (1993). *Arrivano I Barbari. La Lega nel racconto di quotidiani e periodici 1985-1993*. Milano: Rizzoli.

Gallante, Severino ed. (1995). *Dove Va Il Nord-Est? Ipotesi Interpretative e proposte Politiche*. Atti del Convegno tra scienza e politica organizzato dal gruppo consilire Veneto del

PRC: Padova.

Galli, Giorgio (1958). *Storia del Partito Comunista Italiano*. Milano: Swarz Editore.

Galli, Giorgio (1966). *Il Bipartitismo Imperfetto. Comunisti e Democristiani in Italia*. Bologna: Il Mulino.

Galli, Giorgio (1978). *Storia della DC*. Bari: Laterza.

Galli, Giorgio (1993). *Mezzo Secolo di DC 1943-1993. Da De Gasperi a Mario Segni*. Milano: Rizzoli.

Galli, Giorgio (1994). *I Partiti Politici in Italia 1943-1994*. Torino: Utet Libreria.

Galli, Giorgio and Prandi, Alfonso (1970). *Patterns of Political Participation in Italy*. New Haven and London: Yale University Press.

Gellner, Ernest (1983). *Nations and Nationalism*. Ithaca, NY: Cornell University Press.

Ginsborg, Paul (1990). *A history of contemporary Italy. Society and Politics (1943-1988)*. London: Penguin Books.

Giovagnoli, Agostino (1996). *Il Partito Italiano. La Democrazia Cristiana dal 1942 al 1994*. Bari: Laterza.

Gobetti, Daniela (1996). 'La Lega. Regularities and Innovation in Italian Politics'. *Politics and Society*, vol. 24, no. 1, March 1996.

Gourevitch, Peter Alexis (1979). "The Reemergence of 'Peripheral Nationalisms': Some Comparative Speculations on the Spatial Distribution of Poitical Leadership and Economic Growth'. *Comparative Studies on Society and History* no. 3: 303-322.

Gramsci, Antonio (1951). *La Questione Meridionale*. Ediozioni Risnascita: Roma.

Grecco, Massino and Bollis Alberto (1993). *Carrocio a Nord-Est. Storia Programma e uomini della Lega Nord del Friuli-Venezia Giulia*. Trieste: MGS Press Editrice.

Gremmo, Roberto (1992). *Contro Roma. Storia, Idee e Programmi delle Leghe Autonomista del Nord*. Aosta: Collana Il Grial.

Gutman, Amy ed.(1992). *Multiculturalism and the Politics of Recognition*. Princeton: Princeton University Press.

Hainsworth, Paul ed. (1992). *The Extreme Right in Europe and the USA*. New York: St. Martin's Press.

Handler, Richard (1888). *Nationalism and the Politics of Culture in Quebec*. Madison: University of Wisconsin Press.

Hechter, Michael (1975). *Internal Colonialism. The Celtic Fringe in British National Development 1536-1966*. Berkeley: University of California Press.

Heraud, Guy (1963). *L'Europe des Ethnies*. Paris: Presses d'Europe.

Heraud, Guy (1978). *Fédéralism et Communautés Ethniques*. Edition Istitut Jules Destrée (A.s.b.l.).

Heraud, Guy (1993). *L'Europe des Ethnies*. Paris: Bruyant-Bruxelles.

Herzfeld, Michael (1992). *The Social Production of Indifference. Exploring the Symbolic Roots of Western Bureacracies*. Chicago: The University of Chicago Press.

Herzefeld, Michael (1996). 'Essentialism' in Alan Barnard and Jonathan Spencer eds. *Encyclopedia of Social and Cultural Antrophology*. London: Routledge.

Hetcher, Michael, and Levi, Margaret (1979). 'The comparative Analysis of Ethnoregional movements'. *Ethnic and Racial Studies*.

Hobsbawm, Eric (1990). *Nations and Nationalism since 1780. Programme, Myth, Reality*. Cambridge: Cambridge University Press.

Hobsbawm, Eric and Terence Ranger eds. (1978). *The Invention of Tradition*. Cambridge: Cambridge University Press.

Huber, John and Ronald Inglehart (1995). 'Expert Interpretations of Party Space and Party

Locations in 42 Societies'. *Party Politics* 1\1 Sage: 73-111.

Hueglin, Thomas O. (1986). 'Regionalism in Western Europe: Conceptual Problems of a New Political Perspective'. *Comparative Politics*, vol. 18, no. 4, July 1986, pp. 439-457.

Iacopini, Roberto and Bianchi, Stefania (1994). *La Lega ce l'ha Crudo. Il linguaggio del Carroccio nei suoi slogan, comizi e manifesti*. Milano: Mursia.

Ignazi, Piero (1992). *Dal PCI and PDS*. Bologna: Il Mulino.

Istituto Guglielmo Tagliacarne (1993). *Il Reddito Prodotto in Italia. Un'analisi a livello Provinciale*. Anni 1980-1991. Milano: FrancoAngeli.

Istat (1997). *Note Rapide*. Roma, Istat.

Istat (1999) *Italia in Cifre*. Roma, Istat.

Istat (2000). *Bilancio Demografico Nazionale*, Roma, Istat.

Iversen, Torben (1994). 'The Logics of Electoral Politics'. *Comparative Political Studies* vol. 27, no. 2, July 1994: 160.

Jean, Henri (1992). *De l'utopie au Pragmatisme? Le mouvement occitan 1976-1990*. Perpinya: Llibres del Trabucaire.

Jenkings, J. (1983). 'Resource Mobilization Theory and the Study of Social Movements'. *Annual Review of Sociology* no. 9: 527-53.

Katz, Richard (1996). 'Electoral reform and the Transformation of party politics in Italy'. *Party Politics* 2\1. Sage: 31-53.

Katz, Richard S. and Peter Mair (1991). *Party Organizations. A Data Handbook on Party Organizations in Western Democracies 1960-1990*. London: Sage Publications.

Keating, Michael (1988). *State and Regional Nationalism. Territorial Politics and the European State*. Hertfordshire: Harvester-Weatsheaf.

Kertzer, David I. (1980). *Comrades and Christians. Religion and Political Struggle in Communist Italy*. Cambridge: Cambridge University Press.

Kertzer, David (1988). *Ritual, Politics and Power*. New Haven: Yale University Press.

Kitschelt, Herbert, (1989). *The Logics of Party Formation. Ecological Politics in Germany and Belgium.*

Kitschelt, Herbert (1995). *The Radical Right-Wing in Western Europe: A Comparative Analysis* in collaboration with Anthony J. McGann. Ann Arbor: University of Michigan Press.

Klandermans, Bert (1988). 'The Formation and Mobilization of Consensus'. *International Social Movement Research*, vol. 1: 173-196.

Klandermans, Bert and Tarrow, Sidney eds. (1988). 'Mobilization into Social Movements: Synthesizing European and American Approaches'. *International Social Movement Research* vol. 1: 1-38.

Klandermans, Bert and Tarrow, Sidney (1988). 'Mobilization into Social Movements: Synthesizing European and American Approaches'. *International Social Movement Research*, vol. 1: 1-38. JAI Press.

Kymlicka, Will (1995). *Multicultural Citizenship*. Oxford: Clarendon.

Koopmans and Statham, Paul (2000). 'Political claims-making Against Racism and discrimination in Britain and Germany' in Ter Wal and Verkuyten eds. *Comparative Perspectives on Racism.*

La Lega Nord attraverso I manifesti. Un percorso di 14 Anni con I principali veicoli di communicazione del movimento leghista. Editorale Nord, Milano 1996.

La Vera Storia della Lega Nord 'Federalismo e Libertà' Dalle Origini ad Oggi. Lega Nord.

Lafont, Robert (1974). *La Revendication Occitane*. Paris: Flammarion.

Lago, Giorgio (1996). *Nordest Chiama Italia. Cosa Vuole L'area del Benessere e della Protesta*. Vicenza: Neri Pozza Editore.

Laitin, David (1986). *Hegemony and Culture. Politics and Religious Change among the Yoruba*. Chicago: The University of Chicago Press.

Lange, Peter (1975). 'The PCI at the Local Level' in *Comunism in Italy and France*. Blackmer, Donald and Tarrow, Sidney eds. Princeton: Princeton University Press.

Larana, E. and Gusfield, J. (1994). *Los Nuevos Movimientos Sociales: de la Ideología a la Identidad*. Colección Academia. Madrid, CIS.

Laurence, Jonathan (1998). *The Accession and Dethronement of a King: Umberto Bossi's Lega Nord and the Italian News Media*. Cornell University. Honors Thesis, May.

Lega Nord. Italia Federale. Organo Ufficiale della Lega Nord.

Lega Nord. Organo Ufficiale della Lega Nord.

Legge 25 Marzo 1993, no. 81. '*Elezione diretta del sindaco, del presidente della provincia, del consiglio comunale e del consiglio provinciale*'.

Lenguereau, Marc (1968). *La Vallée d'Aoste. Minorité Linguistique et Région Autonome de la République Italianne*. Grenoble: Editions des Cahiers de l'Alpe.

Lijphart, Arend (1977). 'Political Theories and the Explanation of Ethnic Conflict in the Western World: Falsified Predictions and Plausible Postidctions' in Esman, Milton ed. *Ethnic Conflict in the Western World*.

Linz, Juan (1973). 'Early State building and Late peripheral nationalism' in Eisendstad, S.N. and Rokkan, S. eds. *Building States and Nations. Models, Analysis and Data across three Worlds*. Vol. II. Beverly Hills, Sage.

Linz, Juan (1982). 'From Primordialism to Nationalism' in Tiryakian, Edward and Rogowski, Donald eds. *New Nationalism of the Developed West*.

Lipset Seymour, M. and Stein Rokkan (1967). *Cleavages Structures, Party Systems and Voter Alignments: An Introduction*. New York: The Free Press.

Mack Smith Denis (1988). *The Making of Italy*. New York: Holmes and Meier Publishers Inc.

Maddens, Bart, Billiet, Jack, and Beerten, Roeland (2000), 'National Identity and the attitude towards foreigners in multinational states: the case of Belgium' in *Ethnic and Migration studies*, vol. 26, no. 1 January 2000: 45-60.

Manconi, Luigi (1989). 'Due Tempi, due Ritmi. La direzione Democristiana, 1973-1986'. *Polis*. Anno III, no. 1, Aprile 1989.

Maneri, Marcello (1998a) 'Lo Straniero Consensuale. La devianza degli immigrati come circolarita di pratiche e discorsi' in A. Dal'Lago ed. *Lo Straniero è il Nemico. Materiali per l'etnografia Contemporanea*. Genova: Costa and Nolan.

Maneri, Marcello (1998b). 'Immigrati e Classi pericolose. Lo statuto dell'Extracomunitario' nella Stampa Quotidiana' in M. Delle Donne ed. *Relazioni Etniche, Stereotipi e pregiudizi, Fenomeno migratorio ed esclusione sociale*. Roma, Edizioni dell'Università Popolare.

Mannheimer, Renato (ed) (1991). *La Lega Lombarda*. Milano: Feltrinelli.

Mannheimer, Renato (1994). 'Il Mercato Elettorale dei Partiti tra il Vecchio e il Nuovo' in Renato Mannheimer and Giacomo Sani, *La Rivoluzione Elettorale. L'Italia tra la prima e la Seconda Republica*. Milano: Anabasi.

Mannheimer, Renato and Sani, Giacomo (1994). *La Rivoluzione Elettorale. L'Italia tra la Prima e la Seconda Repubblica*. Milano: Anabasi.

Maraffi, Marco (1994). 'Charisma and Organization in Political Parties: The Case of Italy's Lega Nord'. European Consortium for Political Research. Madrid, 18-22 April 1994.

McAdam, Doug, McCarthy, J. and Zald, M. eds. (1996). *Comparative Perspectives on Social Movements*. Cambridge: Cambridge University Press.

McCarthy, J., Zald Mayer (1977). 'Resource Mobilization Theory and Social Movements: A

Partial Theory'. *American Journal of Sociology* vol. 82, no. 6.

Melotti, Umberto (1996). Immigrati e autoctoni in Italia: conflitti etnici o sociali? Univesita degli Studi di Trento. Associazione Italo-Tedesca di Sociologia, no. 12, 1996-I-II.

Melucci, Alberto (1985). 'Movimenti Sociali negli anni 80: Alla Ricerca di un oggetto perduto?'. *Stato e Mercato*, no. 14, Agosto.

Menapace, Lidia (1974). *La Democrazia Cristiana, Natura, Struttura e Organizzazione*. Milano: Mazzota.

Messina, Anthony (1987). 'Postwar protest Movements in Britain: A challenge to Parties'. *The Review of Politics*. vol. 49, no. 3, 410-428.

Messina, Patrizia (1997), 'Persistenza e mutamento nelle subculture politiche territoriali' in Gangemi, G. and Riccamboni, G. *Le Elezioni della Transizione*. Torino, UTET.

Miglio, Gianfranco (1994). *Io, Bossi e la Lega. Diario Segreto dei miei quattro anni sul Carroccio*. Milano: Arnaldo Mondadori Editore.

Mingione, Enzo (1993). 'Italy: The Resurgence of regionalism'. *International Affairs* 69, 2 (1993): 305-318.

Moran, Gregorio (1982). *Los Espanoles que dejaron de serlo. Euskadi 1937-1981*. Madrid: Planeta.

Morlino, Leonardo (1997). 'Crisis of Parties and Change of Party System in Italy'. *Party Politics* 2\1. Sage 1996: 5-30.

Mudde, Cas (2000). *The Ideology of the Extreme Right*. Manchester: Manchester University Press.

Nairn, Tom (1977). *The Break-Up of Britain. Crisis and Neo-Nationalism*. NLB.

Natale, Paolo (1997). 'Mutamento e stabilità nel Voto degli Italiani' in Bartolini and D'Alimonte, *Maggioritario per Caso*. New York: Archon Books.

Newell, James J. and Bull, Martin (1997), 'Party Organisations and Alliances in Italy in the 1990s: a Revolution of Sorts' in Bull and Rhodes. *Crisis and Transition in Italian Politics*.

Panebianco, Angelo (1982), *Modelli di Partito*. Bologna, Il Mulino.

Pansa, Giampaolo (1975). *Bisaglia. Una Carriera Democristiana*. Milano: SugarCo Edizioni.

Parisi, Arturo (1979). *Democristiani*. Bologna: Il Mulino.

Pasquino, Gianfranco (1995), 'La societá contro la politica: un nuovo qualunquismo' in Il Mulino anno XLIV numero 3611, 5795 Settembre/Ottobre: 801-809.

Pasquino, Gianfranco (1997). "No Longer a 'Party State?' Institutions, Power and the Problems of Italian Reform' in Bull and Rhodes eds. *Crisis and Transition in Italian Politics*.

Pearson, Paul (2000). 'Increasing Returns, Path Dependency Analysis and the Study of Politics', APSR, June 2000, vol. 94, no. 2, pp. 251-267.

Pellegrini, GianBattista (1986). *Minoranze e Culture Regionali*. Padova: CLESP.

Peri, Pierangelo (2000). 'Italy. An Imperfect Union' in Hagendoorn et al. *European Nations and Nationalism. Theoretical and Historical Perspectives*. Ashgate: UK.

Piattoni, Simona (1996). *Local Political Classes and Economic Development: the Cases of Abruzzo and Puglia in the 1970s and 1980s*. M.I.T. doctoral thesis.

Piattoni, Simona (1997). *Clientelelismo virtuoso. Le basi immorali di un'economia in sviluppo*.

Pizzorno, Alessandro (1966). 'Introduzione allo studio della partecipazione politica'. *Quaderni di Sociologia*. vol. XV, Luglio-Dicembre.

Pizzorno, Alessandro (1993). *Le Radici della Politica Assoluta ed altri saggi*. Milano: Feltrinelli.

Poggi, Gianfranco (1967). *Catholic Action in Italy. The Sociology of a Sponsored Organization*.

Stanford: Stanford University Press.

Putnam, Robert (1993). *Making Democracy Work. Civic Traditions in Modern Italy.* Princeton, Princeton University Press.

Rampini, Federico (1994). 'Come Berlusconi ha inventato il Primato di Milano' in *Limes. Rivista Italiana di Geopolitica.* A Che Serve l'Italia. Perche' Siamo una Nazione. 4\94, p 45 y ss.

Revelli, Marco (1996). *Le Due Destre.* Torino: Bollati Boringhieri.

Riccamboni, Gianni (1992). *L'identità Esclusa. Comunisti in una subcultura bianca.* Vicenza: Liviana.

Riccamboni, Gianni (1997). 'Ritorno al Futuro? La Transizione nell'ex-subcultura bianca'. *Le elezioni della transizione.* a cura di G. Gangemi and Gianni Riccamboni. Torino: UTET.

Ricolfi, Luca (1995). 'Il voto proporzionale e il nuovo spazio politico Italiano' in Stefano Bartolini and Roberto D'Alimonte eds. *Maggioritario Ma non Troppo.* Il Mulino: Bologna.

Ricolfi, Luca (1997). 'Politics and the Mass Media in Italy' in Bull and Rhodes. *Crisis and Transition in Italian Politics.*

Rokkan, Stein and Urwin, Derek (1983). *Economy, Territory, Identity.* London: Sage Publicatons.

Ross, Marc Howard (1997). 'Culture and Identity in Comparative Political Analysis' in Mark Irving Lichbach and Alan Zucherman eds. *Comparative Politics.* Cambridge: Cambridge University Press.

Rousseau, M. and Zariski, M. (1987). *Regionalism and Regional Devolution in Comparative Perspective.* New Yord: Praeger Publishers.

Rusconi, Gian Enrico (1993). *Se Cessiamo di Essere una Nazione.* Bologna: Il Mulino.

Ruzza Carlo and Schmidtke, O. (1993). 'Roots of Success of the Lega Lombarda: Mobilisation Dyanmics and the Media'. *West European Politics*, vol. 16, April 1993, no. 2: 1-23.

Sagredo de Ihartza, Fernando (Federico Krutvig) (1978). *La Vasconie et L'Europe Nouvelle.* Anglet: IPSO.

Said, Edward W. (1978). *Orientalism.* Penguin Books.

Said, Edward (1993). *Culture and Imperialism.* London: Chato & Windus.

Salvi, Sergio (1975). *Patria e Matria. Dalla Catalogna al Friuli Dal Paese Basco alla Sardegna: Il Principio di Nazionalità nell'Europa Occidentale Contemporanea.* Firenze: Vallechi.

Salvi, Sergio (1978). *Le Lingue Tagliate. Storie delle Minoranza Linguistiche in Italia.* Milano: Rizzoli.

Sani, Giacomo (1994). 'Dai Voti ai Seggi' in Ilvo Diamanti and Renato Mannheimer eds. *Milano a Roma. Guida all'Italia elettorale del 1994.* Roma: Donzelli Editore.

Sani, Giacomo and Paolo Segatti (1996). 'Programmi, Media e Opinione Pubblica'. *Rivista Italiana di Scienza Politica.* Anno XXVI. Dicembre 1996: 459-483.

Sartori, Giovanni (1994). *Ingenieria Costituzionale Comparata.* Bologna: Il Mulino.

Schlesinger, Joseph A. (1984). 'On the Theory of Party Organization'. *The Journal of Politics* vol. 46: 369-400.

Shepsle, Kenneth (1991). *Models of Multiparty Electoral Competition.* Harwood Academic Publishers.

Sidoti, Francesco (1986). 'The Extreme Right in Italy: Ideological Orphans and Countermobilization' in Hainsworth ed. *The Extreme Right in Europe and the USA.*

Smith, Anthony (1986). *The Ethnic Origins of Nations.* Oxford: Blackwell.

Smith, Anthony (1991). *National Identity.* Middlesex: Penguin Books.

Smith, Anthony D. (1995). *Nations and Nationalism in a Global Era.* Cambridge: Cambridge Polity Press.

Sniderman, Paul, Peri, Pierangelo, de Figueiredo, Rui J.P., Piazza, Thomas, J.R. (2000). *The Outsider. Prejudice and Politics in Italy.* Princeton, Princeton University Press.

Snow, A. and Benford, R. (1988). 'Ideology, Frame Resonance, and Participant Mobilization'. *International Social Movement Research* vol. 1 pages 197-217.

Snow, A., Burke, Rochford, Worden, S., Benford, R. (1986). 'Frame Alignment Processes, Micromobilization and Movement Participation'. *American Sociological Review* vol. 51, August: 464-481.

Sosyal, Yasemin (1996). 'Boundaries and Migrants in Europe'. Department of Sociology. Harvard University.

Soysal, Yasemin (1997). 'Changing parameters of Citizenship and Claims-Making. Organized Islma in European Public Spheres'. *Theory and Society* vol. 26/4. August 1997: 509-527.

Stella, Schei Gian Antonio (1996). *Dal Boom alla Rivolta: Il Mitico Nord-Est.* Milano: Baldini and Castoldi.

Stern, Alan J. (1971). 'Local Political Elites and Economic Change: A Comparative Study of Four Italian Communities'. Yale University, PH.D 1971. University Microfilms, A Xerox Company. Ann Arbor: Michigan

Stern, Alan (1975). 'Political Legitimacy in Local Politics: The Communist Party in Northeastern Italy' in Blackmer, Donald L. and Tarrow, Sidney eds. *Communism in Italy and France.* Princeton, Princeton University Press.

Streek, Wolfgang (1992). 'Inclusion and Secession: Questions on the Boundaries of Associative Democracy'. *Politics and Society* vol. 20, no. 4, December.

Swyngedouw, Marc (1992). 'L'Essor d'Agalev et du Vlaams Blok'. *Courier Hebdomadaire* no. 1362, Crisp: 1-42.

Swyngedouw, Marc (1995). 'The 'Threatening immigrant' in 'Flanders, 1930-1980: Redrawing the Social Space'. *New Community. Journal of the European Research Centre on Migration and Ethnic Relations* vol. 21, no. 3, July: 325-341.

Swyngedouw, Marc (1998). 'L'ideologie du Vlaams Blok: L'Offre Identitaire. Revue International de Politique Comparée' vol. 5, no. 1.

Tarrow, Sidney (1994). *Power in Movement. Social Movements, Collective Action and Politics.* Cambridge, Cambridge University Press.

Ter Wal, Jessica and Verkuyten, Maykel (2000). *Comparative Perspectives on Racism.* Aldersshot. Ashgate.

The De Gasperi-Gruber Agreement on the Alto Adige (1960). The Presidency of the Council of Ministers, Rome.

Thelen, Kathleen and Sven Steino (1992). 'Historical Institutionalism in Comparative Politics' in Sven Steinom, Kathleen Thelen and Frank Longstreth eds. *Structuring Politics. Historical Institutionalism in Comparative Analysis.* Cambridge Studies in Comparative Politics. Cambridge: Cambridge University Press.

Todesco, Claudio (1992). 'Governanti in Carriera. Ministri e Sottosegretari Italiani delle Prime Dieci Legislature'. Tesi di Laura. Universita degli Studi di Milano. Facolta di Scienze Politche.

Todesco, Fabio (1994). 'Marketing Elettorale E Comunicazione Politica'. Il Caso Lega Nord. Università Commerciale Luigi Bocconi.

Trigilia, Carlo (1986). *Grandi Partiti e Piccole Imprese. Comunisti e Democristiani nelle Regioni a Economia Diffusa.* Bologna, Il Mulino.

Trigilia, Carlo (1992). *Sviluppo Senza Autonomia*. Bologna: Il Mulino.

Trigilia, Carlo (1994). 'Nord e Sud, se il Belpaese si Spezza'. *Limes* no. 4: 91.

Trigilia, Carlo (1994). 'Nord e Sud, se il Belpaese si spezza'. *Limes* no. 4\1994.

Trigilia, Carlo (1997). 'Regionalism in Italy: Politichal Change in the North and in the South'. Paper presented at the Workshop Political and Institutional Change in Contemporary Italy. Center for European Studies. Harvard University. February 7-8.

Urwin, Derek (1983). 'Harbinger, Fossil or Fleabite' in Mair, Peter, *Western European Party Systems. Continuity and Change*. Beverly Hills CA: Sage Publications.

Van der Brug, Wouter, Fenemma, Meindert and Tillie, Jean (2000). 'Anti-Migrant Parties in Euorpe: Ideological or Protest Vote?'. *European Journal of Political Research* 37:77-102.

Verzichelli, Luca (1996). 'La Classe Politica della Transizione'. *Rivista Italiana Di Scienza Politica*. no. 3, Anno XXVI, Diciembre.

Waters, Sarah (1994). 'Tangentopoli and the Emergence of a New Political Order in Italy'. *West European Politics* vol. 17, no. 1, January: 169-182.

Waters, Sarah (1994). 'Tangentopoli and the Emergence of a New Political Order in Italy'. *West European Politics*, vol. 17, no. 1, January.

West European Politics (1997). vol. 20, no. 1, Frank Cass: London.

Wolleb, Enrico and Wolleb, Guglielmo (1990). *Divari Regionali e Dualismo Economico. Prodotto e Reditto Disponibile delle Regioni Italiane nell'Ultimo Ventennio*. Bologna: Società Editrice Il Mulino. Colana della Svimez.

Woods, Dwayne (1992). 'The Crisis of the Italian Party-State and the Rise of the Lombard League'. *Telos*. Fall, no. 93: 111-126.

Zucchini, Francesco (1998). 'La genesi in parlamento della legge sull'immigrazione'. *Il Rapporto ISMO*. Milano, Franco Angeli.

Party Journals

Arnassitaa Piemonteisa

Assion Piemonteisa

Autonomie Valdotaine

Ethnie

Lombardia Autonomista

Quaderni Padani

Union Piemonteisa

Veneto Libero

Vento del Nord